# LIFELINE

The moment of truth had arrived. I removed my knife from the pocket of my foul-weather gear and opened the blade. Bruno said, *"Maintenant!"* and Marc turned the helm of the 86-foot-long, 45-foot-wide catamaran hard to port and into the wind and waves. Catamarans tend to go backward almost as fast as they go forward. If this boat started backward, I thought, the rudders on the back of each hull would break in an instant.

"She's holding!" I said with an explosion of breath. "She's holding!" Then Marc and Bruno, working together, turned the helm hard to port and then lashed the wheel to hold us closer to the wind. We all started breathing again. I closed my knife and put it back in my pocket. Only then did I notice that Marc and Bruno were doing the same thing. Each of us was afraid the catamaran would go over as we turned into the wind and waves, and we'd be trapped under the trampoline and under the water by our safety lines. With our knives we could cut the safety lines and, perhaps, not drown. . . .

Also by Michael Levitt

LEARN TO SAIL (coauthor Dennis Conner)
AMERICA'S CUP 1851–1992: THE OFFICIAL RECORD
  (winner of a 1992 Benjamin Franklin Award)
SAIL LIKE A CHAMPION (coauthor Dennis Conner)
THE ART AND SCIENCE OF SAILS (coauthor Tom Whidden)
UPSET: AUSTRALIA WINS THE AMERICA'S CUP (coauthor Barbara Lloyd)
A TISSUE OF LIES: NIXON VERSUS HISS (coauthor Morton Levitt)

# AROUND
# THE WORLD
## IN
# SEVENTY-NINE
# DAYS

CAM LEWIS
AND MICHAEL LEVITT

DELTA
EXPEDITION

A Delta Book
Published by
Dell Publishing
a division of
Bantam Doubleday Dell Publishing Group, Inc.
1540 Broadway
New York, New York 10036

Grateful acknowledgment is made to reprint the following:

Excerpts from Jules Verne's *Around the World in Eighty Days* were taken from a Bantam Classic copyright 1984 and used with permission of the publisher.

A quote is used from George Day's and Herb McCormick's *Out There* copyright 1983 by Seven Seas Press and used with permission of the authors.

A quote from Jon Bowermaster's article "Has the Great Lamazou Missed the Boat?" published in the November 1993 issue of *Outside* magazine is used with permission of the publisher.

Several quotes were taken from Christian Février's article "Around the World in 80 Days (or Less)" published by *Multihulls* magazine April/May 1993 and used with permission of the writer.

A quote was taken from Frank Rosenow's article "The Fire Still Burns" published in the May 1990 issue of *Sail* magazine and used with permission of the publisher.

Several quotes were taken from Sir Robin Knox-Johnston's book *A World of My Own* published by Morrow in 1970 and used with permission of the author.

Library of Congress Cataloging in Publication Data
Lewis, Cam.
    Around the world in seventy-nine days / by Cam Lewis and Michael Levitt.
        p.    cm.
    "A Delta book"—T.p. verso.
    Includes bibliographical references (p. – ) and index.
    ISBN 0-385-31326-8 (pb)
    1. Commodore Explorer (Catamaran)  2. Voyages around the world.
I. Levitt, Michael.  II. Title.
G440.C373L48   1996
910.4'1—dc20                                                        95-32565
                                                                          CIP

Manufactured in the United States of America
Published simultaneously in Canada

April 1996

10  9  8  7  6  5  4  3  2  1

BVG

To my father, who shared with me his love of the sea,
and for Molly and Max, who waited for me.
Also, to my shipmates,
Bruno, Marc, Jacques, and Chinois.

—Cam Lewis

The authors are most indebted to Skip Novak and Peter Stalkus for their cheerful willingness to make comments and corrections on this manuscript. Novak, a veteran of four Whitbread Round the World Races, is currently skipper and owner of *Pelagic*, which takes adventurers, the media, and scientists to Antarctica. Stalkus, an America's Cup sailor in his free time, is captain of the *Green Wave*, the resupply vessel for the U.S. Antarctic Research Program. Brian Doyle, of North Sails Cloth, was ever ready and willing to answer technical queries, as he has so generously done in the past. The text from Jules Verne's *Around the World in Eighty Days* was taken from a Bantam Classic and is used with permission of the publisher. Our book could not have been written without the collection of the Redwood Library in Newport, Rhode Island. Also, we wish to thank Meredith Bernstein of the Meredith Bernstein Literary Agency, and Jacob Hoye, our editor at Dell.

Chris Hartley, Nancy Keefe, Ruth Dunseath, and Daniel Forster were helpful in translating the French. Also, we wish to thank *Sailing World* magazine's Sean McNeill for providing research material and translations done primarily by Marie Lésure. Charles Chiodi, of *Multihulls* magazine, provided valuable information. Writers, such as Robin Knox-Johnston, Herb McCormick, George Day, and Christian Février, and the magazine *Outside*, allowed us to use quoted materials. Paul Mirto drew the maps of the world.

And certainly we wish to acknowledge the love and support of our families: Molly and Max Lewis and Linda and Molly Levitt.

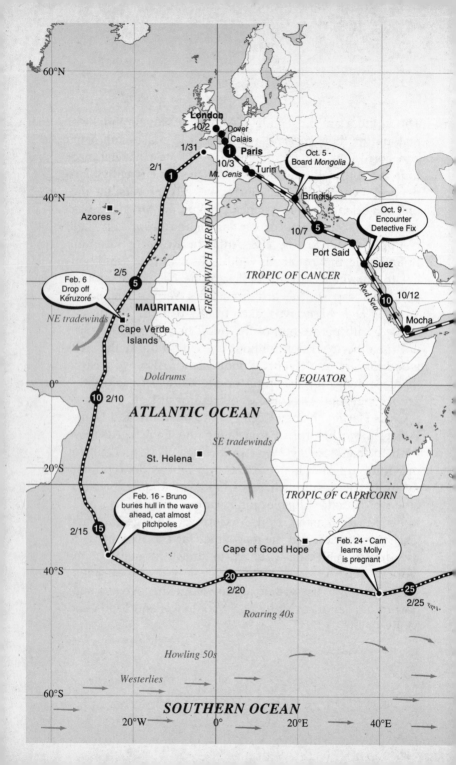

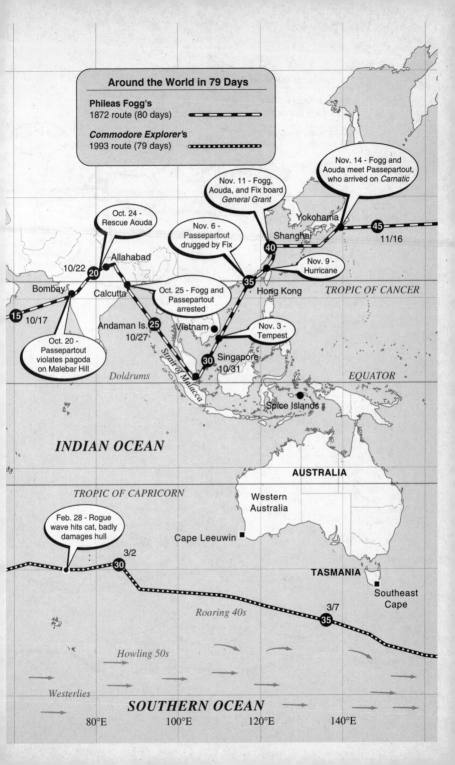

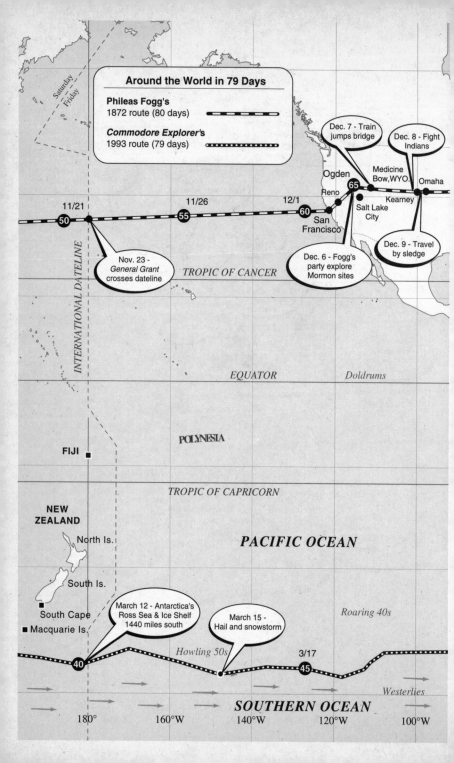

# CONTENTS

With but its bit of sail, the *Tankadere* was lifted like a feather by a wind an idea of whose violence can scarcely be given. To compare her speed to four times that of a locomotive going on full steam would be below the truth. The boat scudded thus northward during the whole day, borne on by monstrous waves, preserving always, fortunately, a speed equal to theirs. Twenty times she seemed almost to be submerged by these mountains of water which rose behind her; but the adroit management of the pilot saved her. The passengers were often bathed in spray, but they submitted to it philosophically.

—Jules Verne, *Around the World in Eighty Days*, 1873

## INTRODUCTION

This is a book about a voyage around the world taken in 1993. It is also a book about a famous if fictitious voyage around the world taken in 1872. It will tell how we got here from there.

# In which a fax from France finds me in rural Maine inviting me to sail around the world

---

On March 25, 1993, it was as if we had wandered into the wrong novel. We had started this adventure in Jules Verne's *Around the World in Eighty Days*, a book I treasured as a child, and had suddenly found ourselves in Joseph Conrad's *Typhoon*, a book that terrified me as an adult.

I was the sole American with four Frenchmen, and all of us riding an out-of-control boat on an empty edge of the earth. On a night without heavenly lights, I was driving the 86-foot-long, 45-foot-wide catamaran *Commodore Explorer* toward Cape Horn, at the foot of South America. I hadn't seen another boat, airplane, person, or land since we'd hurtled past the Cape Verde Islands on February 6. We'd been at this for 53 days, and two thirds of the world was behind us. At this point, sailing around the world in under 80 days was possible but far from assured. The forecast was benign: it called for winds in the 8-to-12-knot range. Forecasts lie.

For sailors, Cape Horn, at about 56 degrees south latitude, is a rite of passage, but few pass this way unscathed. Frankly, I would have been disappointed if we had, but there is a lifetime of difference between unscathed and scathed.

As we got within 200 miles of Cape Horn, the wind continued to build. Soon we found ourselves under bare poles, surfing downwind relentlessly at 28 knots, with the wind screaming at 70 knots. The wind from the west was pushing us inexorably toward land, to the east. Such a lee shore is the absolute last place a ship at sea wants to be, and the absolute worst place to be off a lee shore is at Cape Horn.

This latitude band is characterized as the "Howling Fifties" because of the tenor, or voice, of the wind. The wind was a constant siren song that hurt my ears and weakened my resolve. My foul-weather gear was pressed against my back like a vacuum bag, and my arms were cramped from the pressure of resisting the wind trying to wrap me around the wheel.

Like a "watched pot," dawn was slow to arrive in front of us. When it finally came, we could see what we were in —not just sense it—which made matters worse. Bruno Peyron, the skipper, grew concerned. The wind was consistently over 70 knots. He came over to the port hull to check with Marc Vallin, my watchmate, now at the helm. Marc, who had once sailed this catamaran across the Atlantic in under seven days, to set a world record, shrugged. "A little hairy for the first ten minutes. It's okay now, though."

As he said that the mast shuddered as if to disagree. Immediately, all of us looked up at it. This boat has a carbon-fiber wing mast that towers 110 feet above the water; even without sails and with the rotating mast feathered into the wind to depower it, it presents considerable surface area to a typhoon-worth of wind. The mast was carving angry circles in a bruised sky.

I went below to organize breakfast and was cooking pan-cakes on my humble one-burner stove. Life goes on. After a while, Bruno stuck his head down into my galley and said in his French-accented English, "Hey, Lewie, what do you think about parking this beast?" Not a bad idea, I said, but how? While a monohull is capable of parking, or heav-ing-to, and waiting out the weather, no one, as far as I know, had ever tried to park a tennis-court-size multihull in such conditions.

We scrambled about the net, hung between the two hulls, preparing for a maneuver that had never been tried before. There was no script; it was all ad hoc. Here and there the 40-foot waves heaved up through the net, strung between hulls. If you're not careful, or are unlucky, the waves can knock you off your feet and even off the boat. Each of us knew this was likely the pivotal moment of this voyage, perhaps the pivotal moment of our lives.

Then Bruno shouted, *"Maintenant!"* and Marc, without looking back at the waves that threaten to capsize or crush the boat, turned *Commodore Explorer* into the wind. We lashed the helm over. This turned us into a cork floating at the mercy of the gods. Then we huddled belowdecks, in survival suits, waiting for the mast to fall down, our world to turn upside down, or our boat to run aground on Cape Horn.

What had brought us to Cape Horn on March 25, 1993, was a meeting on a barge on the Seine River in Paris, in August 1990. That year several sailors, most of whom were French, had the audacious idea to try to sail around the world in under 80 days, to chase the fictitious record of Phileas Fogg and Jean Passepartout in Jules Verne's 1873 novel *Around the World in Eighty Days*.

It was audacious because in 1990, the fastest circumnavi-gation in a sailboat belonged to Titouan Lamazou, a

Frenchman who had girded the globe in the monohull *Ecureuil d'Aquitaine II* in 109 days, 8 hours, and 48 minutes, or an average speed of about 9.5 knots. To sail around the world in 80 days, one would have to sail a full 27 percent faster.

Those attending the meeting in Paris included my friend and occasional shipmate Bruno Peyron; Bruno's younger brother Loïck; Titouan Lamazou, the world-record holder; Yves Le Cornec; Florence Arthaud; Peter Blake; and Robin Knox-Johnston.

Knox-Johnston, an Englishman, had been in 1969 the first person to sail alone nonstop around the world. It took him 313 days, for an average speed of about four knots. It was a veritable snail's pace, but in the world of adventuring it's always best to be the first. After that the themes grow more murky: you can be fastest, or the first with red hair.

Blake, of New Zealand, had just returned from winning the 1989–90 edition of the Whitbread Round the World Race on *Steinlager II*. Lamazou, who would set his around-the-world mark in 1989 as part of the Vendée Globe Challenge, would be given a ticker-tape parade down the Champs Elysées for this accomplishment. That same year he was named "World Champion of Open Sea Racing, 1986–1990."

Bruno would go on to break the solo transatlantic record that had previously belonged to Florence Arthaud. This was Bruno's second solo transatlantic record, as he had previously set the record in 1987—the one Florence broke. (Bruno's record would be broken in 1994 by Laurent Bourgnon.) Loïck Peyron had won the 1987 two-handed 3,200-mile La Baule–Dakar Race and would later win the 1992 Europe 1 Star, a single-handed race across the Atlantic, from Plymouth, England, to Newport, Rhode Island. These are the daring young men—and women—and their flying machines: Extreme boats designed to break records. Failing that, they often break themselves and occasionally they break bodies and even end lives.

This group competes on the oceans and in boardrooms for sponsors, movie deals, and even signature-clothing lines. In France, these are the Michael Jordans and Nancy Kerrigans. When Florence, the exotic siren-of-the-sea, set her transatlantic record in 1990, for example, she ranked second to French President François Mitterrand in popularity polls in France.

George Day and Herb McCormick wrote in their book, *Out There,* "In France, single-handers are among the sporting elite. They are rewarded with fame and money and adoring sponsors. Such carrots might be incentive enough to drive French sailors to excellence. But, in characteristic French fashion, they have devised a second level of the game. In it, challenges are encountered, like mountain peaks, for their own sake—because they are there. A solid financial support system has grown to spur these sailors on in their quest—physical and philosophical—of solo adventure. Together, the money and the philosophy form the French imperative."

Professional jealousies and Eiffel Tower–size egos are rampant in this rarefied world, and such a meeting of the minds was practically unheard of. Nevertheless, the summit gave rise to the Trophée Jules Verne, for the first person to sail around the world in under 80 days. The French minister of culture provided $60,000 for a trophy. A million-dollar prize for the first one to break the fictitious record was donated by PMU, a French lottery organization. This prize disappeared after Florence Arthaud and Titouan Lamazou objected to their names being used in advertisements without permission, and, presumably, compensation.

The rules for the circumnavigation weren't complex. The

start was to be between the Lizard, the southwest corner of England, and l'île d'Ouessant, an island off Brest, France. It is this imaginary line that separates the English Channel from the Atlantic. Competitors were to keep the Cape of Good Hope, at the foot of Africa, Cape Leeuwin, in the southwest corner of Australia, and Cape Horn on their left, or port side.

To know the French, it is no surprise that this idea first occurred to several of them. First, they absolutely dominate this type of ocean adventuring. The French also have as great an affinity for the sea as anyone. Could Jacques Cousteau, for example, be anything but a Frenchman?

More than anywhere else, risk-takers are prized in France. Then, Verne was French. Who better to break this fictional milestone penned by a Frenchman than other Frenchmen? Also, Jean Passepartout, Fogg's servant, who reluctantly accompanies his English master on the voyage and is an integral part of it, was French.

It is all of a piece: Verne was a sailor. He and his brother Paul used to rent a leaky old boat for a franc a day at Chantenay, a village near Nantes, where their father owned a summer cottage. As he wrote in *The Youth's Companion,* a magazine published in Boston, "What hopeless sailors we were! Tacking down river on the ebb-tide against the westerly breeze, how many times we capsized disgracefully owing to a misjudged shove at the helm, a botched manoeuvre, an ill-advised tug on the sheets when a swell rose to ruffle the broads of the Loire off our Chantenay! . . . And as our hired boat floundered along between the shores we cast looks of envy on the pretty pleasure yachts skimming past and around us."

When Verne was twelve, he attempted to run away to sea. His father, a prosperous lawyer and apparently the model for the punctilious Fogg, tracked his adventurous son to the ship, the *Coralie,* at its next and last port before departing for the West Indies. He hauled him home. Not one to spare the rod and spoil the child, he delivered a severe caning. The result was, the twelve-year-old promised never to stray again. And he rarely strayed very far, even as an adult and an eminently successful author. Verne strayed, however, often, and as effectively as anyone, in his imagination.

When Verne, an unhappy stockbroker turned author, first tasted the fruits of literary success, he bought a small sailing yacht, the *Saint-Michel*, named in honor of his son, Michel, which he kept at Le Crotoy, a French seaport. As his grandson Jean Jules-Verne wrote, "The importance of the *Saint-Michel* in his life and works cannot be overstated. Even though he visited few of the faraway places frequented by his heroes, he was a sailor."

This was replaced by a much larger sailboat, *Saint-Michel II*, a 43-footer, and then the larger still (92-foot) and much grander steam yacht, *Saint-Michel III*. In it, Verne toured the Mediterranean. To show the distance he had traveled, professionally if not actually, he steered the yacht into the same dock that he had attempted to stow away from forty-four years before.

Verne wrote novels that were anthems to the "Machine Age," a time when scientists left the theoretical and focused on the practical. First, there was the steam engine, invented in 1712, to run pumps to remove water from coal mines in England. Later in that century, it was recognized that the up-and-down motion of the coal-fired steam engine could be converted to circular motion through a crank or gears. Then, the wheels of the "Industrial Revolution" in Europe and America began to turn. This led, for example, to the locomotive in 1804 and the steamboat driving a paddlewheel, around the same time. Later, it would be a steam engine turning a screw propeller on steamships.

When Verne wrote *Around the World in Eighty Days*, in

1872, steam-driven locomotives could travel 80 mph, and steamships were already sounding the death knell for sail-powered vessels. The telegraph was already connecting distant cities in Europe and America; the telephone would be invented four years later. The locomotive, steamship, and telegraph figure prominently in this novel. This was a time when people were leaving their farms to find work in factories in crowded cities.

If *Around the World in Eighty Days* celebrates the present —in this case, the nineteenth century—Verne, the most popular French author, also anticipated, even provided the blueprints for, the machines of the twentieth century. He is considered the "man who invented the future"—the father of science fiction. Verne's book *Twenty Thousand Leagues Under the Sea*, written in 1869, inspired Simon Lake, an American, who went on to invent the submarine twenty-eight years later, says Franz Born, a Verne biographer.[1]

Other Verne literary inventions, most of them described before the turn of the century, include the atomic bomb, television, moving pictures with sound, a flight to the moon, which departs from Florida, air-conditioning, Aqua-lung, helicopter, and synthetic materials.

Verne's books also influenced generations of adventurers, which in France, in particular, still strikes a resonant chord. His book *The Adventures of Captain Hatteras* is said to have inspired American Captain Robert S. Peary to conquer the North Pole, the earth's mathematical top, in 1909. It also provoked the famous race between Roald Amundsen, a Norwegian, and Robert Falcon Scott, an Englishman, to conquer the South Pole, the earth's mathematical bot-

---

[1] The submarine actually dates back to 1620. Simon Lake's contribution was to combine the internal-combustion engine for surface operation with battery power for underwater operation. The fundamental Lake design, which also included a floodable superstructure, an airlock, and a periscope, continued for fifty years.

tom. The Norwegian, incidentally, won the race, on December 14, 1911, by a thin month. Captain Scott and his four-man team never made it back to their base camp. Their frozen bodies were found but eleven miles from a food and fuel cache that certainly would have saved their lives.

As a ten-year-old, Richard Evelyn Byrd read and reread Verne's *Twenty Thousand Leagues Under the Sea*. He was particularly fascinated by the chapter where Captain Nemo reaches the South Pole. He would fly over both the North and South poles—being the first one to do that—and lead four other American expeditions to Antarctica. In 1934, he spent five months alone near the South Pole in the long winter's night. This sojourn is described in his book *Alone*. He nearly died of carbon-monoxide poisoning, and the effects of this awful gas never fully left him.

Admiral Byrd has been called the "Last Explorer." He pioneered naval aviation and extended the territorial claims of America to Antarctica. He helped to fill in the blanks of the map in the polar regions and advanced the science of meteorology and the art of survival.

My second cousins Harry, Leverett, Ames, and Dickie Byrd are grandchildren of Admiral Byrd. They are older than me and a spirited bunch. They taught me about women—we called them "girls" then—beer, sharp knives, and smoking corn silk in corncob pipes. I don't know what, if anything, that makes Admiral Byrd to me, but I like to think of him as my distant relative.

Men like Byrd, Amundsen, Scott, and Peary, as well as those who climb mountains, go rocketing into space, or circle the globe in wind-powered vessels, are also proof of how life sustaining—how consuming—adventuring can become. These men did it, I'm sure, because they loved doing it, even if they never said it so plainly.

*Around the World in Eighty Days*—the most successful

novel of the nineteenth century—traces the peripatetic adventures of Phileas Fogg, a most proper Englishman, and Jean Passepartout, his newly hired French servant, as they circle the earth in 80 days.

For Verne, the inspiration for this tale was a Thomas Cook and Son prospectus that he chanced to see at the travel agency on the Boulevard des Italiens in Paris. It promised an around-the-world voyage in 90 days. The basis for this was the completion of the Union Pacific Railroad, 3,300 miles across America, in 1869, and the completion of the Suez Canal that year. Verne thought he could reduce that voyage in his mind's eye to 80 days. The result is an action-packed 80 days. Had Verne only stuck to the original script, sailing "Around the World in 90 Days" would have been a far easier goal to attain.

Thomas Cook organized such an around-the-world tour in 1872, when Verne's novel *Around the World in Eighty Days* was being serialized in a Paris newspaper. It took him and his party 220 days.

Practically each chapter of Verne's novel begins with the words *dans lequel*—which translates to "in which"—a device used in this book too.

The world has grown "smaller," maintained Phileas Fogg, a man of most regular habits, to his whist partners at the stuffy Reform Club in London's Pall Mall district. In 1872, regularly scheduled steamships and rail service across India and America had made it possible, averred Fogg, to round the world in exactly 80 days, or "in nineteen hundred and twenty hours, or a hundred and fifteen thousand two hundred minutes." Fogg wagered £ 20,000—half his fortune—that such a journey was possible.

" 'Twenty thousand pounds!' cried Sullivan. 'Twenty thousand pounds, which you would lose by a single accidental delay!'

" 'The unforeseen does not exist,' " quietly replied Phileas Fogg. Of course, the unforeseen does exist, and that makes Verne's adventure in time and travel so compelling even 121 years later.

Fogg and Passepartout—pronounced Pass-par-TWO—traveled by trains, steamships, elephant, yacht, and iceboat as they journeyed from England, France, Italy, through the Suez Canal, the Red Sea, the Arabian Sea, across India, Singapore, Hong Kong, Shanghai, Japan, across the Pacific Ocean to San Francisco, Chicago, New York, across the Atlantic to Ireland and then England, and back to London where they had begun.

They stopped a suttee, a human sacrifice, in India, and as a result the wooden, lifeless, and apparently chaste Fogg found love: the fair Aouda—the widow about to be burned at the funeral pyre; nearly fought a duel with a rude American politician in San Francisco; fought Indians in Nebraska; and almost always managed to escape the clutches of a detective who was certain Fogg was responsible for a £ 55,000 heist at the Bank of England. All of this was played out under the inexorable tick-tock of the clock.

The book was first serialized in the French newspaper *Temps*, for which Verne was paid a fabulous sum. Beyond France, Verne's tale captured the world's imagination. For example, foreign correspondents would keep their newspaper readers in New York and San Francisco apprised of Fogg and Passepartout's progress with summaries.

The popular edition of the novel sold 110,000 copies in France and the illustrated version 300,000 more. Eventually it was translated into English and continues in print to this day. A successful play was made of the book, and an Oscar-winning "Best Picture," starring David Niven as Phileas Fogg and Cantinflas as Passepartout, was made in 1956.

\* \* \*

Like Fogg, I believe the world is getting smaller too. I returned to my cousin Dickie Saltonstall's apartment in rural Waldoboro, Maine, one night in October 1992, where I was on an extended visit, to find the fax machine spitting out a message for me from Paris from Bruno Peyron. He'd found me.

Like a good penny, Bruno keeps turning up in my life, tempting me with unlikely sailing adventures. This isn't difficult to do, as my attachment to the straight-and-narrow life is loose at best. Bruno and I had talked about this pursuit of Phileas Fogg in a large multihull during the previous summer. He had 50 percent of the budget. "Call me when you get what you need," I said.

An absolute master at doing large deeds with little money, he faxed me when he had reached that goal. Or so he said. In fact, we'd sail off the edge of the earth three months later with no financial safety net: Bruno impossibly in debt. This forced him to dial for dollars or francs by ship-to-shore radio in the Southern Ocean. Talk about your "cold call."

If getting rich doesn't count, Bruno Peyron has accomplished much in his thirty-seven years. He has sailed across the Atlantic twenty-nine times—eleven times were solo. Until 1994, he held the single-handed west-to-east record of this ocean crossing: 9 days, 19 hours, and 22 minutes. *Seahorse* magazine, in England, described him as the "best big-cat[amaran] sailor on the planet—period."

An adventurous lot are these Peyrons: Bruno's younger brother Loïck won the 1992 Europe 1 Star and the 1987 La Baule–Dakar Race. When Bruno was twelve, he and Loïck would sail all winter in France, training in small Olympic dinghies. They'd pee on their hands to get them warm enough to work. Bruno's father, Hervé, skippered the 554,000-ton supertanker *Bellamya*, and another brother, Stéphane, windsurfed alone across the Atlantic Ocean in

*Liberté de Timex* in 1987. For the uninitiated, that means Stéphane stood up and held up—without the benefit of rigging—a 60-square-foot sail 3,300 miles across the ocean. This is the sailing equivalent of walking on water—walking across an ocean. He's windsurfed around the magnetic north pole near the top of the world, and around Cape Horn near the bottom.

In sailing, count the hulls. It is as true a read—a Rorschach test—into the hearts and minds as are messages on T-shirts. Sailboats come in one-hulled "monohulls" and "multihulls," which can be divided into two-hulled "catamarans" and three-hulled "trimarans." When it comes to monohulls and multihulls, rarely the twain do meet.

To the yachting establishment, multihulls are a "third world"—or biker boats for speed freaks. That has been true since 1876, when the legendary American yacht designer Nat Herreshoff, who would go on to pen five winning America's Cup monohulls, crashed the supposedly "open" Centennial Regatta of the New York Yacht Club with a spidery 30-foot catamaran. Despite two victories that day over the ninety-boat fleet, Herreshoff's *Amaryllis* was disqualified for a lack of accommodations, meaning a toilet. There have been precious few accommodations between the two worlds since. Forced to play alone, *Amaryllis,* later that summer, challenged and beat the steamer *Richard Borden,* the fastest boat on Narragansett Bay in Rhode Island.

Large multihull racing and high-speed adventuring are primarily a French phenomenon. Multihull sailing tends to be much, much faster, but much closer to the edge than monohull sailing. As Dick Newick, a multihull designer from America, once said, *"Macho* should have been a French word."

The list of those who have lost their lives in such high-strung crafts is sobering. For example, Loïc Caradec, a Frenchman, was lost off the 85-foot *Royale,* in the 1986 singlehanded 3,700-mile Route du Rhum race, from Saint Malo, on France's northern coast, to Pointe-à-Pitre, Guadeloupe—roughly the reverse course of the rum trade. Daniel Gilard, also a Frenchman, was lost off *Jet Services V*, in the 1987 La Baule–Dakar Race. Olivier Moussy, a Frenchman, was lost off *Laiteries Mont Saint-Michel* in the 1988 Quebec–Saint Malo Race. Rob James, an Englishman, was lost off a trimaran, *Red Star, Night Star*, in Salcomb, England. Alain Colas, a Frenchman, was lost in 1978, off *Manureva*, in the Route du Rhum Race. In that same 69-foot trimaran in 1973–74, Colas had sailed alone around the world in 169 days, to set a record. Jean Castenet, a Frenchman, was lost off *Jet Services IV*, an 85-foot catamaran, in 1986. Mike Mc-Mullen, a former Royal Marine commando, disappeared on a Dick Newick–designed trimaran, *Three Cheers*, in the 1976 Observer Singlehanded Transatlantic Race (OSTAR). Yacht designer Arthur Piver, sailing on a qualification run for the OSTAR in 1968, disappeared off the coast of California in *Nimble One*, a 25-foot trimaran of his design.

Eric Tabarly, a Frenchman and the first star of this world, told journalist Jon Bowermaster, in an article in *Outside* magazine, "The French love somebody who does something unusual. These are not golfers. They risk their lives; they go out there and do something that is the most dangerous sport. When they go off into the Southern Ocean, there is no one on the sidelines who can help them, no helicopter that can save them. If they go over, they're dead."

Americans, by way of contrast, seem to prefer their sailing in monohulls. Also, they prefer doing it in boats kept upright with lead keels, rather than exaggerated beam—the multihull solution. A lead keel represents a brute-force solution to the problem of the weight of the wind in sails. It is in some ways very American, like Manifest Destiny. A monohull with a keel is slower and safer than a multihull.

As the weight and expense of something go hand-in-hand, a boat with a lead keel is also more expensive.

My monohull accomplishments are respectable—I'd won two 505 World Championships and two Finn Gold Cups (world championships). The Finn is an Olympic single-handed boat. Wrote A. C. Pye, about the joys of Finn sailing: "The aim of the Finn designer [Rickard Sarby] was to produce a boat that would torture its helmsman to the limit of human endurance while at the same time testing his self-control to the utmost with unusual profusions of unusual gear."

I'd won the Finn world championship in 1979 in Weymouth, England, and in 1980 in Auckland—the latter year coincided with the Olympics. I was well positioned for an Olympic run, but after the Soviets invaded Afghanistan, President Carter canceled America's participation in the 1980 Games. While I understood the politics, most athletes are like flowers—annual flowers. They don't stay in bloom for the four years between Olympics. That opportunity taken away from me has to be one of the most profound disappointments of my life.

After 1980, it was time for a change. I've long been attracted to racing large, powerful, and lightning-quick multihulls. I'd raced in France in the Formula 40 Championship with Randy Smyth, also an American, which we won. Talk about your "Americans in Paris"—so incongruous was this victory that it attracted considerable attention in France. I'd raced with Bruno Peyron before in the oversized multihulls that he prefers. I'd done parts of two Round Europe Races with him in 1987 and 1989. In 1987, we finished second in the two-handed 3,200-mile La Baule–Dakar Race. The winner, as noted, was Bruno's brother Loïck by 34 minutes.

As a result of this multihull exposure, rare for an American, I'd raced in the America's Cup of 1988, with Dennis

Conner on his catamaran *Stars & Stripes 88*, which easily bested a 130-foot monohull, *New Zealand*, fielded by Michael Fay, a combative Kiwi. That was as bitter an America's Cup as there probably ever was, with the battle lines being drawn over the monohull-multihull issue. It was in ever higher courts in New York for two years.

After that, I sailed for a time in Bill Koch's afterguard in the 1992 America's Cup. It was Koch, without me, however, who went on to defend the 1992 America's Cup, against a challenger from Italy. After Koch and I went our "respective ways"—I was fired—I stayed in San Diego to get my airplane pilot's license.

The morning after Bruno's fax found me, I phoned him. He had, he told me, purchased the 75-foot catamaran *Jet Services V*. This boat owned the transatlantic record of 6 days, 13 hours, and 3 minutes and was, until proven different, the fastest wind-powered vessel in the world. To make it even faster, Bruno planned to lengthen it by almost 11 feet.

While the invitation to chase the record as a watch captain wasn't a surprise, my specific duty was—to cook for Bruno and his French crew. "You do remember I'm an American?" I asked. "Okay, I promise no strawberry pasta." I'd made that for him in the La Baule–Dakar Race, when I mistook the frozen strawberries for the marinara sauce. While I'm a fearless cook, I'm uneven.

Later, the French press would enjoy the fact that an American, nurtured on cheeseburgers and French fries—at least in their minds—was cooking for four Frenchmen, with their supposedly sophisticated palates.

Then, too, I don't speak much French. The most I can manage is a little sailing French and enough of a vocabulary to order *le cheeseburgeur et pommes frites* in better French restaurants. "I'll see you soon," I promised. *"Au revoir."*

# "In which a conversation takes place which seems likely to cost Phileas Fogg dear"

---

Jean Passepartout went to work for Phileas Fogg on October 2, 1872. This was the day his predecessor, James Forster, was fired. He was dismissed, "because that luckless youth had brought [Fogg] shaving-water at eighty-four degrees Fahrenheit instead of eighty-six."

Passepartout was hoping for a more tranquil life, courtesy of a settled master. Behind the Frenchman was a checkered past. As he told Fogg during his interview: " 'I have a natural aptness for going out of one business into another. . . . I've had several trades. I've been an itinerant singer, a circus-rider, when I used to vault like Léotard, and dance on a rope . . . [1] Then I got to be a professor of gymnastics, so as to make better use of my talents; and then I was a sergeant fireman at Paris, and assisted at many a

---

[1] Jules Léotard was a French gymnast who invented the flying trapeze. In 1859 at the Cirque d'Hiver, he first wore a leotard, or one-piece garment, still worn by dancers and female athletes today.

big fire. But I quitted France five years ago, and, wishing to taste the sweets of domestic life, took service as a valet here in England. Finding myself out of place, and hearing that Monsieur Phileas Fogg was the most exact and settled gentleman in the United Kingdom, I have come to monsieur in hope of living with him a tranquil life.' "

In many ways, his timing was unfortunate, however. For a final question, Fogg asked, What time is it? " 'Twenty-two minutes after eleven,' " said Passepartout, after drawing an enormous silver watch from the depths of his pocket. It is a substantial watch, particularly for a domestic servant, showing that Passepartout, like Fogg, is a man who takes time very seriously.

" 'You are too slow,' said Mr. Fogg.

" 'Pardon me, monsieur, it is impossible—'

" 'You are four minutes too slow. No matter; it's enough to mention the error. Now from this moment, twenty-nine minutes after eleven, A.M., this Wednesday, October second, you are in my service.' " (Unless it took Fogg three minutes to make that utterance, he, too, is in error. "It's enough to mention the error.")

That settled, Fogg passed out the door and walked off to his newspapers and whist game at the Reform Club, as was his daily custom. According to his schedule, posted over a clock in his mansion in Saville Row, which Passepartout noted immediately, he would not return until midnight.

A punctilious man, Fogg "put his right foot before his left five hundred and seventy-five times and his left foot before his right five hundred and seventy-six times" to get there. Knowing the precise walking distance between places was a favorite exercise of Verne's father.

The robbery at the Bank of England, which had occurred three days before, was a major topic of discussion this day among Reform Club members. Fogg, a voracious reader of newspapers, looked up from one and contributed the fact that " 'the *Daily Telegraph* says that [the robber] is a gentleman.' "

Gauthier Ralph, a director of the Bank of England and a whist

partner of Fogg's, voiced confidence that the robber would be
" 'apprehended and the money returned.' " Learned in the course
of their conversation was that "picked detectives hastened off to
Liverpool, Glasgow, Havre, Suez, Brindisi, New York, and other
ports, inspired by the proffered reward of two thousand pounds,
and five percent on the sum that might be recovered."

As the game of whist began, Fogg's clique discussed where in
the world a gentlemanly appearing robber, now £55,000 richer,
might hide. Andrew Stuart, an engineer, said, " 'The world is big
enough.'

" 'It was once,' " Fogg disagreed. As proof of the diminishing
size of the world, the whist players turned to a story published in
that day's *Daily Telegraph*. The article listed this itinerary, for a
voyage around the world in 80 days:

- From London to Suez via Mont Cenis and Brindisi
  (Italy), by rail and steamboats:                         7 days

- From Suez to Bombay (India), by steamer:                 13 days

- From Bombay to Calcutta, by rail:                        3 days

- From Calcutta to Hong Kong, by steamer:                  13 days

- From Hong Kong to Yokohama (Japan), by steamer:          6 days

- From Yokohama to San Francisco, by steamer:              22 days

- From San Francisco to New York, by rail:                 7 days

- From New York to London, by steamer and rail:            9 days

TOTAL                                                      80 days

Fogg's overweening confidence that an 80-day voyage around
the world was possible became annoying to Stuart, who finally

made him a wager that it couldn't be done. Stuart's original wager of £4,000 was topped, in one fell swoop, by Fogg to £ 20,000.

One of his whist partners pointed out to Fogg: " 'But, in order not to exceed [80 days], you must jump mathematically from the trains upon the steamers, and from the steamers upon the trains again.' "

Fogg said, " 'I will jump—mathematically.'

" 'You are joking,' " said an astounded Stuart.

" 'A true Englishman doesn't joke when he is talking about so serious a thing as a wager,' " said Fogg.

Fogg told his whist partners, who had joined in the bet against him, that he'd be off that very night. " 'As today is Wednesday, the second of October, I shall be due in London, in this very room of the Reform Club, on Saturday, the twenty-first of December, at a quarter before nine P.M.; or else the twenty thousand pounds, now deposited in my name at Baring's, will belong to you, in fact and in right, gentlemen.[2] Here is a check for the amount.' "

The "tranquil life" the world-weary Passepartout coveted would only last eight hours and one minute, because at half past seven that evening, Fogg returned early, contrary to the schedule, and announced, " ' We start for Dover and Calais [France], in ten minutes. . . . We are going round the world.'

"Passepartout opened wide his eyes, raised his eyebrows, held up his hands, and seemed about to collapse, so overcome was he with stupefied astonishment.

" 'Round the world!' he murmured.

" 'In eighty days,' " responded Mr. Fogg. " 'So we haven't a moment to lose.'

[2] This is more correctly Barings, Britain's oldest investment bank, which would fail 123 years later in February 1995 because of derivative positions allegedly taken by a twenty-eight-year-old investor in its Singapore office. In business for 233 years, Barings had financed the Napoleonic Wars and America's purchase of the Louisiana Territory.

" 'But the trunks?' gasped Passepartout, unconsciously swaying his head from right to left.

" 'We'll have no trunks; only a carpet-bag, with two shirts and three pairs of stockings for me, and the same for you. We'll buy our clothes on the way. Bring down my mackintosh and travelling-cloak, and some stout shoes, though we shall do little walking. Make haste!' "

Fogg and Passepartout headed to Charing Cross Station in London, where Fogg purchased two first-class tickets for Paris. Fogg had time, however, to give his day's whist winnings of twenty guineas to a poor and unwashed beggar woman, barefoot with a child in her arms. This gesture touched Passepartout's "susceptible heart."

Before boarding the train for Dover, Fogg was greeted by his five cronies from the Reform Club. " 'Well, gentlemen, I'm off, you see; and, if you will examine my passport when I get back, you will be able to judge whether I have accomplished the journey agreed upon.' " His friends assured him that wouldn't be necessary. They trusted his word as a gentleman.

Once aboard, Passepartout uttered a cry of despair. Asked by his master what the matter was, he said, " 'Alas! In my hurry—I—I forgot . . . to turn off the gas in my room.'

" 'Very well, young man,' returned Mr. Fogg, coolly; 'it will burn—at your expense.' " We learn later that the gas would cost more per day than Passepartout made.

# In which my father,
# for the first time
# in my life, tells me,
# "Be careful"

One hundred and twenty years later, in November 1992, my departure for France to join Bruno Peyron and to chase the fictitious record of Phileas Fogg and Jean Passepartout was not so immediate or so dramatic. But that's an advantage fiction has over fact, or maybe it's the other way around.

I was personally adrift at this point. During the week, I was living in my cousin Dickie Saltonstall's apartment, in Maine, building a DN iceboat in his barn, and looking to buy a small house and some land. As a professional sailor, who was unmarried and often traveling, I didn't require much, just a place that I could come home to that was mine. A place to which I had a greater attachment than a lease. A mortgage, for example.

I was also looking forward to enjoying a real winter in Maine: iceboating, skiing on natural snow, and skating outdoors. Winter was something that the southern coast of

New England, where I lived, had been lacking for years and something that I missed.

I still maintained an apartment in Newport, Rhode Island, a town with which I was growing disenchanted. A sailors' town was well on its way to becoming a party-hearty town, a place for yahoos in Top-Siders. However, my girlfriend, Molly Fitch, lived there, with whom I wasn't disenchanted. While Molly knew of my vague plans to sail around the world, I hadn't told her that a fax from Bruno had found me, and I was off to see the world.

On our return trip from Maine to Newport, she grew suspicious when I stopped at R.E.I., a backpacking and camping store—off Route 128, which skirts Boston—to buy waterproof duffel bags, waterproof flashlights, and Gore-Tex socks, not fashionable in Newport or even rural Maine. "They'll make for happy feet," I told her.

"You're going, aren't you?" she asked. It was a question, more than an accusation. Molly knows I have restless feet, but that doesn't mean she's always comfortable with my penchant for adventuring. She knows the perils.

Sailing around the world involves risks, and sailing around the world in a fragile, if fast, multihull compounds those risks. It is analogous to driving a Corvette or Ferrari automobile in the Mexican 1000 or Paris–Dakar Race, which are primarily off-road events. If you can keep such hybrid sports cars together, if you can keep them from getting stuck in the muck, if you can keep them from beating the drivers to death, you certainly have the horsepower to win. Those are huge ifs, however.

There are many reasons why a multihull is more delicate than a monohull. The simplest way to make something strong is to make it heavy. Overbuild it. However, the quickest way to cripple a multihull is to make it heavy. Therefore, fittings holding up the mast, the mast itself, sails, dagger boards, and the rudders tend to be made of light but strong high-tech composites—as delineated by Verne—which too often fail in the harsh test of the sea. It's a vicious circle: to go fast, you have to go light, but when you go light, things break. At the very least, breaking something can slow you down, even stop you. At the most, it can kill you.

Then, too, since the theme of ocean-girding multihulls is speed, speed-producing factors, such as mast height, sail area, and the depths of the dagger boards and rudders, are exaggerated. Our carbon-fiber mast, for example, was 102 feet off the deck; 110 feet off the water. Further complicating matters, it was designed to rotate at its base to present a cleaner leading edge to the angle of the wind. When numbers get pushed in boat design—particularly when played against the imperative of keeping things light—and when systems get complicated, things break.

Further, while multihulls have good initial resistance to heeling through their exaggerated beam, they don't have good ultimate resistance. (At 45 feet wide and 86 feet long, the boat we would be sailing on was more than half as wide as it was long.) At some mysterious point, some combination of wind speed and sail area, such boats will tip over. It is very hard for sailors to know precisely where that point is, however.

Always in the back of your mind is the cardinal question: Are you pushing the boat too hard? Should a multihull of this size tip over, there is nothing sailors can do to right it, save to wait for help. Depending on where in the world you are, help can come quickly, not so quickly, or not at all. Being prone to capsizing, these boats have escape hatches on the inside of either hull, allowing sailors trapped belowdecks to escape to fresh air.

Also, at 30 knots (34 mph), well within the range of these boats, you travel 50 feet per second or 2,992 feet per minute. Fall off the boat, and if the impact doesn't kill you or your clothes don't sink you, those aboard might be able to turn it around to come back for you in two minutes. That is assuming anyone saw you fall overboard and that there are sufficient people on deck to turn the boat. By that time, you're more than a mile away: a very small target bobbing in a very vast ocean. The chances of anyone ever finding you are not good.

Commodore Explorer, the multihull we would use in our around-the-world attempt, was the former Jet Services V. She had set the transatlantic record of 6 days, 13 hours, and 3 minutes, in 1990, as described. That is an average speed of 19.48 knots. Before this, Daniel Gilard, her skipper, had fallen overboard in the 1987 La Baule–Dakar Race and was lost at sea. While I don't believe in ghosts, I would think of him now and then. I felt connected to him because I was sailing on his boat, of course, and because I had sailed with Bruno Peyron in the race in which he was lost.

I'd think of Mike Plant too. November 1992 was an inauspicious time to be leaving Newport for a circumnavigation in a multihull. That month the town was saddened by the loss at sea of Mike Plant, America's premier single-handed distance racer. Plant, who had lived across the Newport Bridge in Jamestown, was lost while soloing his boat, Coyote, to France, for the start of the Vendée Globe Challenge, a nonstop solo race around the world. I only knew Plant well enough to say, "How are you doing?" when I saw him around town. Once or twice I visited him on his boat, a 60-foot monohull. As I understand it, the 8,400-pound lead keel separated from the hull, and the boat tipped over. Eventually, Coyote would be found upside down 700 miles southwest of Ireland. On November 25, the boat would be boarded, but there was no sign of Plant.

Just before leaving, Molly and I went into the Candy Store, a fashionable Newport restaurant. We overheard people and some acquaintances whispering about my impending voyage. The gist was that I must have a death wish. I felt like tainted meat in a butcher shop. Small talk by small people, I tried to reassure her.

I don't believe I've ever had a death wish; if anything, it is a life wish. I have a substantial appetite for life. I've always enjoyed sailing, competing, adventuring, and getting to know new people. More than a few have said I've enjoyed those things too much. An article by Christian Février in *Multihulls* magazine described me as "Mr. 200,000 Volts." Then this distinguished French journalist went on to say, "He is an easygoing but fast-speaking guy full of real '*joie de vivre*,' full of good fellowship, great helmsmanship skills on these delicate flying machines, is a cook and also a poet." I like that.

A quote I treasure is from Paul Elvstrøm, the greatest sailor of all time and my hero. Elvstrøm, from Denmark and naturally called the "great Dane," won four Olympic gold medals—a record unequaled in sailing. By any measure, he is the giant of this sport. Said Elvstrøm in *Sail* magazine, "If there is someone who does not sail fair, I go off. Sailboat racing is an attempt at perfect seamanship. You keep to the rules, or the enjoyment is gone.

"It is possible to sail very provocatively, to edge a fellow competitor into breaking a rule. You can almost induce a collision if you want to. But what is the use of winning if you don't have a friend or two left to share the pleasure with?

"I remember a celebrity race at Yale University. We sailed in 420's, and Cam Lewis and I fought over the last two places. He's the kind of fellow who keeps a sense of proportion and enjoys his sailing. So you enjoy sailing against him."

I have been blessed with abundant energy, some size and strength, an elemental need for speed, and a desire to see the world and to meet its people. The "tranquil life," which Jean Passepartout longed for in Verne's novel, holds little attraction for me. Movement near the edge—be it high-speed sailboat racing, windsurfing, skiing from helicopters, mountain-biking, iceboating, flying, scuba diving, in-line skating, or adventuring—is what brings joy to my life. While I test the edge, I've almost never really gone over it.

I grew up in Sherborn, Massachusetts, which is about twenty miles west of Boston. My father's mother, my grandmother, was a Saltonstall, a name long prominent in Massachusetts politics and business. Leverett Saltonstall, my great-uncle, was the governor of Massachusetts, from 1938 to 1944—the longest term in Massachusetts in ninety years. Being governor of Massachusetts was practically the family business, as eight other forebears held that position. Leverett Saltonstall later served in the U.S. Senate, from 1944 to 1967, and was the Republican whip in the Senate. Leverett's daughter Emily married Richard E. Byrd, Jr., the son and namesake of the polar explorer.

We all lived near one another, in what amounted to an extended family estate. My great-uncle Leverett had a large farm. He raised his own meat and grew his own vegetables, which he would take with him to Washington, simply because he preferred to eat what he had raised or grown. I remember parties across the river at his farm. At cocktail time, all the children would be expected to disappear. Later, there would be singing around the piano for all ages.

Leverett, his brother, my great-uncle Richard, or my grandmother would host an annual Christmas party. A highlight was an evening excursion on this large wood-hauling sled, called a "pung." Two huge workhorses pulled it. We'd gather on the straw under blankets. Sometimes, it would snow. A rope off the back of the pung would pull skiers along, at the slow pace of the draft horses. It was the winter equivalent of waterskiing. Like a Currier & Ives engraving, it was all completely magical. The brothers Saltonstall had a 60-foot sailboat, an Alden cutter called *Fish Hawk*. Eventually, my father and I took her over.

My father, George, is an investment counselor. He started the company when he got out of the army in 1955. My mother, Laura, was a true southern belle. My father and mother met at the University of Virginia, where she was what was termed a "faculty brat." She was one of twenty-five females in a college of five thousand. Her father was coach of the boxing team and assistant athletic director.

My mother's maiden name was Laura Lewis Carruthers, meaning there are Lewises on both sides of the family. An article in *The Commonwealth*, the magazine of Virginia, written by Dr. Freeman H. Hart, a professor at the University of Florida, describes her family as "Those Fighting Lewises of Frontier Virginia." They were famous Indian fighters, warriors, and explorers. Perhaps it is from my mother's side of the family that I get my energy and wanderlust.

The Charles River, which meanders through Boston before emptying into the Atlantic, was in our front yard. This river, with its "dirty water," made famous in the song, is to Boston what the Seine is to Paris or the Hudson and East River are to New York. Across the street was a spring-fed pond. It was clean, and there were always sailboats and rowboats on which to play. Beyond that, we'd swim there in the summer and skate there in the winter. When my mother and father got divorced, she moved to a house on the pond. For me, it was faster to walk cross-country to her house than to go by road.

There were ponies and horses to ride too. I'd come home from school and hop on my pony, without a saddle or bridle, like an Indian, and ride off if not into the sunset then until sunset. If I wanted to climb a 200-foot tree, I'd climb one. Most often, I'd go sailing. I taught myself to windsurf in the winter, when one day the ice disappeared from the pond. I did it without the benefit of a wetsuit. I don't remember ever being told, "Be careful," or "Don't!" as I learned about myself by testing the edge. My father, in fact, seemed to encourage my adventurous spirit. Safety first! was not a motto we lived by.

I have two sisters, Lisa and Lynnie, and an older brother. My brother, George, fourteen months my senior, was the type of kid who was reading *The Wall Street Journal* when he was in the sixth grade. I have no interest in the financial world, which is the working world of my father. Rather, I've always had a propensity for playing near the water. My father thought my love of the sea and sailing was just fine. He's always enjoyed sailing on weekends and vacations and has taken an interest in my sailing too. He encouraged me to travel and to see the world. Doubtless, these are things he would have liked to do more of himself.

While nothing special as a student, I was the type of kid who devoured maps. I'd stare at them from my bird's-eye view and wonder what the people and land are like in other countries. What do they do? How do they live? While started on the principle of diversity, America has become homogenous. We watch the same television shows, read the same newspapers, listen to the same music, read the same books, and eat at the same places. America has become an endless strip mall of the same restaurants and the same stores. Variety no longer seems to be the spice of life.

Not content to do this to our own country, we merrily export our culture to other countries in a form of cultural imperialism. The French in particular seem unwilling to embrace America. And Americans. As an American, this

promised to make my voyage around the world with four
Frenchmen most interesting.

Sailing is what I do for a living. Sailing as a career is
what tennis was before the Open era. Uneven. At times,
such as during an America's Cup or maxi-boat racing, you
make great money; other times, it's slim pickings. You can
keep your head above water—barely—by writing articles
for magazines and doing similar things. From my father's
perspective, what I do is perfectly acceptable. Perhaps because my father has made a great deal of money, he recog-
nizes that there are other measures—yardsticks—in life
besides the amount of money one makes. I like to tell him
I'm waiting to take over the family business: be the governor of Massachusetts or else an explorer.

Besides Admiral Byrd on my father's side of the family,
who I would say I am "loosely" related to, my mother's
forebears include Andrew Lewis, who explored what is
now West Virginia. This exploration and the subsequent
Indian battles he fought there expanded America's territorial claims to the Mississippi River instead of the Appala-
chian Mountains.

Troops he led won two important battles just before the
American Revolutionary War: the Battle of Point Pleasant
and the defeat of Lord Dunmore, the last colonial governor
of Virginia, at Gwynn's Island in the Chesapeake. Andrew
Lewis was named a brigadier general by the Continental
Congress in 1775. He was even considered for the rank of
commander-in-chief; that title, however, went to General
George Washington. Indeed, Andrew Lewis was Washington's choice; however, Washington was too modest, it was
said, to name himself.

My father always had sailboats when I was growing up,
and I'd race with him whenever I could. He was good
enough at it that he once finished third or fourth in the
Olympic trials in the 5.5 class.

In boarding school, my sport was rowing. However, I tried to join my father whenever I could for Saturday sailboat racing in the spring and fall. This wasn't easy at Middlesex School, in Concord, Massachusetts, because there were classes on Saturday mornings. For me, Saturdays meant math and French, not racing with my father.

I learned to loathe those subjects, which eventually brought me to the attention of the school psychologist. He wondered aloud if I was dyslexic, which might explain my academic difficulties. If I was, I might be excused from these subjects, he told me. He suggested that I be tested in Boston. I didn't know what dyslexia was, but I looked it up and realized it had something to do with the transposition of letters. When I was tested at Harvard, I knew enough to fail the test. Thus, I was free to race with my father. Knowing what I know today, I wish I'd stuck with French. A little more math wouldn't have hurt either.

In my senior year, I was suspended from Middlesex, the day after the night I turned eighteen, for drinking. Eighteen was the legal drinking age in Massachusetts at the time, and a number of us walked two miles down the road to the Colonial Inn, to celebrate my coming of age. Later, I fell asleep in my dorm room with the stereo on. The volume was sufficiently loud to have acted as a birth-control device for adolescents. The master came into my room. A quick study, he rousted me and said, "You're busted!" It had been a rough night, and I asked if we couldn't talk about it in the morning.

My father was a trustee of the school, which, I think, worked against me. They didn't want to appear to be lenient to a trustee's kid. They strongly recommended that I take some time off, do a senior project. I went to work at Hood Sailmakers, then on the harbor in Marblehead, Massachusetts.

After completing high school—eventually—I had no desire to go to college. Butch Dalrymple-Smith, an English-man who was for many years the right-hand man of the noted yacht designer Ron Holland, called and asked me to help him deliver a boat, *Silver Apple,* to Florida from Mas-sachusetts. I did that. Then I returned home for the Christ-mas holidays. While there I bought an oversized red van and tied two Laser sailboats to the top. The van had a big engine, went fast, had a large thirst for gas, and made a lot of noise. It sounds like the description of me in *Multihulls* magazine. In essence, it was the perfect van for me.

In it, my buddy Frank Rosenow, a Swede, and I drove back down to Florida and then sailed the Southern Ocean Racing Conference (SORC), on *Silver Apple.*

When I first met Frank, who has just recently died of cancer, he was a well-known artist, who often contributed to *Sail* magazine. At thirty-six, he was twice my age, but the guy was positively bursting with life—very young at heart. He'd been a wire reporter for the Associated Press and then worked for United Press International in Austra-lia. While there, he started sailing Moths, a small but fairly unruly dinghy. Just the kind of boats I like. He was never at a loss for crazy ideas. Indeed, he was a bigger kid than I was, and I am no slouch in that department.

We worked and raced on *Silver Apple,* and whenever the opportunity presented itself, we'd race our Lasers in Flor-ida. Perhaps the biggest surprise was the realization that I was fast in a Laser, which is a very popular 14-foot single-handed boat. It is like an Olympic Finn dinghy, without, however, an attitude. Like the Finn, it is now an Olympic boat.

The Laser World Championships were in Brazil the next year, and I wanted to go. To do that, you had to qualify. I learned of a qualifying event in Mexico, the grandly named Pan American Championship, and I loaded up the van and drove to this lake west of Mexico City. I had almost no money, and such an innocent was I that everyone was convinced that I was going to disappear off the face of the earth. A friend advised me to buy a machete and—more ominously—learn how to use it.

Differing from Passepartout, my timing was fortuitous. I arrived at the border, and the peso was devalued about 200 percent. I went from being a poor little rich kid to a rich kid pretty quickly. For an instant I thought, the acorn hasn't fallen far from the tree.

I showed up at this lake a couple of weeks early. It was called Valle de Bravo and was described as the little Switzerland of Mexico. And, in truth, it was—a very beautiful place. I drove up to this little club, and no one knew anything about a Laser regatta. While hanging around, I met some Americans and some locals, and by the end of my first week there, I had a house and a housekeeper and more friends than I had back home in Massachusetts. The only rule was you didn't ask anyone what they did for a living. These guys had dirt bikes and endless motorcross trails that we'd ride on, like the Wild Ones.

I'd sail, too, and by the time the regatta started, I knew when and where the wind blew, which is a huge advantage in sailboat racing. It would be a flat calm in the morning, but at 12:15, the wind would come in over the dam and off you'd go. I won the regatta, and after that, my new friends and I drove to Acapulco, where we stayed in a huge house on the water. To play on, there were two Solings—an Olympic keelboat—and a Cal 40, a cruising boat.

The next year, I went to the Laser Worlds in Brazil and finished a credible seventh.

Before leaving for France, to join Bruno Peyron and to meet the crew, I organized the food and the menu. I had only cooked once before on a boat, in the two-handed La Baule–

Dakar Race. That is a two-week sprint as opposed to the 80-day or more marathon upon which we were embarking. You can keep food fresh for two weeks; for three months, you're talking about freeze-dried food. This process sucks all the liquid out of the food and much of the taste.

There was no way this was going to be a Michelin four-star dining experience, as I was limited to a one-burner stove. That's half true, because 40 feet away in the opposite hull was a second one-burner stove.

I talked to friends who had used freeze-dried food on expeditions. I tried the things they recommended. Some of it had food coloring, MSG, and other chemicals. The problem is fat in the food, which turns rancid without the addition of chemicals. Particularly in the southern ocean, you need fat to stay warm. This I learned from reading the books of Roald Amundsen, the great Norwegian explorer who was the first man to stand at the South Pole. Before leaving I read all the books by the famous polar explorers: Amundsen, Captain Robert Falcon Scott, Sir Ernest Shackleton, and Admiral Richard Byrd, my distant relative.

Eventually, I called a friend, Ricky Taubman, who lives in Telluride, Colorado, and who knows about such things as freeze-dried food. It was Taubman, a year and a half later, who was with supermodel Christie Brinkley, when their Jet Ranger helicopter crashed on a helicopter-skiing trip in Colorado. The helicopter belonged to his company. One thing led to another, and eventually, they married, and then separated.

Taubman said, call Alpineaire; here's the president's name. So I called him in Nevada City, California. They sent some samples. It was low-fat and without preservatives, but I figured I could add fat to our diets with powdered oil, which is white and looks like a controlled substance. The Alpineaire food also tasted pretty good.

I'd eat the stuff and make it for friends. Molly, however, turned her nose up at it. Then I'd hop on my mountain bike and take a couple of laps around Newport's Ocean Drive. Next, I'd jump into my in-line skates.

When living in small enclosed spaces, as we would be, "the winds of digestion," as Ben Franklin once put it so well, can ruin a beautiful friendship. To put this another way, I didn't want food that would make us fart. The Alpineaire food proved reasonably palatable and gentle to the digestion.

To please the French tastes, I purchased additional food-stuffs from Quebec and when I arrived in France. I got such things as freeze-dried yogurt, *poisson au fenouil* (fish seasoned with fennel), and *jambon* (ham) and bacon. Then I worked out a twelve-day menu. I figured, between the workload and the cold, we'd need 4,000 calories per man per day. NFL linemen eat, on average, 5,000 calories per day.

Meanwhile Bruno Peyron, the boat's skipper, is telling me, "I just want to eat tuna in a can and plain rice or plain pasta and a little butter."

I had a traditional Thanksgiving dinner with Molly and my family at my father's house in Sherborn. My siblings, Lisa, Lynnie, and George, were there, as were George's wife, Debby, and their son, George junior, and my step-mother, Emmy. While my father tried hard to hide it, he had this look on his face that this was our last supper. No stranger to my world, he knew of Mike Plant, Loïc Caradec, Daniel Gilard, Olivier Moussy, Rob James, Jean Castenet, Mike McMullen, Arthur Piver, and Alain Colas. He was afraid a similar fate awaited me. My father, too, had ghosts.

As Thanksgiving dinner ended, and we said our good-byes, he burst into tears. My father is tall, thin, and ramrod straight—he even wears bow ties. His distinguished forebears all wore bow ties. No one had ever seen him cry before. Less because of my leaving than my father's reaction to it, everyone else started crying too.

As I got in my VW Vanagon camper with Molly to drive to Logan Airport for my departure for France, my father slipped a letter into my pocket before saying good-bye one last time.

We drove to the airport in a light rain. I don't like airports and dramatic good-byes. Molly and I spent some time in the van, where I assured her that everything would be fine. She had some work to do before joining me in France the day after Christmas.

So with "a damp drizzly November in my soul," as Melville once described it, I boarded an airplane in Boston for France. As the plane headed east over the Atlantic, into the late-autumn evening sky, I read the letter from my father. It said:

Bon voyage—you are off on a great voyage and adventure. Your experience with people and boats has brought you a long way, and I hope this round-the-world trip will be more successful than all your past endeavors. There is no place to hide where you are going, so safety first.

The time you have will be consumed by hard work, maximum performance for speed, but with that come risks. Try to balance those things, because finishing the journey is just as important as starting. Your best judgment will be continually challenged.

Your future lies ahead. Use your time constructively to pursue ideas and goals you want to achieve. Write them down. Keep a good diary of your experiences. It should be fascinating and interesting to others.

My fears will be silenced by your return. Godspeed and good luck.

Much love, Dad.

I was thirty-five years old, and for the first time in my life, my father was telling me, "Be careful."

# "In which Fix, the detective, betrays a very natural impatience"

It took Fogg and Passepartout 158½ hours, or six and a half days, to travel east toward the rising sun from London to Suez. It happened this way: By train, they traveled from London to Dover, with its distinctive white cliffs, on the southeast corner of England. It is here that the blind Gloucester intends to commit suicide in Shakespeare's *King Lear*. Gloucester, a parallel character to Lear, plans on throwing himself from the cliff. His son Edgar, who has disguised his voice and thus his identity, has led him there. Edgar pretends they are at the edge. Gloucester jumps, but since he is not at the edge, he survives the "fall." The experience of cheating death changes him: "Henceforth I'll bear affliction till it do cry out itself." That line could serve as an anthem for an adventurer or for anyone who walks near the edge.

By ferry, Fogg and Passepartout crossed the English Channel, some 22 nautical miles to Calais, France.[1] This is the traditional

---

[1] There are errors and ambiguities in some of Verne's distances in the novel. Often it isn't clear if the author is using nautical miles or statute miles. A

route between these two countries, still traversed by millions each year. It is here in the narrow Dover Strait that England and France seem to reach out to one another. Eight thousand years ago, geologists say, the land masses were connected.

A tunnel across the English Channel was first proposed in 1802, much to Napoleon I's amusement. Napoleon was at war with England at the time. England and France actually started building a tunnel in the early 1870s—around the same time as Fogg and Passepartout's fictitious voyage. It was abandoned, however, when the English concluded that there was virtue in keeping Europe at arm's length. They described this separation as "splendid isolation."

England had long been an attractive target for European armies. For example, the island nation was twice invaded by Julius Caesar's Roman legions, beginning in 54 B.C. Caesar built a castle in Dover. The French have tried numerous times to invade England, beginning in 1066 with William the Conqueror. After killing the king, he named himself King William I. King Henry II, in 1153, and King Henry VII, in 1485, followed similar invasion and nearly identical "career" paths. The Spanish Armada tried and failed in 1588. In this century, Hitler tried to invade England in 1940 across the Dover Strait with his Operation Sea Lion. This became known as the Battle of Britain.

In the spring of 1994, as I write this, the "Chunnel," or Channel Tunnel, from Folkstone (near Dover) to Calais, has opened. It cost $15 billion to build.

Fogg and Passepartout traveled by train to Paris and on to Turin, Italy, after passing through the Alps by way of the Mont Cenis Tunnel. This nine-mile-long tunnel, under the Col de

---

nautical mile—sometimes called a "sea mile"— equals 6,080.2 feet, while a statute mile equals the familiar 5,280 feet. There are 60 nautical miles in a degree of latitude, or, to put this another way, one minute of latitude equals one nautical mile, or knot. To convert statute miles to nautical miles divide by 1.15. To convert nautical miles to statute miles multiply by 1.15. See the Appendix for distances in both nautical and statute miles.

Fréjus mountain on the French-Italian border, was the first rail-way-mountain tunnel, built in 1871. Had it not been completed, the fictitious 80-day voyage, begun one year later, would likely not have been possible.

In Brindisi, Italy, on the heel of this boot-shaped country, they boarded the steamer *Mongolia* for Suez and its famous canal. The sea voyage from Italy to Suez is a distance of 925 nautical miles, says the author. Verne describes the *Mongolia* as "one of the fastest steamers belonging to the [Peninsula and Oriental Company], always making ten knots an hour between Brindisi and Suez, and nine and a half between Suez and Bombay."

The hundred-mile-long Suez Canal, connecting the Mediterranean to the Red Sea, was built by Ferdinand de Lesseps, a Frenchman. It shortened the distance from Europe to India, where Fogg and Passepartout would be heading next, by 4,400 miles. French Empress Eugénie, the wife of Napoleon III, opened the canal on November 17, 1869, in the last year of her husband's reign.[2] De Lesseps was hailed as "the greatest Frenchman of his time."

Verne, "the man who invented the future"—an ardent believer in Progress—recognized de Lesseps's contribution to Suez, in particular. He wrote, "This once struggling village now, thanks to the enterprise of M. Lesseps, [is] a fast-growing town."

The date of Fogg and Passepartout's arrival in Suez was October 9, a Wednesday, according to the calendar for the year 1872. According to George Makepeace Towle's original English translation—though not in the original French text—October 9 is a Friday. As Fogg airily said to Passepartout after the servant gave the incorrect time—the crucial question in the job interview—"No matter; it's enough to mention the error."

In Suez, Fogg and Passepartout got their passports visaed, to prove to members of the Reform Club that Fogg had been where he said. At this point, Fogg made a note in his journal that he had

[2] Napoleon III was the nephew of Napoleon I.

neither gained nor lost time but was right on schedule. He would keep this journal meticulously throughout the journey.

There Fogg was espied by Fix, apparently one of the detectives who had been dispatched from England to find the bank robber. "It was his task to narrowly watch every passenger who arrived at Suez, and to follow up all who seemed to be suspicious characters or bore a resemblance to the description of the criminal, which he had received two days before. . . . The detective was evidently inspired by the hope of obtaining the splendid reward which would be the prize of success, and awaited with a feverish impatience, easy to understand, the arrival of the steamer *Mongolia*," writes Verne.

Fogg apparently bore a striking resemblance to the gentlemanly bank robber. Immediately, Fix, who is never given a first name, wired England:

Rowan, Commissioner of Police, Scotland Yard:
I've found the bank robber, Phileas Fogg. Send without delay warrant of arrest to Bombay.

Fix, *Detective.*

# In which after years
# of procrastinating,
# I propose to Molly

Like Fogg and Passepartout, I was traveling east toward the rising sun. I arrived at Charles de Gaulle Airport in Paris early Friday morning, the day after America's Thanksgiving. The flight across the 3,322-mile Atlantic Ocean took six and a half hours for an average speed of 520 mph.

This is a book about an around-the-world voyage in 1872 and one in 1993. One obvious way to compare the world then and now is through transportation. There were no airplanes in Fogg's day. Orville Wright wouldn't fly a self-propelled, heavier-than-air craft, designed by him and his brother, Wilbur, until 1903, at Kitty Hawk, North Carolina.

The first transatlantic flight occurred in May 1919, led by Lieutenant Commander Albert Cushion Read, of the U.S. Navy. The transatlantic leg, from Newfoundland, Canada, to Lisbon, Portugal, took 53 hours and 58 minutes, for an average speed of 87 mph. This included a stop in the

Azores, two thirds of the way across the ocean. U.S. Navy ships were on station along the entire sea route, in case the airplane, an N-C-4, had to make an "unscheduled water landing," as they say these days in the "friendly skies." (If there is a stranger, more disquieting phrase than that, I don't know it.) Also, to increase the odds of success, the Navy used three planes, although only the one flown by Read made it across the ocean.

My distant relative, then Lieutenant Commander Richard Byrd, was a member of the flight team, although he did not make the transatlantic leg. Byrd did, nevertheless, do the first two legs on one of the planes as navigation officer, getting as far east as Newfoundland. The transatlantic flight was, in fact, his idea. Two weeks later, a plane piloted by John Alcock and A. W. Brown, of England, flew from St. John's, Newfoundland, to Clifton, Ireland, in 16 hours.

In 1926, Byrd was the first to fly over the North Pole, which made him a genuine hero in America. After returning, he was awarded the Congressional Medal of Honor. A year later, he was part of an ad-hoc group of aviators involved in what the New York newspapers billed as the "New York-to-Paris Race."

It was never that formal, however. In the spirit of good fellowship, Byrd offered a young airmail pilot, Charles A. Lindbergh, from California, the use of Roosevelt Field, on Long Island, which Byrd had leased for his flight. Byrd improved and lengthened the runway to help in the takeoff of his fuel-laden plane—perhaps the most critical stage of such a flight. Lindbergh took off from Roosevelt Field on May 20, 1927, and arrived nonstop in Paris $33^{1}/_{2}$ hours later. This was an average speed of 108 mph, over the 3,610 miles. Lindbergh became the most distinguished American hero.

Two weeks later, Charles Levine and Clarence Chamberlin left Byrd's Roosevelt Field and reached Germany.

Three weeks later, Byrd made his transatlantic flight. It proved to be a classic example of too little too late. He reached Paris but was unable to land, due to fog, and made an "unscheduled water landing," just off the French coast. He and his three-man crew, who were little the worse for wear, paddled an inflatable to shore. It was late at night, and the only person they could find to help them was a young French boy on a bike. He sped off when the wet and bruised aviators tried to flag him down for directions to someone who might help them. Byrd and his men reached Paris the next day by train.

The Paris I flew into was different from the Paris Fogg and Passepartout might have passed through 120 years before or the Paris Commander Byrd reached 65 years ago. For example, the fastest trains in 1872 traveled a very credible — even shocking— 80 mph. That was almost as fast as the first airplane to fly transatlantic in 1919. The high-speed French Train à Grande Vitesse (TGV) that I boarded at the Montparnasse Station in Paris had a top speed of 200 mph. Land-based transportation can't get much faster than that. Of course, that's probably what they said in 1872.

My destination was le Pouliguen, where Bruno lives in a town house, on the south coast of Brittany. The train passed near Nantes, on the Loire River, where Verne grew up.

After a brief nap at Bruno's, which intensified rather than allayed my jet lag, he hustled me off in a borrowed car to see the boat we'd be using, the former *Jet Services V*. The boat was at the Multiplast Yard, in Vannes, about 60 kilometers (37 miles) away. It was here the boat was born and here it returned to start a new life.

For transportation on land, Bruno prefers a motor scooter or a bicycle. When he needs a car, he borrows one from his friend the local car dealer or a girlfriend. My theory is he doesn't choose a girlfriend unless she has a car.

More to the point, I mention this because all of Bruno's money goes to his boats and projects. While some of the luminaries of this world are apparently rich, like Titouan Lamazou and Florence Arthaud, Bruno isn't. Typically, he has to get financing for the next boat, to pay off the debts on the previous one. It's deficit spending, as practiced by the U.S. government.

I first met Bruno during the summer of 1986, when he raced from France to America in his 75-foot catamaran *Atlantic Liberté*, a boat he and—presumably—the bank still own. He was in America for the centennial celebration of the Statue of Liberty. The statue, a gift of the French people, was given to celebrate America's centennial in 1876. It was an early "hands-across-the-sea" project.

For a hundred years, the Statue of Liberty had welcomed to New York Harbor "your tired, your poor, your huddled masses yearning to breathe free . . ." And it looked it. It was refurbished for 1986—the centennial celebration—and this was its unveiling.

Waiting for the festivities, Bruno was in New York, with his boat tied up to some derelict pier off a street in the Twenties, on the Hudson. I was in New York too. I believe we were introduced by a girlfriend of Bruno's, who ran a fashionable Manhattan nightclub and probably had a car.

When we met, I had already developed an appreciation for the French multihull scene. In 1986, after the 12-Meter Worlds in Perth, Western Australia, where I sailed on *Courageous*, I stopped in Maui to do some windsurfing. There Randy Smyth, an Olympic silver medalist, found me and asked me to sail on a new Formula-40 catamaran that he planned on campaigning in France. We won the series. More important, however, I spent much of that year in France and was dazzled by boats like *Atlantic Liberté*, and the high technology they represented.

One high point of the Statue of Liberty celebration was

the Parade of Sail. That day, the entire week of celebration, for that matter, was likely the finest weather New York has enjoyed in a hundred years. The air was so clear, you could practically break it. Certainly one of the stars of the 22 tall ships and 240 other sailboats in the Parade of Sail was Bruno's futuristic *Atlantic Liberté*, roaring up and down the Hudson River at 20 knots. She seemed like a sailboat on steroids—a serviceable description of this type of craft. I was proud to be part of Bruno's crew this glorious day.

*Atlantic Liberté* sported a 6,000-square-foot spinnaker, featuring Lady Liberty and her flaming orange torch (the symbol of the French-American Committee for the Restoration of the Statue) flying from the top of a 92-foot carbon-fiber winged mast. It was a spectacle witnessed by 40,000 spectator boats, hundreds of thousands on either side of the Hudson River, and 200 million television viewers worldwide.

It was a weekend of unabashed narcissism for America, and Bruno, as an unofficial but highly visible ambassador from France, said to any number of television cameras in his French-accented English, "The boat, like the statue, is a symbol of friendship between our two nations." And he absolutely meant it. There is an innocence and sincerity about Bruno and a love of sailing that is obvious and totally disarming. At least I find it so.

After this, Bruno and his crew brought the boat from New York to Newport, where I lived, and they ended up hanging around. Bruno had this big cat but little else. However, a number of Americans were intrigued by these oversized and overstimulated French multihulls but had never seen one close up, let alone ridden on one. While these boats had been to Newport, such as at the finish of what was formerly called the Observer Singlehanded Transatlantic Race (OSTAR), from Plymouth, England, to Newport, they were—and probably still are—a French phenomenon.

Typically, Americans don't speak French—I'm a perfect example of that—and the French won't speak English. Thus, these boats and this scene are terra incognita to Americans. It is Frenchmen racing other Frenchmen, for the most part. And, as such, fairly parochial.

Bruno was just hanging around, having a good time, giving a lot of people rides. I'd often go with him. Bruno likes Americans; he studied English in school and enjoys speaking it. And Americans like Bruno. I know I was intrigued by Bruno and awestruck by his boat.

Eventually, Bruno and his crew, Denis Horeau, ended up living in my apartment. Soon, Jacques Vincent, who would become Bruno's right-hand man, joined us there too. Jacques would be part of our crew in the around-the-world record attempt.

While Bruno lived in my apartment, he was back and forth to New York, Boston, and Paris looking for money for future adventures and trying to figure out how to pay for the present one. As the French say, *Plus ça change, plus c'est la même chose.*

While living together, Bruno told me a little bit about his life. His lifelong ambition was to build a 30-meter (100-foot) multihull—which would be the fastest boat in the world. To get there, however, he started small.

When he was nineteen in 1977, he designed a boat, for La Mini–Transat Race, but couldn't find sufficient funds to build it. He wished to test the design in a towing tank—an unlikely avenue for a fledgling designer. To afford this, he sold his stereo, guitar, and skateboard.

Thirty days before the start, he had no money and certainly no boat. Not to mention no stereo, guitar, or skateboard. He bought the boat-show issue of a French sailing magazine. Bruno started calling the list of exhibitors who manufactured boats that were 6.5 meters (21 feet) long.

Maurice Edel, a boat manufacturer in Lyon, agreed to see him, so Bruno boarded the all-night train to travel across France to Lyon. Edel was charmed by Bruno's energy and passion and agreed to build him his boat. However, his shop was closed for vacation—something the French take very seriously. Bruno convinced Edel to open it. During the day, he helped work on the boat; at night, he slept on the floor in the shop under a drafting table.

Even though Bruno started La Mini–Transat Race a week late, he finished a very credible thirteenth. This despite capsizing the boat in gale-force winds.

Le Pouliguen, where Bruno hails from, is also the home-town of Marc Pajot—the absolute star of French sailing. After years of racing multihulls, for very generous spon-sors, and winning numerous world championships, Pajot graduated to the America's Cup. In 1986–87, he skippered *French Kiss* into the final four in Western Australia, and in 1992, he skippered *Ville de Paris* into the final four in San Diego. In 1995, he skippered *France 3*. Pajot is the Michael Jordan of France.

Coco Pajot, Marc Pajot's wife, was, at one time, the teen-age Bruno's sweetheart. She commented that "there were times in the beginning when it was very difficult for Bruno to pay the rent. Bruno's whole life was focused on building his big multihull."

Bruno once told me that you have the choice when you get money from a sponsor—even if the sponsor is a very big one: Do you put the money in your pocket and live well or do you buy new sails? During the last ten years, he'd chosen to buy new sails and use the extra money to pay for the big boat that he dreamed about.

Leaving Newport, Bruno attempted to break the solo transatlantic record, from New York to the Lizard in En-gland, with his *Atlantic Liberté*—a record he would later hold. He was dismasted when 925 miles from Portugal.

Before the $250,000 carbon-fiber wing mast could be cut away, it punched dozens of holes in the hull. During the passage, his father, who had never approved of what his sons, Bruno, Loïck, or Stéphane, did for work, died. This information was kept from Bruno, who had troubles enough in the Atlantic.

"After the race, there was that bad news," Bruno told me. "The other bad news was there was no sponsor, no insurance, and no money that had been promised to me by another banker. Also, the Route du Rhum Race started in five weeks."

Somehow Peyron got *Atlantic Liberté* to Saint Malo for the start of the Route du Rhum. The towering wing mast was replaced by a four-spreader aluminum spar. This was done for financial reasons: an aluminum mast was one quarter as expensive as a carbon-fiber wing mast. In the hiatus before the start, however, grim reality took hold of him. He recognized that if anything happened to the boat in this race, he would be ruined financially. He made the difficult decision not to start. He said, as I recall it, "Nobody believed me when I said that I couldn't compete. I told French TV that I can't start. I told the public that I had come in second in this race four years before, and everyone believes that I can do well again; but if I can't get some sort of sponsorship—to pay the new suppliers or to pay for insurance—I can't go."

As a result of his appearances on French TV, he found sponsorship from Ericsson, a telecommunications company with headquarters in Sweden. The French subsidiary made a limited offer of sponsorship: the company would pay the suppliers and the shipyard. The contract was signed at 2:00 A.M. on the morning of the start.

Two days into the race, Bruno learned that another competitor, Loïc Caradec, had been lost overboard from his multihull *Royale*. When he heard that, he almost gave up.

This is a very small world, he said, and everyone is close. The first boat to finish in Guadeloupe was *Fluery-Michon VIII*. Then came Bruno Peyron, who beat the famous Marc Pajot in this race, sailing *Elf Aquitaine*.

A year after that race to the Caribbean, Jacques Vincent brought *Atlantic Liberté/Ericsson* to Newport. Newport had been a friendly port for Bruno and Jacques, and Jacques left the boat on a mooring over the winter. He probably figured no one would notice. However, *Atlantic Liberté/Ericsson* is 75 feet long and as striking a boat as ever appeared on the Newport waterfront.

The next spring, I got a call from Jacques, who asked me to check on *Atlantic Liberté* that he'd all but abandoned on a town mooring. I borrowed a rowboat and paddled to the boat in a gale, to check her lines. Jake Farrell, the harbormaster, spotted me aboard and came over in his patrol boat, like a meter maid to a scofflaw. A lively conversation ensued. It ended amiably enough when I wrote him a substantial check for the boat's rent.

Over the years, Bruno and I have become good friends. However, there's always a great mystery surrounding Bruno—how he manages to get just enough money to do the next project. It never leaves anything in his pocket.

In his book on the around-the-world voyage, Bruno describes himself as an albatross, a long-winged seabird. It means, I believe, he needs room to stretch his wings. It is his sailing projects that give him the space he requires. It has almost nothing to do with money. Knocking on doors in a suit, tie, briefcase, and promising sponsors the world— more than he might be able to deliver—is not his strong suit. I'm sure he considers it a necessary evil.

Somehow Bruno's always managed to satisfy his creditors. I don't know anyone he's truly stiffed. He's a very honest person. He's stuck me for some phone bills and similar things, but I've stuck him for some too. That, I believe, is a reasonable definition of friendship.

In our borrowed car we arrived at the Multiplast Yard. There was our ride: *Jet Services V*. Under this signature, this catamaran set the transatlantic record, between New York and the Lizard, in the southwest corner of England, at an average speed of nearly 19 knots. Nevertheless, the years hadn't been particularly kind to the boat; before Bruno bought her, she was something of a white elephant. A nautical untouchable. I understand that Bruno paid 2,500,000 French francs for the boat, or about $500,000.

I hadn't seen the boat in years or ever seen it out of the water. In the shed the boat looked huge, as she was out of her element, like a beached whale. But at the same time, she looked fine-lined and eminently delicate. The boat also looked months away from being ready for an around-the-world voyage. Money can hurry things along, but, I knew, there wouldn't be money to pay the workers for overtime; perhaps not even regular time. I once heard an American say, "The French buy an eighty-five-foot boat on a sixty-five-foot budget." There's some truth to that, but the French don't think small.

When I saw the boat this day, she was being transformed from *Jet Services V* to *Commodore Explorer*, in honor of Commodore International, Ltd., the American-based international computer company that had given Bruno just enough money to buy the boat, but nothing extra to make the voyage. Nevertheless, he had given them the plum: the boat's name. Once that was gone, Bruno had much less to offer other interested sponsors. In hindsight, he was in financial difficulty from the word *go*. That said, there wouldn't have been a go without Commodore and certainly without Bruno.

In view of our limited finances and Bruno's conservative nature, he described our voyage to the press as a "reconnaissance mission." By that he meant, we were seeing if sailing around the world in 80 days was possible. I don't know whether he believed this or not, but that's what he said. He seemed intent on lowering others' expectations. This is Bruno's strength as a man and as a leader but a weakness when it comes to selling his projects to the corporate world.

The transformation of the boat involved more than just a new name on her transom. For example, the main beams, or "crossarms," were being glassed permanently to the hulls. Before, they'd been bolted and thus could be unbolted, and the two hulls folded neatly together, making for easier transportation of the folded boat on a trailer down the road. This seemed remarkably inappropriate, or makeshift, for a boat of this size—particularly one designed to set records across oceans. Obviously, it made even less sense for a boat poised to make an around-the-world dash over some of the most hostile real estate on earth.

Also, the forward crossarm, one of two that holds the two hulls of the boat together and traveling in the same direction—more or less—was moved forward six feet as the boat was lengthened from 75 to 86 feet. This was in the interest of increased speed.

When traveling as fast as it can go, a displacement boat such as this generates a wave at the bow, called a "bow wave," and a wave off the stern, the "stern wave."[1] These two waves move along with the boat, as if a conveyor belt. Boat speed is absolutely limited by the speed of the "conveyor belt," or the speed of this wave train.

[1] The opposite of a displacement boat is a planing boat. A planing boat is light enough that it can leave its stern wave behind and plane up its bow wave. In essence, it has escaped the hole. With much less of the boat in the water, it goes faster than a similar-sized displacement boat.

Interestingly enough, the greater the horizontal distance between the bow and stern wave, or the longer the boat in contact with the water (called waterline length), the faster the wave train moves. And, so, too, does the boat. It is as if you've sped up the conveyor belt.[2]

Before we leave yacht design, a few other points need be mentioned. First, why is an 86-foot catamaran, which is a displacement boat, faster than an 86-foot monohull, which is also a displacement boat? A monohull with a lead keel, which resists the heeling forces of the wind, tends to be as much as three times heavier than a multihull without one. Obviously, if you're racing horses, you don't carry an extra 25 pounds unless you have to. If you're racing boats, you don't carry an extra 55,000 pounds unless you have to. Lighter is invariably faster.

Know, too, that for every length a displacement boat travels, it must push its weight of water out of the way. This is basically "Archimedes' principle." If, for example, an 86-foot monohull weighs 75,000 pounds, it pushes aside 75,000 pounds of water for each boat length it travels. In an around-the-world voyage of 26,000 nautical miles, that is 137860465116 pounds of water, which is either my credit card number or 138 billion. A multihull, which weighs two-thirds less (*Commodore Explorer* weighed 21,280 pounds or 9.5 displacement or long tons) pushes aside two-thirds less water, or a mere 46 billion pounds. Put that way, it's pretty easy to see which boat works less and, also, goes faster.

Also, a catamaran, with its wide beam—the newly dubbed and newly sized *Commodore Explorer* was 45 feet wide by 86 feet long—doesn't heel as much, at least ini-

---

[2] Yacht designers show the relationship between waterline length and ultimate speed of a displacement boat, termed "hull speed," by the formula: hull speed = $1.34 \sqrt{\text{waterline length}}$.

tially. (Of course, that is until you cross the multihull Rubi-
con, and it capsizes.) All that beam keeps the boat floating
on its lines and faster than a boat like a monohull that heels
ever more to the weight of the wind. Less heel allows a
boat to carry larger sails in the same wind and makes its
speed-producing foils—sails, dagger boards, and rudders
—more vertical and thus more efficient.

All I remember about December 1992, in France, was working and working some more on the boat and getting to
know those members of the crew I didn't already know.
With so much to do and so little time, there was little sleep
for the crew of *Commodore Explorer* in December and even
less in January. For me, there was the constant worry:
What would we have left to give to the record attempt?

One of the crew members I didn't know was Olivier
Despaigne, called "Chinois," or Chinese, for obscure reasons that date back to his callow youth. He has a dramatic
mustache and is a fan of overwrought Harley-Davidson
motorcycles, one of America's most popular exports to
France. Chinois was a holdover from the *Jet Services V*
crew. Age forty-eight, he had been aboard the boat in 1990,
when it set the transatlantic record. He had also crewed for
Loïc Caradec, until Caradec was lost off *Royale*. He worked
as a boatbuilder at the Multiplast Yard when and where
this boat was built.

There, too, was Marc Vallin, another crew member from
*Jet Services V*. Marc, age thirty-five, had raced in the Whitbread Round the World Race on *Kriter IX* and ran Marc
Pajot's wonderfully named *French Kiss* and sailed aboard
the boat in the 1986–87 America's Cup. He was our
onboard sailmaker and spent much of his time when he
was around at the North loft.

At the same time, he was working on getting his license
to fly helicopters. So Marc was often here today and gone

tomorrow and the next day. At two o'clock on December 21, when he was here but fast asleep, he got a phone call saying his wife, Michelle, an Air France flight attendant, was in labor; this was a couple of weeks premature. He hopped into Chinois's ancient truck, which ran more out of habit than mechanical correctness, and drove as fast as he dared to Le Havre, but missed the birth of son Antoine by two hours. He was back at work the next day, hammering away at his to-do list. Such lists fairly dominated our lives.

Also working on the boat, with a similar if not greater list, was Jacques Vincent, whom I had first met through Bruno in 1986. Jacques, known as Tick-Tock Jacques, because he is so organized, had crossed the Atlantic nine times—usually with Bruno. With Bruno, he won the Lorient–St. Barts Race. Age thirty in 1992, he'd also sailed around the world in 1989–90 on *The Card*, in the Whitbread Round the World Race. He calls the sea his home. When he's not at "home," he has an old diesel truck, a gift from Bruno, full of wet suits, windsurfers, and tools, which he more or less lives in.

Later I would learn from Bruno's book that my place on the boat wasn't assured. He was concerned that my energy level—you remember, "Mr. 200,000 Volts"?—might be off-putting to the French crew during a voyage of this length. I didn't know this was a test, which is likely why I passed it. It isn't easy for me to bank the fire.

France is full of government ministers, and I was dubbed the "Minister of the Interior," whose portfolio was to keep the crew well fed, safe, happy, and comfortable—responsibilities that I took seriously.

Our work moved from Vannes, where the boat was being refitted, to la Trinité-sur-Mer, which is considered the Multihull Capital of the World. Here, North Sails, our sailmaker, had a loft. We put a container there to hold all the stuff, which was growing inexorably, but at the same time was emptying the exchequer. Obviously, this was a mounting concern to Bruno, the Minister of Finance, who kept asking: "Do we really need that?" Beyond the cost, there was always the concern that taking too much stuff would slow the boat down.

I had a list of things to do that numbered in the high hundreds. Others had comparable lists. I'd cross one item off the list, having completed the task, and three more would appear. Readying this boat was the nautical version of Sisyphus. We were constantly pushing rocks uphill and constantly worrying that they would sink us—be it financially or actually.

During this period my thoughts often turned to Fogg, whose departure consisted of instructing Passepartout, "We'll have no trunks; only a carpetbag, with two shirts and three pairs of stockings for me, and the same for you. We'll buy our clothes on the way."

One of my more interesting assignments from Bruno, who was away in Paris looking for money much of the time, was to design or find a whale-avoidance system. Running into a blue whale, which can be a hundred feet long and weigh 286,650 pounds, can "ruin your entire day," as the common saying has it about any collision at sea. This is not just free-floating anxiety—the nautical version of things that go bump in the night. Boats have run into whales, and the results have been catastrophic.

I went to the Paris boat show. While there, I talked to a guy who used to work for Jacques Cousteau who had heard that if you transmit the sounds of an Orca, or killer whale—the "bully boys" of the whale set—other whales will steer clear. I asked Bruno if he really wanted me to pursue this, and he did.

Ultimately, I called a friend who works at the Monterey Bay Aquarium, in California, and he knew one of the world's leading authorities on Orcinus, or killer whales.

The expert said he knew more about trying to attract whales through sound, to study them, than repelling them, but it might be possible to do it. We'd need to find some way to transmit an Orca's sound from a transducer in the hull, and yet, at the same time, not slow the boat down too much. Anyway, it was beginning to account for a number of international phone calls and consume a number of francs, and eventually Bruno called me off.

The world is a big place, he reasoned, and the odds of one 86-foot catamaran and one hundred-foot whale occupying the same piece of ocean at the same instant are pretty remote.

For me, America seemed a long ways away. I can remember before Christmas shopping for my family and friends in this sleepy little French town of la Trinité-sur-Mer. A summer resort, it seemed practically shuttered tight for the winter. I seriously considered buying Molly an engagement ring for Christmas. While I'd long planned to do this someday, perhaps it was the season, the distance from home, or what lay ahead that made me think about actually doing it then. Mostly, it was Molly. I got cold feet and did nothing about it that day, however.

Also, before I'd left America, there had been some tension between us. I didn't want to live in Newport anymore. As mentioned, I wanted to move to Maine. Maine seemed a little foreign—a little sleepy—to her. So I really didn't know where we were going. Besides, first I was going around the world.

Molly finished work, waitressing and modeling, before Christmas and joined me in France the day after. If this seems a diverse résumé, let me explain. When Molly Fitch was fifteen and playing the flute in a recital in North Kingston High School, in Rhode Island, a fashion photographer who happened to be there approached her about modeling. This wasn't the first time this had happened, but her mother thought she was too young and the business just a bit unsavory. A couple years later, Molly did some modeling in Providence and later in Boston.

A photographer who had taken photographs of her in Boston, ended up moving to New York and showing these pictures to Eileen Ford, head of the famous Ford Models. Eileen Ford went to Boston to meet her at the Ritz. She told Molly, then just out of high school, that she should enter the Super Model of the World Contest. But before that there was the New England edition of the contest. She intimated that Molly would win that, which she did. Then Molly entered and won the Super Model of America contest, which was on national television. There were limousines and parties, bright lights and big cities.

The morning after she was named Super Model of America she was to appear on *Good Morning America*, and be interviewed by Joan Lunden. Also, Eileen Ford wanted her to move to New York.

Molly was days out of high school, and it was all happening too fast. She's from Jamestown, a small town across the bridge from Newport, and wanted to be playing with her friends more than working in big-time modeling. She cried all night in her hotel room and woke up the morning of her national-television appearance with a bloody nose. She got through it, however.

The bright lights, big city, and big salary beckoned, and she moved to New York to work for Ford Models. Molly lived with several other models in the top floor of Ford's brownstone, on Manhattan's Upper East Side. She was making as much as $2,000 a day, but hated New York, which is no place for an innocent. She found it a shifty-eyed city, where merely meeting someone's eyes is construed as an invitation or worse. In 1987, Molly moved to Madrid, Spain, where her blond, well-scrubbed, all-American looks were in great demand. She appeared on the covers of several fashion magazines and had a large photo spread in *Elle*.

Eventually, she returned home to New England and enrolled in Emerson College, in Boston, to study mass communications. She wanted to be behind the camera, not in front of it. Eileen Ford told her she was stupid to go to college. Molly paid for Emerson through modeling and waitressing and graduated. She still models occasionally. She smiled in honor of Doublemint gum, in a long-running television commercial. And appeared in a brief bathing suit in a popular Foster's beer poster. Most recently she was in the L.L. Bean catalog. Molly waits tables on occasion, too, when the need for money or the mood strikes her.

The day she arrived in France we went to a post-Christmas party at Stéphane Peyron's house. Stéphane, you will recall, is Bruno's brother, the transatlantic windsurfer, who now is a television producer in France. He produces a program about adventuring and adventurers. Also there were Bruno's daughter, his mother, and her brother, Jean-Yves Terlain. All in the family, Terlain sailed the 128-foot three-masted *Vendredi 13* (Friday the thirteenth) in the 1972 Observer Singlehanded Transatlantic Race (OSTAR).

Missing, however, was Bruno's brother Loïck. As I understand it, Bruno had hoped that the brothers Peyron might make this around-the-world voyage. Stéphane was enthusiastic about this, as was Loïck—at least that's what he said. Later, Bruno learned Loïck was trying to buy another multihull, to mount his own around-the-world record attempt. Bruno was furious.

Much of my time was spent trying to purchase things, which in France wasn't easy. Not all of this had to do with my lack of French. For example, I found it remarkably hard to locate items: big thermoses and big teakettles, and especially insulated cups, like the kind you can find in every Dunkin' Donuts in America.

With my one-burner stove, my culinary arts were limited to little more than boiling water and rehydrating freeze-dried food. Thus, it seemed a good idea to buy such cups, to keep water and food hot. This way we'd save on fuel, as I wouldn't be boiling water every time someone was hungry. Ultimately, my father had to send me several from America.

Similarly, service people in France would agree to help us, but you never knew if that meant today, this month, or this year. It was impossible to pin anyone down. Besides it was Christmastime, and the French take holidays seriously.

For example, between the two hulls on a catamaran such as this is a net, strung taut like a trampoline. It is several thousand pounds lighter in weight than a solid deck, as found on a monohull, but moving about the boat is relatively precarious. Anywhere and anytime, the seas can erupt through the trampoline like a tidal wave and knock you over, even off the boat.

To keep you attached to the boat should you lose in the nearly constant game of "dodgeball" are safety lines, running across, from hull to hull, and forward, where the headsails are set, and aft. To this you attach a harness, which you wear over your clothing or foul-weather gear. It wasn't until the day before we left that Jacques got the safety lines attached. He'd hired a rigger to help him, but this was France and the rigger went off skiing for two weeks. Jacques didn't want anyone to do the splices except for him and this other guy, so at the last minute he had to do it.

If "*macho* should have been a French word," so, too, should *mañana*.

Besides us, two other multihulls were ready and would

be departing around the same time as we would: One was *ENZA New Zealand,* a nine-year-old 85-foot catamaran sailed by Peter Blake, of New Zealand, and Robin Knox-Johnston, of England. *ENZA,* by the way, stands for Eat New Zealand Apples. Once on the ocean, we became fast friends with the crew of *ENZA,* chatting on the radio almost every day.

No such friendship developed between us and the French crew on *Charal,* the other boat poised to leave. *Charal* was a seven-year-old trimaran, sailed by Olivier de Kersauson, who had to his credit a solo-multihull circumnavigation record of 125 days, 19 hours, and 32 minutes in this boat. This included two stops, at Cape Town and Punta del Este, Uruguay. His sponsor was Charal, a meat-packing company that belonged to Raul Gardini. His budget was reported to be a generous $3.6 million.

It was Gardini who led *Il Moro de Venezia,* the Italian America's Cup boat, which lost to Bill Koch's *America³* in 1992. De Kersauson met Gardini during that America's Cup and persuaded him to lend his support.

In 1993, as Gardini's financial empire began to crumble, and he stood accused of bribing government officials in Italy, to the tune of $140 million—what the *New Yorker* described as "the mother of all bribes"—he put a bullet through his head.

In France, de Kersauson hosts an intellectual and popular radio program called *Les Grosses Têtes,* or big heads. A man who dances to his own drummer, if he'll forgive me that cliché, de Kersauson was unwilling to ante up the $16,000 entry fee to join the Trophée Jules Verne competition. Blake and Knox-Johnston paid it, as did Bruno; this was a hard decision for Bruno, I know, because he didn't have an extra $16,000 lying around.

De Kersauson was asked by a journalist before he left

what he thought about Bruno Peyron's chances to sail around the world in under 80 days? "Who?" he said.

Molly learned from a journalist friend that de Kersauson had his food vacuum-bagged. In essence, each day's food was stacked neatly in a brick and then vacuum-bagged to protect it from water, condensation, and dirt and to make it the smallest possible package. This seemed a wonderful idea to me. I made several telephone calls to try to find someone who could do this for us. The best I could come up with from my English-French dictionary was *le sac du vide.* Later I found out this meant the bag of emptiness. Close but no cigar. If only I hadn't lied my way out of high-school French.

Eventually, Molly and I practically tied Jacques to a chair and made him make some telephone calls. He reached this guy who said, "Come right over."

As Minister of the Interior, it occurred to me that we should also vacuum-bag some clothes, in particular long underwear and Gore-Tex socks, which would go a long way toward keeping us warm and happy.

Marc got excited about this idea, too, and he helped Molly and me load up a truck, which belonged to Bruno's accountant, and together with ninety-three bags of food— one for each day—and sundry clothes, off we went to this huge meat-packing factory, Métro Boeuf. It was a typical Breton winter day, raining hard, and practically dark. At this time of the year and in this latitude—about the same as that of Newfoundland—the sun doesn't make its timid appearance until about eight in the morning. Because of the weather, Molly wore a polar-fleece baseball-style hat I'd given her for Christmas. Not exactly an engagement ring.

In the front is a retail shop, but in the back is this food-processing plant. The place is refrigerated and immaculate. There are all these sides of meat, and guys in impeccable white coats are slamming cuts of meat into vacuum bags—

about the size of body bags. The vacuum packing is so efficient that the meat is actually compressed.

We get a couple of dollies and start bringing the food in. It wasn't in any particular order. I'm trying to organize things and to get Molly to write down day 1, day 2, until she gets to 93. This guy is helping us stuff one day's worth of food into a big plastic bag, and then he brings over the vacuum machine. I shout, "Not too much pressure!" but whether he heard me or understood is unclear. He sucks the air out of the bag until it's under about eight atmospheres of pressure. It's of sufficient pressure to mold a carbon-fiber America's Cup mast. Suddenly, there's an explosion, BOWANG! And I hear, "*Mon Dieu! Une catastrophe!*"

I whirl around and there's Gatorade dust, carrots, chicken, food powder everywhere. It's amazing someone wasn't impaled by a chicken wing. By this time, Molly has erupted in hysterics, but I'm fighting to control it, because we need the help of this guy.

Orders are shouted, and workers descend upon us to help clean up the mess. Instead of being angry, the guy in charge is now challenged by it. He wants it to be all scientific. Perfect.

We get the food finished by 11:45. In France, work stops at 12:00 for a two-hour lunch. It's impossible to get anything done then. So with fifteen minutes to go I say, "Marc! Get the clothes."

Marc's organized and meticulous. He's putting the right number of socks for each day, but I'm racing the clock and just jamming stuff into these clear plastic bags. Then the guy vacuum-bags the clothes. It's otherworldly to see what a Hawaiian shirt looks like under eight atmospheres of pressure. Given sufficient time, it would likely turn into a diamond.

On Wednesday, January 27, the work on the boat was

completed, and we moved it from La Trinité, to Brest. It's about a hundred miles up the coast. Bruno wasn't with us for the passage. It occurred to me then, how little we'd sailed the boat. Maybe we'd been out in her five times.

At Brest, I bought fresh produce at this large wholesaler there. Marc came along again because he's an apple expert; he eats about eight of them a day. We purchased apples, onion, bananas, tangerines, oranges, carrots, and garlic, and by the time we're through there's pallets' worth of the stuff. I'm wondering where in the world we're going to put it. Then I decided never mind, it will keep us healthy.

Molly drove to Brest to meet us there in a borrowed and beat-up *deux-chevaux*, a typical French no-frills automobile. Since her arrival at Christmas this hadn't been the most romantic time. Life was getting up at 5:00 A.M. and taking a shower; making some breakfast and then running off to the boatyard and working until 11:00 P.M. I'd throw Molly a to-do list like the rest of us. She'd do her jobs without complaining. We'd fall into bed at about midnight. Nevertheless, our relationship was great; we didn't fight. We were too tired.

Around New Year's I thought about asking her to marry me again, but got cold feet—again. I had this notion that if I encumbered her with a proposal of marriage and she accepted and then I died on this voyage, it wasn't fair to her. It's one thing to lose a boyfriend, people lose boyfriends for one reason or another all the time. It's another to lose a fiancé or husband.

On January 30, the night before we were to leave, the voyage was no longer an abstract idea, living somewhere in the future. It was tomorrow. The weather looked good. *ENZA*, our competition, was docked next to us. We'd had a gentleman's agreement to depart on the same day. This, we believed, would make the contest more like a race and thus more interesting and comprehensible to the public. De Kersauson and crew on *Charal*, however, were long gone at this point, having departed on January 22.

As he said as the boat was christened in Brest, "I will comply with nothing. The program of *Charal* is very simple, and I will start the day when I decide after January 11." His early departure forced us and, perhaps, the crew of *ENZA* to leave earlier than we would have liked. Our original plan was to leave February 5, and a few extra days of rest would have done the crew of *Commodore Explorer* a world of good.

Most of the crew of *Commodore Explorer* had gone to dinner with friends or loved ones or to bed, but Molly was still handing me apples and bunches of bananas, while I'm trying to find places for them aboard the boat and for a few books I've decided to squirrel aboard. I had a copy of Verne's *Around the World in Eighty Days* (there was a second copy aboard in French that I would try to read); Richard Henry Dana Jr.'s *Two Years Before the Mast*; Admiral Byrd's *Alone*; Sir Ernest Shackleton's *South*; Bruce Chatwin's *In Patagonia*; and the *Antarctic Pilot*. It was mostly adventure reading for my adventure.

I'd finished loading the food and food for thought, all my clothes were aboard, and there was only one thing left to do. "Molly?" I asked. "Will you marry me?" She looked at me like I'm crazy. Then said, "Yes." There were tears, and not all of them were hers.

We had a nice dinner with champagne to celebrate. Bruno was at a table nearby with family and friends, and he seemed delighted by the news. Then Molly and I returned to our room in the Hôtel du Parc in Brest to celebrate some more. I was leaving and yet we were to be married—two more antipodal states I couldn't imagine, yet it felt right. Complete.

Then before we fell asleep Molly cut my hair, as there aren't barbers where I'd be going. Tomorrow.

# In which
# *Commodore Explorer*
# is off to see
# the world

---

Most races start with a bang—a cannon on a committee boat sends you on your way in appropriate style. Our race around the world against the ghosts of Phileas Fogg and Jean Passepartout, as well as the very real Peter Blake and Robin Knox-Johnston on *ENZA* and Olivier de Kersauson on *Charal*, began "not with a bang but a whimper," as T. S. Eliot once said about the end of the world rather than a voyage around it.

I stuck my head out of the port-hull cabin, where I'd been cleaning up after making lunch and packing away food and gear and asked, "When do we start?"

"About a minute ago," came the reply.

Unbeknownst to me, we'd crossed that imaginary line between the lighthouse at l'île d'Ouessant, in France, and the lighthouse on the Lizard in England, and were off to see the world.

A journey of a thousand miles—or 27,000 nautical miles

---

—begins with one step, as the saying has it, and I'd just missed the first step. Some of those steps, like this one, are more important than others, I believe.

Bruno had placed a lawyer in the lighthouse at l'île d'Ouessant to record our official departure time, which was 13:02:27 (1:02 P.M.) Greenwich Mean Time (GMT) on Sunday, January 31, 1993, or 14:02:27 (2:02 P.M.) local French time. To beat the record, we'd have to cross this line again from the opposite direction in less than 80 days, or, to use Verne's math, in "nineteen hundred and twenty hours, or a hundred and fifteen thousand two hundred minutes." (And I'd already missed the first minute.) That would mean we would have to be back before 13:02:27 GMT on April 21, a Wednesday. Even a second later would be too late.

This is a book about time, as was *Around the World in Eighty Days*, so a brief discussion of time is warranted. Time as well as longitude begins in Greenwich, England— near London. Placing Greenwich, England, at the center of the world has been official for the British since 1675, when that nation's important *Nautical Almanac* was first published. The book showed angular measurements between the moon and a few select stars, which, at the time, was of critical importance in celestial navigation.[1] Greenwich Mean Time became the world's standard in 1884.

The apparent movement of the sun in the sky has long been used to fix time. I say "apparent" because the sun doesn't move in the sky, of course; the earth rotates on its axis and around a fixed sun. When the sun is on your longitude line, or directly north or south of you, it is local-apparent noon or "high noon." The latter is a good descriptive name for this phenomenon, because the sun is as

---

[1] Greenwich was the site of the Royal Observatory established by King Charles II on the Thames in 1675. It is now in Sussex.

high as it gets in the sky. The moment that the sun crosses your longitude line, shadows point toward either of the poles, or due north or south. When the sun is 180 degrees from one's longitude, it is local-apparent midnight.

The rotational speed of the earth on its axis is about 1,044 mph at the equator. One revolution of the earth takes about 24 hours: a day. Other than the apparent movement of the sun or stars across the sky, from east to west, that speed is not obvious to those who ride this planet. It's analogous to sitting on a train at a railway station with another stationary train next to you. When one starts to move, you often can't tell which one it is without looking at a fixed point, like a tree.

The earth rotates toward the east; that is why it's later to the east of anyplace and earlier to the west. In fact, for every degree you travel to the east—the direction Fogg and Passepartout were traveling, and the direction we would be traveling once we rounded the Cape of Good Hope, at the bottom of Africa—the sun rises four minutes earlier. Every degree you travel to the west, the sun rises four minutes later.

Beyond a complete rotation of the earth, which is about a day, time is measured by the earth's complete revolution around the sun. This orbit takes about a year, or about 365 days. On this elliptical journey around the sun, the earth travels in a counterclockwise direction at about 66,000 miles per hour, but, again, we don't notice it. Actually it takes the earth about 365.2422 days to rotate around the sun, and that fraction complicates matters mightily.

For example, it is very important that the calendar accurately reflect such things as when spring comes to the northern hemisphere, that is, when the sun appears to cross the equator on its apparent journey north. This occurs on or about March 21. If you live in the northern hemisphere, planting seeds before then might be a waste of time, effort, and money. Similarly, it is important to know when the sun reaches the Tropic of Capricorn, at 23.5 degrees south, on or about December 21. That's top-down weather Down Under; ski season in the northern hemisphere.

However, to account for the fact that the sun takes 365.2422 days to round the earth—not 365—mathematical corrections are applied to the calendar. For example, any year evenly divisible by four is a leap year, meaning that February is given an extra day, February 29, so there are 366 days that year. Every year that ends in 00, however, must be evenly divisible by 400 to be a leap year. This means the year 2000—just on the horizon—is a leap year, but 1800 and 1900 were not.

Beginning in 1928, GMT was also called "Universal Time" (UT). In 1964, Greenwich Mean Time was largely replaced by coordinated Universal Time (UTC). Its second is based on the vibration of the cesium atom but its year is based on the earth's orbit around the sun. As the earth is actually slowing in its orbit, a leap second is added about once or twice a year.

Time and longitude are intertwined. The Greenwich Meridian, also known as the Prime Meridian, is designated 0 degrees. From Greenwich, the earth is divided into 180 degrees of longitude to the east of Greenwich, and 180 to the west, for a total of 360 degrees. With Greenwich as the center, or reference point, everything on earth is either east or west of Greenwich, or on the same longitude line.[2]

Earlier I noted for every degree you travel to the east, the

[2] The French, in fact, were never enthusiastic about centering time and longitude in England, just as the English were never enthusiastic about the metric system—a French idea first proposed in 1793. For the French, Paris was the center, and they set their clocks nine minutes and twenty-one seconds ahead of English clocks. *Et tu.* Americans, however, favored Greenwich. In an international conference in

sun rises four minutes earlier. Another way to say this is that the sun shines *directly* on each line of longitude for four minutes. The most a degree of longitude can represent is 69.17 statute miles at the equator. Since longitude lines converge at the poles, the distance is 1.21 miles at 89 degrees and nothing, depending on how fine you draw the lines, at the North and South Pole. So rather than changing time zones every 69 miles, or less, when traveling east or west, we divide the earth into 15-degree time zones—each of which equals one hour (15 [degrees] × 4 [minutes] = 60 [minutes]). Thus, there are 12 time zones to the east of Greenwich and 12 to the west. That is a total of 24 time zones, or 24 hours.

Starting at 0 degrees, or the Greenwich Meridian, the zones are centered on the numbers evenly divisible by 15. The zone then spans $7^1/_2$ degrees on either side of these whole numbers.

Those time zones to the *east* of Greenwich are labeled –1, –2, –3, et cetera. If you're in France, which is –1, you *subtract* one hour from the local time to get GMT; you add one hour to GMT to get local time. Those zones to the *west* of Greenwich are labeled +1, +2, +3, et cetera. Zone 12 is centered on 180 degrees, which is also called the international dateline. Newport is +5, so when the east coast of the United States observes standard time, it is five hours later in Greenwich, England, than in Newport, six hours later in France.

When traveling on the ocean east or west, navigators typically adjust their local time at noon, to keep pace with the time zones, which, again, span 15 degrees. Thus when traveling to the east, toward the sun, some days may have fewer than 24 hours. *"Tempus fugit,"* as Caesar, who, inci-

---

Washington, D.C., in 1884, the principal nations voted for Greenwich, with the French abstaining.

dentally, gave the world leap year, might have put it. When traveling to the west, which I like to think of as running away from the sun, some days may have more than 24 hours. A slow day, as I put it.

Time zones over the oceans are nearly perfectly scribed bands. It is when they pass over land, that things get messy. For example, France is an hour ahead of England, even though the Greenwich Meridian passes directly through it. In fact, most of Western Europe shares the same time zone: −1, save for Portugal and England—the latter country has always been ambivalent about whether it is part of Europe. Using GMT or UTC obviates many of these complications.

Perhaps I've spent too long on time. Verne addresses it in about half as much time, but time as well as the times, I believe, were simpler in 1872.

Having missed the start by a minute, I turned around, and there was the black-and-white-painted Créac'd lighthouse on Ouessant. Here the Spanish Armada was becalmed in 1588, depriving the warships of the element of surprise in their attack on England. This is a threatening piece of water, with adverse currents and tricky winds that have claimed many ships. It sticks out in the Atlantic Ocean like a sore thumb and receives the full weight of the wind and waves, including what's left of the Gulf Stream, which usually comes at it from the west: the direction of the predominant winds. A French expression has it, Who sees Ouessant sees his blood.

This wasn't our problem this day, however. *Commodore Explorer* danced merrily along at 20 knots—almost 6 knots faster than the "magic number" of 14 knots, which we would need to break the around-the-world record—and some 5 knots faster than the speed of the wind. Sailing faster than the wind is a trick beyond the capabilities of a displacement monohull.

I asked Bruno for the course, and he pointed vaguely to the southwest—close to the direction we were heading. If his aim was correct, that would allow us to clear Spain's Cape Finisterre. To me it all seemed remarkably informal, but Bruno had passed this way many times before.

Above us were six helicopters with members of the press. The helicopters were making their awful rat-tat-tat. It was reminiscent of the Vietnam movie *Apocalypse Now*. The only thing lacking was Wagner's high-energy "Ride of the Valkyries."

It had not been an auspicious beginning, however. When I saw Bruno that morning in the Hôtel du Parc, he had a cellular phone glued to one ear and was surrounded by attorneys. As I understand it, it was a shell game of sorts: To get the bank loans he needed to pay his yard bills, and to finish paying for the boat, he needed insurance. However, he couldn't get insurance until he paid his bills and had title to the boat. It all came down to who was going to blink first. Whoever it was, it wouldn't be Bruno.

We left Bruno with his lawyers, and Molly and I were the first ones to arrive at the boat. It was 7:30 on a foggy morning, and the red-and-white aggressively painted *ENZA*, which had been moored next to us the night before, was gone. The only other life at this hour was a couple of guys walking their French poodles.

I was to cook and sleep in the port hull with Marc Vallin and Chinois Despaigne. For the first week, we'd be joined there by filmmaker and photographer Jean-René Kéruzoré, who was going as far as the Cape Verde Islands. Bruno told us about this addition at the last minute, which was fine, except I hadn't planned on feeding another mouth, and Kéruzoré proved to be one hungry filmmaker.

This catamaran was set up like a duplex: 40 feet across the boat was the starboard hull, in which Bruno and Jacques would be living. (The distance was significant enough that we communicated between hulls by VHF radio.) *Living* is perhaps too grand a word for what all of us would be doing. The dimensions of either hull were six feet wide with a height of five feet three inches. I'm six feet four, so there was no standing headroom for me. In fact, the hulls were so narrow and so short, one more wore them than lived in them.

While our port side of the world looked fairly orderly on this the morning of our departure, their side of the boat was chaos. There went the neighborhood.

There had been a problem with grounding the antenna for the single-sideband radio, which we would need for long-distance ship-to-ship and ship-to-shore communications. Jacques and some electronics technician had torn out a bunk, to try to fix it. Bits and pieces of this emergency surgery were everywhere. Also, there was a spare fractional spinnaker, which had come out of its bag, that was draped throughout the cabin. It would be there for days—I'm sure Bruno and Jacques ceased to see it after a while—and like a strange life-form, it seemed to be growing inexorably and demanding more and more space.

Then, too, Bruno had a fair amount of duplicate electronics, which never really found a place to live. Bruno gave them his bunk and slept on an impossibly small cot, under the *casquette*, which translates to "crash helmet" but is a plastic aerodynamically shaped hatch-cover. There was a *casquette* over each hatch in either hull to keep the water from going down below, or so the theory went. By being so close to the action, Bruno could constantly monitor the progress of the boat—a holdover from his single-handed sailing. It would make sleep, however, practically impossible.

The chaos in that hull and its persistence was not typical of Bruno. Like the rest of us, he hadn't had much sleep in the past two months. Also, Bruno was distracted by money problems and related worries. If the boat broke—a new mast and sails would cost $250,000—he was broke. The blackness of his mood would grow like the blue folds of the spinnaker that choked his and Jacques's starboard hull.

Soon the rest of the crew was there, and we emptied the boat of extraneous gear: sail covers, extra mooring lines, unneeded fittings, and garbage. My newly anointed fiancée, wives, girlfriends, and interested spectators—there would be hundreds of them—lined the dock, which made moving the stuff no easy task.

I'd tried to call my father to tell him I was getting married, but was forced to leave the message on his answering machine. I did, however, reach my sister Lynnie, who lives in Newport. She was delighted by the news. I'm sure in her mind, Peter Pan had taken a bride.

Bruno announced, "We're out of here!" I grabbed Molly and said take care. I told her that I loved her; and that I'd do my best to get back as soon as possible but in any event in one piece. I told her that for me, the underlying principle of this voyage was Don't break the boat. She seemed reassured; doubtless my newly cautious father would have approved of this safety-first sentiment too. We held on to one another until, at Bruno's behest, the crew of *Commodore Explorer* slipped the ties that bound us to land.

As we left the dock, I had an empty feeling: an overwhelming sense that I didn't know what was waiting for us over the horizon. At least I knew the earth was round. What must it have been like, I wondered, to sail over the horizon being unsure of that?

Of the three boats in pursuit of the record in 1993—*Charal*, *ENZA*, and *Commodore Explorer*—ours was given the least chance of success. An editorial in *Seahorse* magazine, published after our return, put it this way: "Bruno and his crew left France on 31 January aboard what was the lightest and seemingly the most fragile of the three Jules Verne Challengers. Many of their supporters admitted that their hopes for the *Commodore* crew lay more for their safety than in any realistic chance of their breaking the 80-day benchmark. . . ."

After the start, Kéruzoré placed the tape and film he'd burned up to that moment in a plastic bag and tossed it over the side. The container had little floats attached to it. Earlier in this century, adventurers waved the flag of scientific exploration, technological advancement, manifest destiny, or all of these things. Heaven forbid they should say, "It beats a day at the office."

Sometimes actions speak louder than words, however: Sir Ernest Shackleton, the famous Antarctic explorer, once drove a golf ball through the office window of the Royal Scottish Geographical Society. He worked there in 1905 in his first and only real job, after returning from his first expedition to Antarctica and getting married. In due time, he followed the golf ball out onto the street.

Today adventuring is "show biz," and our sponsors anxiously awaited the videotape, so it could appear "Live at Five" or *"En Direct à Cinq Heures."* As planned, a helicopter swooped out of the sky to grab it with a grappling hook. It was all very impressive until they couldn't fish it out of the sea. As we disappeared over the horizon at 20 knots, we saw the helicopter still trying to make contact with the elusive tape cache. Later we learned by radio from Michel Horeau, our press agent, that they'd finally snagged it.

After the videotapes were set adrift, I suggested that we put up a spinnaker, as the wind was behind us. Setting a spinnaker is something each of us had done thousands of times separately, if almost never together, due to the dearth of practice time. No big deal, my idea was to go get it and pull the spinnaker up. *Voilà.*

Jacques Vincent was in charge of the bow, and thus in charge of the spinnaker sets. We hadn't had enough practice to determine whose job it was to put the halyard on the sail; who was responsible for clipping on the sheets; who was charged with leading the sheets aft and putting them on the winch.

To contain it during the hoist, this huge spinnaker is packaged within a sail-sock device, but we'd packed the spinnaker incorrectly. So we had to lower the sail and sock again and start all over. I'm getting impatient. I'm easily readable, and doubtless it's written boldly across my face. Above are the flying journalists, and we can't be impressing them. Jacques turns to me a couple of times and grumbles, "This is not the America's Cup, you know?" It takes us an hour and a half to get the spinnaker flying, when it should have taken five minutes.

Shortly after that, Bruno is driving the cat easily with one hand. With the other, he's on a VHF radio, giving a you-are-there style interview to Radio France—one of our sponsors.

He's not paying much attention to sailing the boat and suddenly it accidentally jibes, or turns its back ends through the eye of the wind. Then the huge 3,400-square-feet (299-square-meter) mainsail, stretched wide by eight full battens and a 35-foot carbon fiber boom, smashes across the boat with sufficient force to murder or maim. We were lucky that no one was in the way.

Unfortunately, the leeward traveler line, which controls power in the mainsail, wasn't cleated. All this force—unarrested by the traveler—takes its revenge on the bottom three feet of track, which unzips from the mast. It is this track that holds the mainsail's luff to the rotating carbon-fiber mast that reaches 100 feet off the deck—110 feet above the water. We've been at this less than two hours, I think, and have already broken the boat and made a mockery of a spinnaker set. No wonder the press wrote us off.

There was, supposedly, extra track aboard for this contingency, but somehow it got unloaded in the chaos of the morning. It would take us three days to fix the track, by scavenging bits and pieces from other places. We had to redrill the holes for the track on the mast, but the charger for the drill crapped out. By the time we got the sail track fixed we were off Portugal. We're lucky that we didn't have to reef, or shorten, the mainsail, as we could not have done it with the broken track.

This kitty cat was a thoroughbred, however. On February 2, for example, we outpaced some dolphins at 22 knots. I could almost hear them say: "Who are these guys?" We did 1,400 miles in the first three and a half days. This was an average distance of 400 miles per day—a respectable distance even in your car. As we only needed to make 324 miles per day to sail around the world in 80 days, we were comfortably ahead of schedule—ahead of Fogg and Passepartout.

I kept finding wonderful notes and small gifts, like favorite CDs or chocolates, that Molly had hidden for me. They were sweet reminders of what waited for me at home —sweet home.

The days weren't easy, however. Sailboats are raced day and night. To allow time for sleeping, eating, cleaning the boat and yourself, reading a book, et cetera, the time is divided into watches. Certainly, the simplest watch system is four hours on and four hours off. That means you're on deck and on duty a total of twelve hours a day, for seven days a week. There is no time off for holidays or good behavior. This is slave labor by any measure. Know, however, that there are a lot of ways to divide those twelve hours on, twelve hours off.

Marc was my watchmate, so he shared the deck time with me, alternately steering, trimming sails, and making certain things didn't break. Beyond standing a watch, I was charged with cooking for everyone, which happened often and often at odd times. Jacques and Chinois were on the other watch. As skipper, Bruno didn't stand a watch, but navigated, worked out strategy in view of the wind direction and weather, communicated, and filled in on deck as needed.

Our watch system was not so simple, however. It was established by Dr. Jean-Yves Chauve, a French physician, who had been a consultant to Vendée Globe sailors who left France a couple of months before we had. He became famous when Bertrand de Broc, a French competitor, saw his boat, *Group LG*, accidentally jibe, as we had done. The boom hit him in the head, and he nearly bit his tongue off and split his eyelid. As noted, the Vendée Globe Challenge is a solo race and by telex (de Broc couldn't talk to use the radio) Dr. Chauve instructed him how to sew his tongue back on and his eyelid together. It was successful, which is a credit to both men.

The watch system he proposed for the crew of *Commodore Explorer* was very scientific—it had to do with circadian rhythms: our waking, sleeping, and eating cycles— but it proved much too complex to follow. It went something like you're on for fifteen minutes, off for forty-five, on for an hour and twenty-seven minutes. And you were supposed to eat before and after. Also, I had to cook for everyone, which left little time for sleep.

Thus, for the first two weeks, we actually had no firm watch system. You just took the watch when you felt you could, or when you felt you were stronger than someone else, which ensured no one got adequate rest. This was exacerbated by the fact that all of us departed France wholly emptied by our preparations and exhausted by the lack of sleep. It was a race just to get into the race.

A two-man watch on an 86-foot boat is adequate, barely, as long as you're just steering and trimming sails to stay in harmony with the wind. As soon as you had to tack, reef, jibe, change sails, or repair something, it required "all-hands-on-deck." So you'd be off watch, maybe having just fallen asleep, and you would often be awakened for a maneuver. It was taking a toll.

I can remember during the first week being alone on deck at night, and hallucinating from the lack of sleep. The 86-foot boat was galloping into the dark abyss at 18 or 20 knots. A misstep, I might bury the bow into the wave ahead and trip the boat. The consequences of that could be disastrous. I tried splashing bitter salt water on my face to stay awake.

We had left France in winter, and in three days we'd sailed sufficiently south toward the equator that it was spring. In another few days, it would be summer, and a few days later, autumn. By the third week, at this speed, we'd be in the Southern Ocean, starting to work down to at least 56 degrees south latitude for our trip around Antarctica and to clear Cape Horn. At this latitude, it is winter even though the calendar says summer. Extreme latitude can make a liar of the calendar. As I saw it, I needed to fatten these guys up and get them rested, healthy, happy, and strong again for the rigors that lay ahead. Before we left on the voyage, I'd read Roald Amundsen, the Norwegian explorer who was the first to stand on the South Pole in 1911. Amundsen believed that explorers, like an army, travel on their stomachs. I subscribed to this.

I heard myself saying things like "Eat! Eat like a pig. Sleep! Sleep like a bear. Wash yourself. Do you have sunblock on? Have you brushed your teeth? Put on warm clothes." More than once I heard the reply, *"Oui, ma mère."*

On a boat of this type, you bathe outside or you don't bathe at all. When the days were too cold to wash yourself comfortably, I'd encourage the crew to wash with lanolin-soaked towelettes, or baby wipes. I'd brought a ton of them along. You could wash under your arms and around various folds of skin and feel, if not clean, then cleaner. And do so without freezing to death.

When we sailed into summer, I'd start shower parties for the *cochons volants* (flying pigs), as we'd begun to call ourselves, for very obvious reasons. I'd get things moving, mostly by disrobing and starting to wash with the saltwater soap we used. Once one guy got naked, the rest would often follow suit too. It was almost as if someone had to break the ice. What strange creatures we are. Then since we had a desalinator, to convert salt water to fresh water, we could rinse off with sweet water.

Summertime sailing was also a good time to wash clothes. We would dry them off the martingale, which was forward of the bow wave, and thus the driest spot on the boat. It gave the boat, however, the look of a Fall River triple-decker on laundry day.

To use the New York Yacht Club's vernacular, there was a "lack of accommodations" on *Commodore Explorer*, as there was on *Amaryllis*, the Herreshoff-designed catamaran that the august club, of which I happen to be a member, disqualified from its Centennial Regatta in 1876. With no toilet, or head, we used the big one off the back beam of the boat when the weather was decent. When the weather was awful, we'd use a bucket and then wash it out. However, the idea was not to go to the toilet in the boat if you could avoid it.

At night, Marc, Chinois, and I used pee jars, like mountain climbers in their tents. I had to pee all the time, so did the others. At first we thought it was the desalinator not working properly—not removing all the salt from the seawater; later, we concluded it was the constant motion of the boat that seemed to turn the contents of your bladder to froth. Like a steam engine, pressure built up. After standing a watch, it took some time to unwind; I'd read or listen to music through headphones. Then when I just started to get sleepy, I often had to leave the bunk to pee in the jar. To get into or out of my bunk, I had to climb behind Marc. This would invariably wake him. However, he never complained. Once back in my bunk, I'd have to start the unwinding process anew. Peeing into a jar where you slept could not be managed, as the bunks were too small.

While using the ocean as a toilet amounted to a drop in the proverbial bucket, I believe, it was about the only trail left in the oceans by the crew of *Commodore Explorer*. The entire crew agreed that we should not throw any of our garbage overboard. We stored all trash in the back sections of the hulls, where they'd been lengthened.

However, later in the Southern Ocean, I threw three wine bottles over the side. In them, I noted our latitude and longitude at that moment and offered a cash reward to anyone who found them. I was inspired to do this by Kéruzoré, our filmmaker, who told me a story about how the heiress to the Singer sewing machine fortune once placed a note in a bottle, which she dropped into the Atlantic, pledging 10 percent of her fortune to the person who found it. Fifty years later, someone from Japan found the bottle and collected the prize. Whether this is apocryphal or not, it appealed to me. I didn't pledge 10 percent of my net worth but a hundred dollars.

On the sixth day, it was time to jettison Kéruzoré at the Cape Verde Islands. While I liked him, I was glad to see him go because, as mentioned, he wasn't using the opportunity to lose weight. Besides that, Bruno had told him to pack light, so he was wearing a lot of my clothes.

Michel Horeau contacted the port captain in the Cape Verde Islands, to arrange for Kéruzoré's pickup. To that end, Kéruzoré had brought along a little inflatable, like something you'd buy for thirty dollars at a filling station. It looked as if it could hardly hold air, let alone Kéruzoré. I

wouldn't go across a swimming pool in it. The raft also had
these silly insubstantial paddles.

Also dispatched to Cape Verde was Dominique André
from Radio France, who was to conduct an interview with
Bruno as we sailed past the island of Saint-Vincent. Only
Chinois was familiar with the area; he'd stopped there once
following the La Baule–Dakar Race.

On the chart, it looked like a nice sheltered place to drop
the photographer over the side. When we got there, however, there was a riot of wind. These high volcanic islands
of the l'Archipel du Cap-Vert, as the French name it, focused the wind as a magnifying glass focuses the sun. It
reminded me of the Molokai Channel in Hawaii. You could
see this arid red earth, blowing horizontally. It looked to
me as if another day of this assault by the wind would
return the place to the sea.

By the time we reached the harbor, we had changed
from a fractional-rigged spinnaker and a full main, to a
staysail and mainsail reefed to the third reef point. We
managed to get Kéruzoré's raft inflated with a foot pump.
However, we had to tie it to the trampoline to keep it from
blowing away. Meanwhile this huge tugboat comes roaring out to meet us, with Dominique aboard, leading the
charge.

We turned into the wind to stop the cat, and the tug
comes straight for us. Try to stop a catamaran in forty
knots of wind, and it starts heading backward almost immediately. Afraid of a collision, we're shouting at the tug
to stay away. The boat missed us by inches. As our cat was
heading backward at 3 or 4 knots, we placed the raft over
the side; however, it kept flipping over in the wind. Finally, Kéruzoré, in desperation, jumps in with all his expensive and bulky cameras, still film and videotapes, and
personal gear. Apparently he's seen enough of the world

from the deck and cabin of *Commodore Explorer*. We immediately cut him loose.

As I looked behind us, there's Kéruzoré bent over trying awkwardly to paddle with his hands, while this huge tugboat, belching dense black diesel smoke, is chasing after him. He's being blown toward a beach, so I know he won't get in trouble provided he doesn't capsize or the tug doesn't run him down. It's all very funny until I notice he's wearing my extra set of foul-weather gear.

We trimmed sails and got out of there. Meanwhile, Bruno's conducting an interview on the hand-held VHF with Radio France. Later we learned Kéruzoré lived to tell the tale. While he appropriated my extra suit of foul-weather gear, he left three bottles of wine, which were appreciated. It was Kéruzoré's empty bottles that I later tossed over the side, in my quest for pen pals.

# "In which Passepartout talks rather more, perhaps, than is prudent"

The British consul at Suez, who stamped the travelers' passports, told Fix, the detective, that he was not convinced that Fogg was the gentlemanly bank robber. " 'Well, he looks and acts like a perfectly honest man,' " he said.

Fix remained unpersuaded. " 'Possibly; but that is not the question. Do you think, consul, that this phlegmatic gentleman resembles, feature by feature, the robber whose description I have received?'

" 'I concede that,' " said the British official. " 'But then, you know, all descriptions—'

" 'I'll make certain of it,' " interrupted Fix, who decided to question Passepartout: " 'The servant seems to me less mysterious than the master; besides, he's a Frenchman, and can't help talking.' "

Without identifying himself as a detective or sharing his suspicions, Fix engaged the voluble Frenchman in a discussion. In the course of their conversation, Passepartout said he was amazed to be in Egypt, which he suddenly realized is in Africa. " 'In Africa!

Just think, monsieur, I had no idea that we should go farther than Paris; and all that I saw of Paris was between twenty minutes past seven and twenty minutes before nine in the morning, between the Northern and the Lyons stations. . . .'

" 'You are in a great hurry, then?' " asked Fix.

" 'I am not, but my master is. By the way, I must buy some shoes and shirts. We came away without trunks, only with a carpet-bag.' " From this, Fix concluded that they were on the run, likely from the law.

Fix agreeably offered to show Passepartout an appropriate shop. The Frenchman was appreciative but worried about missing the steamer, which was to depart that evening for Aden and then India. Don't worry, Fix assured him; there was plenty of time. " 'It's only twelve o'clock.' "

Passepartout is nonplussed. He pulls out his impressive watch. " 'Twelve! . . . Why, it's only eight minutes before ten.' "

For the second time in a week, Passepartout was told his watch was slow. To this Frenchman, can there be a greater insult? " 'My watch? A family watch, monsieur, which has come down from my great-grandfather! It doesn't vary five minutes in the year, it's a perfect chronometer, look you.' "

" 'I see how it is,' " replied Fix. " 'You have kept London time, which is two hours behind that of Suez.[1] You ought to regulate your watch at noon in each country.'

" 'I regulate my watch? Never!'

" 'Well, then,' " says Fix, " 'it will not agree with the sun.'

" 'So much the worse for the sun, monsieur. The sun will be wrong, then!' "

Passepartout was all innocence, while Fix was cynical—hard boiled. This dissimilarity characterized their relationship.

In his naïveté, Passepartout revealed several other items to the detective, which the latter found incriminating: The first was that

---

[1] The longitude of Suez is about 32:14:53 E, meaning they have crossed *two* 15-degree time zones.

they had left England shortly after the robbery. Said Passepartout, " 'Last Friday at eight o'clock in the evening, Monsieur Fogg came home from his club, and three quarters of an hour afterwards we were off.' " It also means that the translator has again erred on the date, because October 2, 1872, the day they departed, was a *Wednesday*. But again, "it's enough to mention the error."

Passepartout also said that he didn't believe his master's cover story, that they were really going around the world because of a wager. " 'That wouldn't be common sense. There's something else in the wind,' " he speculated.

To Fix's question: Is Fogg rich? Passepartout said, " 'No doubt, for he is carrying an enormous sum in brand-new bank notes with him. And he doesn't spare the money on the way, either: he has offered a large reward to the engineer of the *Mongolia* if he gets us to Bombay well in advance of time.' "

Then Passepartout said he didn't know his master very well, having only been in his employ since the day they left London.

Fix was fairly bubbling with excitement. He was sure he had his man. At this point, the author summarizes the compelling circumstantial evidence provided by the loose-lipped Frenchman: the hasty departure from London soon after the robbery; the large sum of money carried by Fogg; his eagerness to reach distant lands; the pretext of an eccentric and foolhardy bet; and the fact that his servant knew little or nothing about him.

Fix hatched a plan and shared it later that day with the British consul: " '[I will] send a dispatch to London for a warrant of arrest to be dispatched instantly to Bombay, take passage on board the *Mongolia*, follow my rogue to India, and there, on English ground, arrest him politely, with my warrant in my hand, and my hand on his shoulder.' "

That evening the travelers, including Fix, were aboard the *Mongolia*, heading the length of the Red Sea for Aden, a distance of 1,310 miles, according to Verne. The steamship company allotted the *Mongolia* 138 hours, or almost six days, to make the passage. Fogg paid no attention to the exotic world that slipped past his ship. Verne describes him as "one of those Englishmen who are wont to see foreign countries through the eyes of their domestics."

Despite boisterous seas, in which the *"Mongolia,* with her long hull, rolled fearfully," Fogg ate four meals a day and indefatigably played whist. His partners included a tax collector on the way to Goa, a port city south of Bombay; the Reverend Decimus Smith, returning to his parish at Bombay; and an unnamed brigadier general of the English army, who was about to rejoin his brigade at Benares, on the Ganges River Plain, in India. Later, we learn that this was Sir Francis Cromarty, who would join Fogg and Passepartout on the rail passage across India.

As for Passepartout, he proved himself to be an able and hungry seaman too. He was delighted to renew his acquaintance with Fix, who, by coincidence, in Passepartout's mind, just happened to be on the *Mongolia.* Fix frequently bought the Frenchman a glass of whiskey or pale ale in the steamer barroom. Such kindness Passepartout "never failed to accept with graceful alacrity," writes Verne, "mentally pronouncing Fix the best of good fellows." The detective also used their good fellowship to ask Passepartout seemingly innocent questions about his master.

At Aden, Fogg and Passepartout went ashore to get their passports visaed. They were followed surreptitiously by the detective. After which, Verne tells us, "Mr. Fogg returned on board to resume his former habits; while Passepartout, according to custom, sauntered about among the mixed populations of Somalis, Banyans, Parsees, Jews, Arabs, and Europeans who comprise the twenty-five thousand inhabitants of Aden. He gazed with wonder upon the fortifications which make this place the Gibraltar of the Indian Ocean, and the vast cisterns where the English engineers were still at work, two thousand years after the engineers of Solomon.

" 'Very curious, very curious,' said Passepartout . . . on returning to the steamer. 'I see that it is by no means useless to travel, if a man wants to see something new.' "

The *Mongolia* arrived early in Bombay, India, on October 20, 1872. Since leaving London, Fogg had traveled eighteen days and was at this point two days ahead of schedule. He "calmly entered this fact in the itinerary," writes Verne.

Once off the *Mongolia*, the travelers have three and a half hours until the train to Calcutta leaves, at 8:00 P.M. Fogg got his passport visaed, and then went immediately to the train station. Fix reported to police headquarters, where he learned the unhappy news—for him—that no warrant for the arrest of Phileas Fogg had arrived. He resolved to follow Fogg on the train to Calcutta.

Passepartout went off to buy "the usual quota of shirts and shoes." After that he wandered the streets. Verne writes, "It happened to be the day of a Parsee festival. These descendants of the sect of Zoroaster—the most thrifty, civilized, intelligent, and austere of the East Indians, among whom are counted the richest native merchants of Bombay—were celebrating a sort of religious carnival, with processions and shows, in the midst of which Indian dancing-girls, clothed in rose-coloured gauze, looped up with gold and silver, danced airily, but with perfect modesty, to the sound of viols and the clanging of tambourines. It is needless to say that Passepartout watched these curious ceremonies with staring eyes and gaping mouth, and that his countenance was that of the greenest booby imaginable."

After following the carnival for a while, Passepartout saw the "splendid pagoda on Malebar Hill," writes Verne, "and was seized with an irresistible desire to see the interior." He was ignorant of the fact that Christians were forbidden to enter certain Indian temples, such as this one, and that even Indian visitors had to leave their shoes outside. Passepartout found himself lost in the "splendid Brahmin ornamentation," when he was jumped by three outraged priests, who tore off his shoes.

Never fear. "The agile Frenchman was soon upon his feet again, and lost no time in knocking down two of his long-gowned adversaries with his fists and a vigorous application of his toes; then, rushing out of the pagoda as fast as his legs could carry him, he soon escaped the third priest by mingling with the crowd in the streets." However, he was shoeless and hatless and had lost his packages.

In this sorry condition, Passepartout reported his misadventure to his master, who was not pleased. " 'I hope that this will not happen again,' " Fogg said coldly. This conversation was over-heard by an eavesdropping Fix, who had an inspiration and changed his plans. " 'No, I'll stay,' " he muttered to himself. " 'An offence has been committed on Indian soil. I've got my man.' "

# In which we travel rather faster, perhaps, than is prudent

After we'd departed the Cape Verde Islands, leaving Kéruzoré in the volcanic dust, flying fish began making their aerial assault on *Commodore Explorer*. You'd hear them go *thump! thump! thump!* into the hulls and often onto the trampoline, or net strung between hulls. It was like bugs hitting your car's windshield in Nebraska in the summer, only the bugs were fifteen inches long and weighed a couple pounds. While this isn't as much of a problem on monohulls, the two hulls of the catamaran seemed to confuse the fish and herd them at or onto the boat. One late night I was on deck with Marc, both of us slightly unfocused due to lack of sleep. Occasionally, we heard the *thump!* of flying fish. With a flashlight, I went around harvesting them; they were still quivering with life. I cut off their heads and fried them up in my galley, which I had taken to calling the "Flying Pig and Commodore Café on the Rive Gauche." Marc and I ate *poisson volant* at three in the morning, while drinking a bottle of Kéruzoré's wine. As I wrote in my log, "One life for another."

Another night, Jacques got hit in his manly center by a flying fish. It was *poisson volant* smack-dab in his balls. It took him a full five minutes to stand tall again.

An essential element for an adventurer, I believe, is to "bear affliction," as Gloucester says in *King Lear*, "till it do cry out itself." All of us suffered in those early days, but Jacques suffered the most. Normally he's the most phlegmatic, easygoing, amusing guy imaginable. "Tick-Tock" Jacques is the perfect shipmate. He'd sailed around the world once before on a maxi called *The Card*, in the 1989–90 Whitbread Round the World Race, so this wasn't new to him.

Yet this was Jacques from another planet. He was physically and mentally fried when we started, and no matter what the crew or I did to help him, he couldn't seem to reestablish himself. I brought him extra food; the crew and I also stood parts of his watches so he could get some extra rest.

Jacques's mood was caused, or at least exacerbated, by an angry skin condition that erupted the first week of the voyage and never went away. These hives, what the French call *boutons*, flared up around his wrists, for example, where the elastic of his foul-weather gear ate into his skin. The salt water, which blew into the boat at the combined speed of the boat and the wind, made it worse. Often, it was as if facing off with a fire hose. Also, the sun baked down, frying his already damaged skin. His hives became infected.

For Jacques, there was little relief belowdecks either. He slept in what we called the *"dérive chambre,"* or daggerboard room, in the starboard cabin.

The electronics were on the starboard side. This is Jacques's forte, and so it seemed appropriate that he be close to them. Also, he'd sailed thousands of miles with Bruno, who lived on this side too. I think Jacques wanted to sleep in the back, behind Bruno, but it was too difficult to crawl past him. Besides Bruno and all his stuff, which ranged from electronics to wet clothes, the spare spinnaker blocked the way. Then, too, Jacques's feet smelled, and Bruno wanted him forward—not in his cabin. Such was the privilege of rank for Bruno and the curse of being rank for Jacques.

For Jacques, however, the *dérive chambre* must have been like living in the bucket of a dehumidifier, as the uninsulated dagger-board case was several degrees cooler than the air in his tiny cabin. It would condense all the humidity from the air and drip on him. There was also an ineffectual Dorade vent, which would deliver fresh air, as it should, but also a shower of water, which it shouldn't. Further, the dagger board in his cabin would stick anywhere from five to twelve feet into the water, depending on the boat's angle to the wind. It hummed at various, if all-awful, pitches like a 20-square-foot tuning fork. As such, these cabins (there was one on the port side too) were, also, the noisiest spots on or in the boat.

Doubtless, he was uncomfortable there. A couple times I'd caught him sleeping headfirst, which is a cardinal sin in a boat, particularly one traveling at 20 or more knots. Hit something, like a whale or a log, and the boat will stop in its tracks. However, the crew members keep going at the speed of the boat until friction stops them or they hit something. Better your feet lead the charge than your head.

I can pinpoint, I think, the moment when Jacques had short-circuited ashore. Molly and I were at what I dubbed "the little blue ship shop," in La Trinité. It was run by two sisters, who were delightful and helpful, provided you got there before about noon. After that, the *vin ordinaire* would take a toll. Cheap wine aside, they were very sincere and very dear ladies, who would open up for us anytime of the day or night.

One day, Jacques showed up there while we were looking for fishing tackle and shouted that the compass adjuster was at the boat, and we'd have to leave that instant. He bundled us out of the store and down to the boat, where we spent three hours removing magnetic deviation from our compasses. Meanwhile Jacques has talked the port captain into giving us a tow out; there's no engine on our boat. This guy thinks it's going to be a fifteen-minute job and then he can get back to work, but Jacques keeps him out there with us for the entire time. He's pissed and Jacques is aware of it but trying hard to ignore it.

That day, I mouthed to Molly, "Who is this guy?" I'd known Jacques for years and had never seen this overwrought side. In the evening, Bruno appeared, and I told him, "Jacques hit the panic button." We all had a good laugh about it. However, as the voyage progressed, Jacques seemed unable to find his personal "true north."

One night, when we'd been out a week, I was running across the trampoline. I wore a baseball cap pulled low, to keep the spray from my eyes and the flying fish, I hoped, from my face. At full tilt, I ran into the boom with my head. Ah, to be in London, I thought. When the fog finally subsided, I was lying flat on my back. I got up and finished my traverse.

This cloud had a silver lining, however. Back in France, I'd been having trouble with a pinched nerve in my neck. It was causing my hands to go numb. Finally, I'd gone to an osteopath, who worked on my neck for an hour a day. His hands-on treatment seemed to help. After I ran into the boom, the pinched nerve in my neck never bothered me again.

North of the equator lies a trap: the doldrums. This area, more formally known as the "intertropical convergence

zone," is where the northeast trades of the northern hemisphere and the southeast trades of the southern hemisphere meet and tend to cancel one another out. The wind
is typically light and confused—it can trap a sailing vessel
for days—but at other times it can show thunderstorms
and an abundance of wind. Then the squalls pass and then
you park. And you fry in the near-equatorial sun.

Joshua Slocum, who made the first solo circumnavigation beginning in 1895, in his 37-foot sailboat *Spray*, described this alternately breathless and tempestuous area
this way in his classic book *Sailing Alone Around the World:*
"On the following day heavy rain-clouds rose in the south,
obscuring the sun; this was ominous of doldrums. On the
16th [of September 1895] the *Spray* entered this gloomy region, to battle with squalls and to be harassed by fitful
calms; for this is the state of the elements between the
northeast and the southeast trades, where each wind,
struggling in turn for mastery, expends its force whirling
about in all directions. Making this still more trying to
one's nerve and patience, the sea was tossed into confused
cross-lumps and fretted by eddying currents. As if something more were needed to complete a sailor's discomfort
in this state, the rain poured down in torrents day and
night. The *Spray* struggled and tossed for ten days, making
only three hundred miles on her course in all that time. I
didn't say anything!"

Since we'd dropped Kéruzoré off at the Cape Verde Islands, just off Africa, we were committed to cross the doldrums to the west. Peter Blake and Robin Knox-Johnston
on *ENZA* went east. *ENZA,* you will recall, had crossed the
starting line more than six hours ahead of us.

By this time, we were talking to them almost daily on the
single-sideband radio. We'd usually exchange positions
and pleasantries. One day, Robin Knox-Johnston told me
that he had to get off the radio because Peter Blake had just

removed two fresh loaves of bread from the oven; if he didn't move quickly they'd be gone—picked clean by the crew. I thought about my one-burner stove that could do little more than heat water and wondered for a moment about my lot in life.

For me, it felt good to be talking English with native speakers. It was also good to know that there was another boat out there who knew where you were and was willing and able to come to your rescue should you need it. This is the nautical version of the buddy system. I'm sure our proximity and friendship were reassuring to them, too. Somewhere out there lurked Olivier de Kersauson and his crew on *Charal*, which at this point was rigged for silent running.

This day, I started the "chat hour" by asking if they'd seen any camels, since they were so far east, so close to the desert of Africa in the country of Mauritania. Then we exchanged positions. I plotted theirs and realized we'd passed them that day. Thank you, Kéruzoré, I thought to myself, for forcing us to go west.

I didn't say anything, however, to them. The world is a very big place, and there were 24,000 miles to go at this point.

After 8 days, 19 hours, 26 minutes of voyaging, we crossed the equator, at 0 degrees, on February 9, 1993, at 08:22:24 GMT. This was my first crossing of the equator under sail, and this step is considered a milestone—a rite of passage—for sailors. The others had crossed the equator dozens of times.

I thought there was going to be some sort of celebration. There are pictures of the Whitbread crews getting dressed up as King Neptune, his court, and court jesters, and welcoming initiates, like me, into the club. It's kind of a "Hell Night" for inductees where various indignities—mostly innocuous—are performed. The "Neptunian ceremonies," as this is called, date back at least to the clipper-ship days.

We just kept going, however. It was a little disappointing. While I believe that some steps are more important than others, maybe other people don't. Or maybe they were just tired. Jacques made a joke about how crossing the equator was a function of your navigation, and that there are several equators floating around out there.

Anyway, the GPS said by way of its chilly liquid-crystal display that we had crossed the equator and were now in the southern latitude bands. The night before, Polaris, or the North Star, had disappeared below the horizon.

The next night I saw the Southern Cross constellation, or Crux. It is this constellation, in the shape of a cross, that appears on the Australian and New Zealand flags. Like the Big Dipper that points to the North Star, and thus the North Pole, the Southern Cross's long arm points directly to the South Pole. As such, it has some import for navigation.

We'd beaten *ENZA* to the equator by about 20 miles. Bruno got on the single-sideband (SSB) radio and asked Michel Horeau, our press agent back in France, to check the record for sailing from the English Channel to the equator. He reported back, the record now belonged to us.

After Bruno's ship-to-shore call, I got through to Molly and then my father, for the first time after many tries. Apparently, the ionosphere—a mirror or reflector for radio waves—decided to cooperate with my need to communicate. That day, the world seemed a smaller—more manageable—place.

While my math skills were never much, on the day we crossed the equator I did some figuring. Our consumption of alcohol for the two cooking stoves was far greater than I had anticipated. At this rate of consumption, we'd be out of fuel long before we returned to France. While we could probably live on rehydrated but uncooked freeze-dried food, who would want to? I asked the crew to waste not, want not.

There were two man-overboard modules (MOM) on *Commodore Explorer*—one on the transom of either hull. The modules were deployed from the cockpit so if your watchmate saw you go overboard, all he had to do was pull this string, or ripcord. They had a little life raft that would inflate automatically, and you could actually climb onto it to get out of the water—away from the cold that could kill you in an hour or two in the icy Southern Ocean. Also to help those aboard find you, they had flares, strobe lights, and whistles.[1]

Just south of the equator, *Commodore Explorer* labored in lumpy seas. I turned around and noticed this large frigate bird, flying low toward us. With their long wing span, up to forty inches, and light weight, they are graceful soarers. I am a pilot, which doubtless influenced my appreciation of this bird's aerial derring-do. As I wrote in my journal, "Their wings are from God's drawing board, so precise in their maneuvers, graceful, effortless wave-skimming ground-effect dives, only to pull in their ailerons, zoom up into a stall, then full rudder and nose down to fight the stall and spin. Perfect in all respects of design and efficiency. Incredible creatures."

In some ways a catamaran like *Commodore Explorer* re-

---

[1] The assumptions here are that your watchmate saw you fall overboard, and that you could swim to the MOM. Considering that a boat going 20 knots travels 34 feet per second, and that swimming in foul-weather gear is practically impossible, those are daunting assumptions. But you do the best you can. If your watchmate saw you go overboard, there was a switch at each wheel that would sound an alarm in each cabin, as well as a switch to freeze the position on the GPS.

sembles a frigate bird—a graceful soarer. I was enjoying the visit, until I noticed that one of the safety modules was missing. I had seen it there fifteen minutes before.

This isn't good, I thought. We're losing equipment that could conceivably save someone's life. I also thought that perhaps the bird had come to warn us of our loss. After all, we were birds of a feather.

On February 12, we crossed the Tropic of Capricorn with barely a thump. Like the equator or the Greenwich Meridian, this is another imaginary line on earth but one with added significance. At $23\frac{1}{2}$ degrees south latitude, this is as far south as the apparent sun gets. The sun "arrives" there on or about December 21 (the "winter solstice"), which is winter in the northern hemisphere, summer in the southern hemisphere. The Tropic of Cancer, at $23\frac{1}{2}$ degrees north latitude, is the northern equivalent. The sun arrives there on or about June 21 (the "summer solstice"), which is summer in the northern hemisphere, winter in the southern.

Actually, the sun doesn't "arrive" anywhere. Rather the earth revolves around the sun in a counterclockwise direction along a fixed path, at an unvarying angle of $23\frac{1}{2}$ degrees to the plane of the earth's orbit.[2] In December, the southern hemisphere is tilted toward the sun. Like a sunbather who props him- or herself up in a lounge chair to be more perpendicular to the sun's ray, this gives the southern hemisphere several more hours of daylight than dark, and thus more energy from the sun or more "cooking time." On December 21, for example, Antarctica (or any area within the "Antarctic Circle" beginning at $66\frac{1}{2}$ south latitude) has total daylight; the Arctic (or any area within

[2] If the earth weren't tilted at $23\frac{1}{2}$ degrees, there would be 12 hours of daylight and 12 hours of night everywhere on earth and all the time.

the "Arctic Circle" beginning at 66½ north latitude) is totally dark. In June, the northern hemisphere is tilted most directly at the sun. Thus it is summer there. Time to tan at the beach.

Two days before, on February 11, we'd passed the sun going north toward spring at the equator at its leisurely pace of ¼ degree a day. We were heading south and in a hurry, doing more than six degrees a day. It felt like ships passing in the night.

If the eighteenth day, on October 20, 1872, was a satisfying one for Phileas Fogg, as he stepped ashore in India, with two full days comfortably deposited in his journal, the eighteenth day, on February 16, 1993, was an awful one for the crew of *Commodore Explorer*.

Since leaving France, it had taken us eight days to get to the equator, to set a record, and another eight days to get into the Roaring Forties. That is an average speed of 343 nautical miles a day, or 14.32 knots. If Fogg banked two days for his 80-day tour of the world, at that point we could bank one in our attempt to break that record. On that fateful February day, we were about 1,640 miles west-southwest of the Cape of Good Hope, at the foot of Africa.

A couple days before, we'd stopped sailing due south and had turned gradually to the left, to the south-south-east, to begin chasing the rising sun. We were now traveling in a similar direction to that of Fogg, Passepartout, and, of course, the cunning Detective Fix.

For us, it was time to roll the dice; to play that endgame for round-the-world sailors: how far south—how close to Antarctica—dare you go?

Most of us imagine the earth as a globe, with the North up, the South down, and the equator in the middle. Certainly a Fogg and Passepartout, whose course around the world would range from about 52 degrees north latitude to about 2 degrees north latitude, would see the earth that way.

Round-the-world sailors, however, envision the earth with Antarctica as the center, and an around-the-world voyage is, to a large measure, a rounding of Antarctica. Turn your globe upside down to see what I mean.

Why is a nautical circumnavigation a rounding of Antarctica? First, until this century, the only opening, or sea route, for such a passage, was between the Cape of Good Hope, Cape Leeuwin, Cape Horn (or alternatively the Strait of Magellan, 214 nautical miles north of Cape Horn) and Antarctica; that is, between 55 and 63 degrees south latitude.[3] North of this path, a significant amount of land intervenes—Europe, Africa, Asia, Australia, North America, and South America, for example—which makes for tough sailing.

Then, once you are forced to go south, the closer you dare sail to Antarctica, the shorter is the distance around the world. This is best explained with an analogy: Give me a bow saw long enough and a prop and arm strong enough, to rephrase Archimedes, and I could cut the earth into 180 parallel circles along the latitude lines. Ninety of

---

[3] While today there are other options—the Suez Canal, which opened in 1869, obviated the need to round the Cape of Good Hope; the Panama Canal, which opened in 1914, precluded the need to round Cape Horn—those shortcuts hold little cachet for adventurers. Even the Strait of Magellan, first traversed by Ferdinand Magellan in 1519 in the world's first around-the-world voyage, is considered a shortcut—less of an adventure. It should be noted that Magellan sailed west, *into* the prevailing westerly winds, the so-called "Roaring Forties" and "Howling Fifties," at the bottom of South America, while we sailed east *with* the wind. Magellan, a Portuguese explorer sailing for Spain, named the Pacific Ocean. He was killed in the Philippines on April 27, 1521, when he got involved in a local war. The voyage was completed by Juan Sebastian del Cano. Of 270 men who started the voyage in September 20, 1519, only 21 returned on September 8, 1522.

those circles would be above the equator, to correspond to the latitude lines, and 90 below.[4]

The circle at the equator would be the largest at 24,902 statute miles, or 21,654 nautical miles. As you go north or south from the equator, the circles get progressively smaller. The smallest circles would be at 90 degrees north latitude, or the North Pole, and 90 degrees south latitude, the South Pole. They would be inches around, or Frisbee-size.

However, a polar circumnavigation isn't possible for sailors, as it is for fliers, like Admiral Byrd, or mushers, like Roald Amundsen and Admiral Robert E. Peary (the American who first reached the North Pole in 1909), because what water there is there is ice.[5] At the top of the world, for example, the drifting ice pack averages ten feet thick over much of the Arctic Ocean, which is 5,541,000 square miles.

At the bottom, there is Antarctica, which is about the same size as the Arctic Ocean. If Antarctica wasn't enough to block your way, on top of the land is 90 percent of the earth's ice, which is up to two miles thick. Winter winds can reach 200 mph, and the winter temperature can drop to −126.9° F (−88.3° C)— that is the coldest temperature ever recorded on earth. It was, as mentioned, in such conditions in 1934 that my distant relative Admiral Byrd chose to winter alone.

[4] Latitude lines are man-made constructions that are *parallel* to the equator; in fact, they are often called "parallels of latitude." Those above the equator, which is 0 degrees, are designated as "north latitude"; those below, "south latitude."

[5] The strict interpretation of a circumnavigation, at least according to *The Guinness Book of World Records*, requires passing through "antipodal points." This means literally passing through two points on the exact opposite sides of the earth. Thus, a sprint around the earth at the North or South Pole would not qualify as a circumnavigation under the formal definition. The antipodal point from the North Pole would be the South Pole. *Guinness* defines *antipodal points* as two points at least 12,429 statute miles (20,000 km) apart.

So the farther south you go, the distance around the world is shorter, but, also, the closer to the "edge" you are. First, there is the weather, which is typically winter, even in the antipodean summer months of December, January, February, and March. Then there is the wind and waves that march around this area practically unimpeded. There is practically no place to run, no place to hide.

Beyond the winter weather, wind, and waves, there are icebergs and associated growlers. While icebergs are threatening, you can usually see them. Growlers can be Mack-truck-sized pieces of ice that have calved off icebergs. Awash much of the time, they are almost impossible to see. Should you hit one, you're history.

An aggressive—more southerly—circumnavigation might get down to 62 degrees south latitude and entail less than 27,000 nautical miles, including the jog south and north, which can be considerable. For example, before we made our gradual left-hand turn to the east, we'd sailed over 5,000 nautical miles to the south. We still had 3,000 miles to go to the Cape of Good Hope. Our return north to France would consume a similar distance: 8,000 miles. So the trip around Antarctica would be 11,000 nautical miles.

Eighty days is 1,920 hours. If you could average 14.0625 knots and go that far south—that close to the edge—you might sail around the world in under 80 days. Of course, some days you'd be in the windless doldrums—that we'd passed the week before—glued to an oily sea; other days you'd be surfing as fast as you dare go. That's the misleading thing about averages; they tell about half the story.

We considered 14 knots our "magic number." If we were above it, we were happy; below it, we were blue. On February 16, 1993, we were way above it, and I was worried. There was a vague but unmistakable end-of-the-world feel to the boat.

We were diving south quicker than I would have liked.

De Kersauson, after 21 days of silent running on *Charal*, had resurfaced and revealed his position. He was south of us—closer to Antarctica—but while ahead, his eight-day advantage was reduced to two.

He had departed more than a week early, without crossing the official Jules Verne Trophée starting line, and without anteing up the $16,000 entry fee. Nevertheless, if he was successful and we failed or if he was first even if we were faster, he would receive—and deserve—the acclaim.

It's like I said before: Everyone knows Charles Lindbergh. Few remember that two weeks later in June 1927, Charles Levine and Clarence Chamberlin reached Germany, having made a significantly longer flight than Lindbergh.

Bruno chose to go after de Kersauson now, despite the fact that an ill-tempered low-pressure system had plagued the South Atlantic for a month. While we made a gradual left turn, Blake and Knox-Johnston on *ENZA*, behind us, made a sharper left-hand turn toward Cape Town. Blake had sailed around the world five previous times in the Whitbread Race, which he won in 1989–90. Also, being from New Zealand, these were, in effect, home waters. He seemed in no hurry to dig south, to confront danger, and thus *ENZA* stayed 200 miles to our north. It was in some ways the around-the-world version of the tortoise, *ENZA*, and the hares, *Charal* and *Commodore Explorer*— or the cautious and the foolhardy.

The day after we went south of east, the wind was behind us. In fact, at this point we'd sailed close to 6,000 miles without tacking, meaning the true wind had never been forward of the beam.[6]

I was driving *Commodore Explorer* at a steady 24 knots.

---

[6] True wind is the wind that an anchored or stationary boat feels. Once a boat starts to move, its speed and angle to the true wind give

From time to time, the boat would pass over the top of one of the waves, which were now about condominium size, and hurtle down its face. It was akin to that first drop of a roller coaster. The one that typically takes you the entire distance.

A couple of times I got going so fast that the bows of the boat seemed about to stick into the wave ahead. My fear was that the boat would trip over its bows. As I later wrote in my log, "Alone on deck. Two huge, terrifying, scary adrenaline-pumping descents. . . ."

When I'd first seen the boat out of the water at the Multiplast Yard in Vannes in November, the day after Thanksgiving, she'd seemed huge. Now, as the waves licked around her, she seemed insubstantial—unequal to the task. I said, "This is crazy; we're going to break the boat." But Marc and Chinois, who had been crew members on this boat for years and had been around the world, weren't troubled by it. It was hard for me to argue with them because I had fewer sea miles on such boats than anyone. So I sat on my fears—a remarkably uncomfortable perch, I found, like the princess and the pea.

What Marc and Chinois neglected to tell me, however, was that after a seven-day dash across the ocean, the boat, then named *Jet Services V*, was trashed. It would require months of healing back in the boatyard and tons of francs to make her whole again.

Finally, Bruno stuck his head out of his starboard-hull cabin and called for a "taxi!" We would steer from the high side, or windward hull, so you would have a long unprotected traverse of the trampoline if you lived or were working in the low hull, or leeward side.

Crossing the trampoline was like running on a water

---

rise to the "apparent wind"—the wind speed and direction as measured on a moving boat.

bed, wearing sloppy seaboots. The waves that penetrated the trampoline here and there made it like running on a water bed that had sprung geyser-size and -strength leaks in random places.

Rule number one was that you notified the boat's driver of your intention to cross the boat. This was no mean task, since the helmsman was typically wearing a hat and hood and often Oakley $H_2O$ goggles to protect his eyes and face from the firehoselike spray of the bow wave. Then there's a constant roar of the boat passing through the water. Also, if you're on the low side, the helmsman is about 34 feet away. With the helmsman upwind of you, your words are often blown back into your face. It's about as effective as spitting into the wind.

We discovered that the word *taxi*—common to French and English—best penetrated the din and the wind. Then, the one calling for a taxi would wait for the helmsman to slow the boat to a safe speed. When the sea was not screaming up through the net or over the windward bow, this person would haul his butt across.

Rule number two was use lifelines and the safety lines that traversed the net. Rule number three was RUN. I remember a couple of times crossing the boat so quickly that I had to slide to a stop, as if I were making a suicide squeeze for home plate. I often shouted, "Safe!" but none of my French shipmates understood.

When safely across, Bruno said, "Maybe a reef in the staysail and another in the mainsail might be in order." It was now blowing 45–55. We did that, and the boat continue sailing at 25 knots. Then we dropped the staysail and put the third reef in the mainsail, and the boat was still doing 25 knots.

To make matters worse, there was this awful cross-sea— waves from several different directions—so you had no idea from where the next assault was coming. Also, the temperature had dropped several degrees in a short time, along with the height of the barometer. This is called a "depression," which mirrored my mood.

Bruno was driving. This was the first real storm we'd been in since leaving France, and Marc was filming him with the video camera. After all, there's no business like show business. The rest of us were down below.

Then Bruno skied down a 40-foot wave that, he later said, suddenly collapsed. *Commodore Explorer* changed from being a boat to an unlikely and ungainly bird until the hulls were planted in the wave ahead. She must have looked like a pelican diving into a wave. Ten tons of catamaran went from Mach speed to nothing, in an instant. It was like running into a brick wall at 30 mph. As the boat stopped, it pirouetted around the leeward-starboard hull. The boat's attitude changed from horizontal to vertical, and both rudders came out of the water. Eighty-six feet of catamaran hung in the air for an awful instant, as if deciding whether to continue going over or not. Life and death were surely held in the balance. It's a miracle we didn't continue going over.

As the boat stopped, Marc, who was in front of Bruno, went rocketing forward, until he took out the NKE instrument display with his head. Later we would watch his backward flight on the video camera, and later we could laugh about it. "Yer out!" I shouted during the video, which again perplexed my four French friends.

I'd been sitting down below cooking corn biscuits in too much hot oil—trying to fatten these guys up for the south. At the same time, I had a cup of hot chocolate held casually, if dangerously, between my bare legs. Also, in my galley was a larger container of hot chocolate for the crew. Suddenly I was launched forward, and chocolate "soup" was everywhere. At the same time, Chinois was propelled from his bunk, behind me, and landed feet-first at my feet.

My first concern was that the hot oil would catch fire, so I quickly turned off the alcohol stove. My second worry was Chinois, whom I asked if he was okay. He was and proceeded to crawl back into his bunk, as if this were just another day at the office. "Hey, Chinois," I said, "can you help?"

I stuck my head into the cockpit. Bruno was wide-eyed and ashen. His tan had been totally erased by naked fear. He was the only one who had seen the whole thing; the only one with a clear view of what a watery white death looks like. Later, he said there was water to the main beam, which is 30 or 40 feet back from the bows. Marc was dazed and bleeding; he was holding his head.

Then I remembered Jacques; I was worried that he'd been sleeping headfirst, as he was wont to do in his endless search to find some comfort. If he was, he's dead, I thought. We went down into the starboard hull, and there were tons of white water, lapping at but not quite reaching Bruno's electronics. We found Jacques, who fortunately had been sleeping feet first.

Next, we took down what was left of the mainsail and ran for a full day under bare poles in 55–60 knots of wind. We'd completely lost our nerve. I remember being alone on deck steering, trying to keep boatspeed under 10 knots. I had never seen waves like that; they were 60-footers, and still confused, and some of them were breaking. As breaking waves break boats—like the flick of a huge locker-room towel—those are the bad ones. It took hours to clean the boat—I found chocolate soup in a hanging locker 18 feet forward of my galley—and to pump out the water. It took many more hours to regain our confidence to fly sails again. After the crash, Bruno wasn't seen on deck. The crew joked he was in his cabin writing his last will and testament.

Also, we headed back to the north, toward the Cape of

Good Hope. Discretion won out over valor; we became a tortoise again.

The night of that awful day, February 16, de Kersauson hit something, perhaps a growler, or a piece of an iceberg. It ripped his starboard hull some 26 feet. He was forced to turn back 1,000 miles to Cape Town. We learned of his troubles from Michel Horeau, our public-relations man back in France.

Recall that when de Kersauson was asked by the press what he thought about Bruno Peyron's chance to sail around the world in under 80 days, he'd said, "Who?" It became a standing joke on *Commodore Explorer*. Every time someone mentioned Bruno's name, someone else would say *Qui?* or who? Bruno, however, was unwilling to forget de Kersauson.

When Bruno was twenty-two, in 1980, he sailed his first Route du Rhum race, from Saint Malo, France, to Pointe-à-Pitre, Guadeloupe. He ran aground after the finish. The only person who came to his aid was Olivier de Kersauson.

On *Commodore Explorer*, we had a Sat-C navigation system. With it, we could send telexes and faxes and could receive telexes. After learning of his difficulty, Bruno sent de Kersauson and his crew a fax, offering them our help. He never responded. In this lonely part of the world, fax coverage was episodic, to be sure, so perhaps he never received it.

"A man who dances to his own drummer," as I've said before, de Kersauson made Cape Town under his own power. At a press conference there, he is quoted by *South African Yachting* magazine as saying, "The [Jules Verne Trophée] organizers are full of bullshit."

And then there were two: *ENZA* and *Commodore Explorer*.

# In which
# Peter Pan learns
# his bride-to-be
# is with child

---

"One, if by land, two, if by sea" was high-tech communications in the eighteenth century, when the unruly child America stood up to the stern parent, England. Alternatively, people who wished to communicate long distances used smoke signals, mirrors, church bells, or the beat-beat-beat of the tom-tom. Of course, you had to see the signal or hear it to understand it. (Also, understanding it assumed you knew the language or code; for example, one could have been if by sea, two if by land.) The need to see or hear it limited the distances that messages could travel.

The steam locomotive, which came first to England in 1804, changed not only transportation but communications. If you lived then and wished to send a message over some distance, you could write it on paper and put it on the train. In other words, the message had to be physically carried by you or by someone else, from source to destination.

By 1829, the wonderfully named *Rocket*, a steam locomotive built by George and Robert Stephenson, could travel at a top speed of 29 mph, or 47 km/h. So 29 mph was the top speed for transportation and long-distance communications.

In the early nineteenth century, there came a revolution in communications, too, which was not piggybacked on transportation. For example, Hans Oersted in 1820 discovered that a wire carrying electricity would deflect a needle. The result was the electric telegraph. By a variation in the timing of the pulses of electricity, numbers and letters, making up the message, could be represented.

The first railroad telegraph was established in England, in 1837. Now messages were no longer limited to 40 mph, the speed of the fastest trains 12 years after the *Rocket*, but were traveling at the speed of light: 186,000 mi/sec (299,000 km/sec).

Samuel F. B. Morse, an artist and inventor from Charlestown, Massachusetts, improved the device wholly with his telegraph receiver, designed in 1831. Here a pulse of current energized an electromagnet, which, in turn, attracted an armature made of iron. The armature could be attracted for a short period of time or a longer one. A short-time became a dot, in the alphabet Morse also developed, and a long-time became a dash. Using dots and dashes, Morse was able to represent letters and numbers, in what became known as Morse Code. For example, S-O-S, or *Save our ship*, is represented by three short dots for S, three long dashes for O, and, again, three short dots for S, or • • • — — — • • •

While Morse experimented with a pencil attached to the armature that scribed the long and short pulses on a moving strip of paper, it proved to be the telltale *click-click-click* of the armature that made his system so accessible. Here, hearing proved keener than seeing.

Morse proved the efficacy of his telegraph and code by sending the message "What hath God wrought," from Baltimore to Washington, in 1844. Soon telegraph wires crisscrossed America and most of Europe. Battery-powered relays reenergized the weak current, sending it ever farther down the line.

Doubtless, if in 1872 a real Detective Fix wired Scotland Yard from the Middle East, about an arrest warrant for a real bank robber, Morse code would have been used. If Fix could only have waited, he could have used a telephone, which was invented by Alexander Graham Bell, in 1876.

Today, electronic ons and offs are the grist—or Morse code—for computers such as the Commodore and Macintosh computers we carried aboard *Commodore Explorer*. Wires aren't needed anymore, as communications satellites, poised high above the earth, receive and then rebroadcast radio signals. Due to the height of the satellites, these signals can penetrate the most out-of-the-way places. Today, there is a rainstorm of electronic information out there, if you're equipped to receive it.

We could send faxes and telexes on *Commodore Explorer* and receive telexes. We could talk ship-to-shore on the single-sideband radio, through the marine operator. We could also receive weather faxes and even transmit digital photographs, taken aboard, which our sponsors found valuable. When de Kersauson's *Charal* dropped out, *Commodore Explorer* was the only French boat trying to sail around the world in under 80 days. It was us versus the Kiwi-Anglo effort of *ENZA*. As the only representative of a sailing-mad nation, photographs from *Commodore Explorer* found themselves in national newsmagazines in France.

On February 24, 1993, those ons and offs from a communications satellite found *Commodore Explorer* in the Indian

Ocean, when north of Prince Edward Island. Bruno Peyron, in his electronic lair in the starboard hull, saw the message first on the computer.

I was driving from the starboard-hull cockpit, and Bruno popped out of the hatch with a full-size grin across his face. "Lewie," he said, "you have to see this telex right now. It's for you, and it's important." I called Marc back from his safety stroll on the bow, where he was looking for anything that might be amiss. After Marc relieved me at the helm, I went belowdecks with Bruno. The message on the computer screen was from Molly, my newly named fiancée. It read: "Dear Cam: I am alone, you are miles away, and I am scared. I do not know if you have heard that I am pregnant! It was confirmed this morning. Hôtel du Parc, I think. So, too, is Nikki [Chinois's wife]. Please call or fax as I need to hear your voice. It is very important for me to know your feelings, as you need to contribute 100 percent as must I. I need to know whether you are prepared to be a father."

It must be something in the water in Brest, I thought. What wonderful news. From the starboard cabin, where the computer was, I called Chinois in the port hull on the VHF radio, which we used as an intercom. "Hey, Chinois!" I said. "You have a telex message, and it is important."

"It's too cold and wet now," he said groggily. "Besides I'm asleep. I'll see you later. . . ."

"No, Chinois. You are pregnant, and so am I." Moments later he appeared and stared at the computer screen. Home in America and home in France, Molly and Nikki were pregnant. A man of few words, Chinois merely beamed. A man of many words, so did I; suddenly my life seemed powered by a new source.

What Molly and Cam have wrought, I thought. Chinois and Nikki too. Peter Pan gets engaged, makes whoopee, and makes a baby. For a slow starter, I was making tracks. For the first time I felt I was forever linked and moving through life with two others. While it would surely put a crimp in my step, it also put a song in my heart. Over a beer a couple days later—the first opportunity we had to toast the news—I shared such thoughts with Chinois.

When I got off watch, I sent Molly a fax. It read: "To Molly and our beautiful baby-to-be. Hi, Sweetpea. I love you, and I hope you are happy today and strong, for we both need to be strong. I hope you are nourishing yourself and keeping strength in your body and soul so that our child will be born with a great personality and have good fortitude and strength for life. Bruno only hopes that she or he does not speak as fast and as much as I do.

"I realize completely the changes our lives will take and that as soon as possible we will have to find a home and prepare a nest for ourselves and the newborn. Where do you want to live? It is important to get our lives in order. It will have to wait, however, until I can get the rest of the way around this planet. . . ."

Although I didn't mention this to Molly, getting around this planet wasn't looking so easy at this point, as bodies, relationships, and the boat were fraying at the edges. For example, a couple of days before Molly's joyful news, Marc sounded a warning as we busied ourselves in the cockpit. "This one's coming aboard," he shouted. I didn't grasp his meaning until a huge wave broke aboard *Commodore Explorer*. As I've commented, breaking waves break boats; this one was like a sneak attack from Niagara Falls.

The waterfall launched me headfirst into the binnacle, designed to protect the compass from, among other things, flying heads. On my way past the binnacle, I smashed my ear, nose, shoulder, elbow, and scraped the remaining two thirds of my body. I was lucky to escape with an awfully sore ear, a bloody nose, and assorted bruises. Fortunately, I have a good solid head that appeared none the worse for wear—at least as I saw it. This followed the first-week blow to my head from the boom that forever cured my pinched nerve.

Marc, while surviving this sneak attack, still had substantial wounds on his head from his meeting with the NKE instruments eight days before, while videotaping Bruno in the storm. His right hip was still mostly discolored by an ugly bruise. He also had a badly bruised hand from when the boat had stuck its nose into another wave. Marc, who'd been working on deck, had had his harness line, which anchored him to the boat, wrapped absentmindedly around his hand. When the boat stopped, he kept going until the harness line ate into his hand.

Then on February 23, the day before Molly's telex, our rudder had hit something. It could have been a log, or even a sizable fish or whale. While there were cracks on deck from the collision, the hull didn't seem to have sustained any damage.

Jacques still had "sore boils from the sole of his foot unto his crown," which gave him the aforementioned appearance and disposition of Job, from the Bible, whence that description comes.

A couple of times I lost my temper and yelled at him. He was often late coming on watch, which meant others had to cover for him when they were tired and cold too. Once or twice, I beat on the top of his cabin with a winch handle to roust him from the sack.

Then I asked him repeatedly to start heating water before it was time to wake me for my 0800 watch with Marc. It would take twenty-five minutes to heat sufficient water to make a freeze-dried breakfast. If Jacques started the water at 0730—all he had to do was light the alcohol stove—I could have breakfast made for him and the rest of the crew before they went off-watch. I don't know if there was a language problem or what, but I couldn't get Jacques to do this; couldn't get him working for the common good. This meant I had to help Marc sail the boat, cook breakfast in the port hull, then carry the food over to Jacques in his starboard cabin, and often wake him to eat it. It meant I was serving him breakfast in bed.

Jacques, however, was like a grizzly bear in his den on a bad day. Never once did he say thank-you—to sound that familiar refrain of the galley drudge, which is what I felt like.

After I yelled at him Bruno said to me, "Look, we've got to take care of Jacques. I've had a talk with him; he's really mentally and physically fried.

"You're an American, and people might take it the wrong way if you're yelling or screaming. Just lighten up."

I said, "I know I've been a little overbearing, but I'm tired too; I've been carrying his load, so have Marc and Chinois."

The boat was breaking too. The first day, you will recall, we broke the bottom three feet of track that held the main-sail to the boom. That took us three days to repair. In the course of that, we forever fried the battery charger for the electric drill. It was back to the hand drill—back to the bad old days and ways.

Also, while *Commodore Explorer* had electronic self-steering at either wheel, as do most around-the-world boats, it never worked very well. The controls were often doused with seawater, which rendered the units inoperable, despite Jacques's best efforts to clean the electrical connections. It meant this boat was being hand-steered around the world, which was demanding of concentration and tiring —even though these boats are much easier to steer than a monohull.

What with the near-constant demands of the helm, you were ostensibly losing one crew member. Thus, anytime a maneuver got the least bit complicated, you had to wake up Bruno or the sleeping off-watch. Waking the off-watch was like emptying a bank account. Each time you did it, there was less left for a "rainy day."

Then the outhaul assembly, which attaches the clew (or back) of the mainsail to the boom, exploded when one of two plates failed. One of the plates was titanium and the other stainless steel. This is a bad marriage, as these two materials stretch differently. The titanium plate, which stretches less and thus was doing almost all of the work, broke in half.

After being repaired, the outhaul worked for a time. Then a shackle on one of the big Harken cars exploded. The pin to release it from the fitting was corroded in place, however. I tried everything, even cooking it on my alcohol stove, to get it to release through the differential in heat. Finally, I had to cut it off with a hacksaw, which took forever. Next, the man-overboard module (MOM), made its break for freedom.

We had two small diesel heaters, one in either cabin. This was as luxurious as things got on *Commodore Explorer*. The heater in Bruno's starboard cabin worked fine—Bruno often turned it down, although this had less to do with the fact that he was overheating than that at some critical temperature Jacques's unwashed body began to ripen. (Jacques had moved into Bruno's cabin at the end of the first month.) The heat seemed to accentuate the negative. Turning the heater down was the same principle as refrigerating garbage—not aesthetically pleasing, perhaps, but it keeps it from stinking.

Comparatively, the heater in the port hull, where Marc, Chinois, and I slept, seemed a poor relation. It wasn't thought out or executed very well; at the most it could raise the temperature inside our cabin by five or ten degrees over the temperature outside. Nevertheless, if you placed wet foul-weather gear or boots near it, they would dry. If there is a more wretched feeling than donning wet foul-weather gear and damp boots for a chilly 2:00 A.M. watch, it's beyond my experience. Also, the boat leaked everywhere, and the heat tended to dry things out, at least a little.

The port heater needed frequent attention, however. This fell to me, probably because the others, Marc and Chinois, were more stoical about the lack of heat than I was. Then, too, I'd seen my second suit of foul-weather gear paddle awkwardly away from *Commodore Explorer* on the bulky body of Jean-René Kéruzoré, our filmmaker, at the Cape Verde Islands.

Certainly up to now, none of this proved life threatening, just inconvenient or uncomfortable. Know, however, that in sailing little things can turn into big things in an instant. That can be the savage accounting of the sea.

Or maybe the piper need not be paid. For example, it took us three days to fix the track on the mast. That could have been a disaster if we had had to reef, but we didn't. Similarly, the loss of the MOM might be a disaster if someone should fall overboard, but if no one did, then it wouldn't be.

Know, too, that all of these breakdowns—the "unforeseen" to Phileas Fogg—were eating away at our bank of time and of physical energy.

# In which
# Phileas Fogg finds
# love on a funeral pyre

---

If the fourth week of our around-the-world voyage in February 1993 brought electronic news of the next generation of Lewises and Despaignes, Phileas Fogg's fourth week in October 1872 would lead to love.

In the first-class railroad car that departed Bombay on October 20, at 8:00 P.M., were Fogg, Passepartout, and the aforementioned Sir Francis Cromarty, a brigadier general of the English army and Fogg's whist partner from the *Mongolia.*

The British, who assumed control of this country in 1757, through the powerful East India Company, built the railroad network, making it the largest such system in Asia. While Verne doesn't mention it, the likelihood is that no Indians shared this first-class railroad car with our protagonists. A curious book, *Days in North India*, written by Norman MacLeod, D.D., in 1870, two years before Fogg and Passepartout's fictitious voyage, puts it this way: "I never saw any native gentlemen traveling in the same [train] compartment with Europeans. The circumstance, however, arises not so much from any repugnance of race, as from the customs and habits which make the native repugnant to the European, and the European equally repugnant to the native."

Verne tells us that Sir Francis "made India his home, only paying brief visits to England at rare intervals, and was as familiar as a native with the customs, history, and character of India and its people."

The author then contrasts Fogg's impassive and disinterested personality to that of Sir Francis: "But Phileas Fogg, who was not travelling, but only describing a circumference, took no pains to inquire into these subjects ['the customs, history, and character of India']; he was a solid body, traversing an orbit around the terrestrial globe, according to the laws of rational mechanics."

Verne also allows Sir Francis to speculate on Fogg's character. "Sir Francis . . . questioned himself whether a human heart really beat beneath this cold exterior, and whether Phileas Fogg had any sense of the beauties of nature."

Sir Francis, we learn, did not approve of Fogg's wager, regarding it as a "useless eccentricity." As Sir Francis saw it, "The way this strange gentleman was going on, he would leave the world without having done any good to himself or anybody else."

As Passepartout slept, Sir Francis told Fogg what a serious offense his servant had committed, that is, his violation of the Indian temple. The British government "takes particular care that the religious customs of the Indians should be respected," he said.

While that is Sir Francis's view, Verne offers his own: "Everybody knows that the great reversed triangle of land, with its base in the north and its apex in the south, which is called India, embraces fourteen hundred thousand square miles, upon which is spread unequally a population of one hundred and eight million souls. The British Crown exercises a real and despotic dominion over the larger portion of this vast country.[1]

[1] In 1993, when we traveled around the world, the estimated population of India was 886,362,180—an eightfold increase in 120 years. It is expected to exceed a billion people by the end of this century. As such, India is second only to China, which has a population of 1,165,800,000 people. The United

Fogg, however, wasn't concerned with his government's enlightened or despotic treatment of its subjects or the population of the country he was passing through or any of its individuals. He commented to Sir Francis, if his servant Passepartout had been caught and convicted, he would have cut him loose. "I don't see how this affair could have delayed his master."

As for Passepartout, he purchased Indian slippers for his bare feet when the train stopped later at Burhampoor. Shod again, he also experienced a philosophical transformation: "His old vagabond nature returned to him; the fantastic ideas of his youth once more took possession of him. He came to regard his master's project as intended in good earnest, believed in the reality of the bet, and therefore in the tour of the world, and the necessity of making it without fail within the designated period. . . . He recognized himself as being personally interested in the wager and trembled at the thought that he might have been the means of losing it by his unpardonable folly of the night before."

Passepartout and Sir Francis had one significant conversation, Passepartout was asked the time by Sir Francis. This is the third time Passepartout was asked this question and the third time he was told his weighty watch was wrong, this time by four hours. Writes Verne, "Passepartout obstinately refused to alter his watch, which he kept at London time. It was an innocent delusion, which could harm no one."

Their train stopped unexpectedly some 15 miles beyond Rothal, in the hamlet of Kholby, in central India. There the conductor ordered all passengers off. For Fogg, the unforeseen had just raised its ugly head.

Sir Francis conferred with the conductor, while Fogg listened intently. " 'Do we stop here?' " asked Sir Francis.

" 'Certainly. The railway isn't finished. . . . There's still a matter of fifty miles to be laid from here to Allahabad, where the line begins again.'

---

States is a surprising if distant third with a population of 255,600,000. India is, however, one third the size of the United States.

" 'But the papers announced the opening of the railway throughout,' " said Sir Francis.

" 'What would you have, officer? The papers were mistaken. . . . The passengers know that they must provide means of transportation for themselves from Kholby to Allahabad.' "

Strangely, Fogg appeared unshaken by this news. " 'I knew that some obstacle or other would sooner or later arise on my route. Nothing, therefore, is lost. I have two days which I have already gained to sacrifice. A steamer leaves Calcutta for Hong Kong at noon, on the twenty-fifth. This is the twenty-second, and we shall reach Calcutta in time.' "

As all other means of transportation had been spoken for by other passengers, Fogg and Passepartout attempted to rent an elephant to take them the 50 miles. This is supposedly a journey of 15 hours on an elephant.

First Fogg offered the elephant's owner £10 an hour for the loan of the beast, which would amount to £600, for the trip there and back, including rest periods. This extremely fair offer was refused by the price-gouging owner. Then Fogg offered to purchase the elephant for £1,000. Eventually, they settled on £2,000. " 'What a price, good heaven!' cried Passepartout, 'for an elephant.' "

Once he owned an elephant, Fogg hired a guide, "a young Parsee, with an intelligent face," who, beyond knowing the route, was experienced in the ways of elephants. Fogg also offered Sir Francis a lift, which the brigadier general gratefully accepted.

In what remained of the first day, they traveled 25 of the 50 miles separating Kholby from Allahabad. They camped that night. By four in the afternoon of the next day, October 23, Allahabad was only 12 miles distant, and the journey appeared all but accomplished. The elephant, named Kiouni, stopped, however, as if sensing danger. Eventually, a "confused murmur" became a "distinct concert of human voices accompanied by brass instruments."

The Parsee guide said, " 'A procession of Brahmins is coming this way. We must prevent their seeing us, if possible.' "

First came the priests with miters on their heads. They were surrounded by men, women, and children singing a lugubrious psalm. Then came a car pulled by four richly appointed oxen. In it was a statue of the goddess Kali, which Sir Francis identified as the goddess of love and death. She had four arms, haggard eyes, was dull red in color, showed disheveled hair, protruding tongue, and lips tinted with betel. Passepartout thought her representation hideous and found her dual role, as goddess of love and death, incongruous. " 'Of death, perhaps, but of love—that ugly old hag? Never!' "

Then, there came a woman, who "faltered at every step." As the eventual love interest for that most proper English gentleman Phileas Fogg, Verne's description of this Indian woman is curious —ethnocentric—particularly in these more "politically correct" times. Verne's problem is: If the English and the Indians can't even share a railroad car due to a mutual "repugnance," as Reverend MacLeod framed it, how can they share a life? Also, Fogg, if not the most straitlaced man in the world, is at least the most puritanical man in England.

Verne writes, "This woman was young, and as fair as a European. Her head and neck, shoulders, ears, arms, hands, and toes were loaded down with jewels and gems . . . while a tunic bordered with gold, and covered with a light muslin robe, betrayed the outline of her form." Thus, we learn that she was young, fair skinned, rich, and—presumably—shapely.

She was trailed by armed guards, and then came a palanquin with the corpse of an old man, gloriously robed. Sir Francis whispered, " 'A suttee.' "

Once the funeral procession has passed, he explained that a suttee was a human sacrifice, " 'but a voluntary one. The woman you have just seen will be burned tomorrow at the dawn of the day.' "

Her dead husband, said the Parsee guide, was " 'the prince, an independent rajah of Bundelcund.' "

Passepartout was outraged by this barbarous custom. " 'Oh, the scoundrels!' " he said.

She would be burned alive, said Sir Francis, at the pagoda of Pillaji, two miles from where they stood. If she were not burned, Sir Francis continued, " 'you cannot conceive what treatment she would be obliged to submit to from her relatives. They would shave off her hair, feed her on a scanty allowance of rice, treat her with contempt; she would be looked upon as an unclean creature, and would die in some corner, like a scurvy dog.' "

The guide said, " 'The sacrifice which will take place tomorrow is not a voluntary one.' " Asked how he knows that, the guide says, " 'Everybody knows about this affair in Bundelcund.' "

Sir Francis found her lack of resistance curious. The Parsee explained that she had been intoxicated by her captors with fumes of hemp and opium.

At this point, Fogg turned to Sir Francis and said, " 'Suppose we save this woman.' "

Sir Francis was stunned by this offer. " 'Save the woman, Mr. Fogg!'

" 'I have yet twelve hours to spare; I can devote them to that.'

" 'Why, you are a man of heart!' " said Sir Francis.[2]

" 'Sometimes,' replied Fogg, quietly; 'When I have the time.' "

Passepartout was utterly charmed by his master's decision to rescue the young widow. Writes Verne, "He perceived a heart, a soul, under that icy exterior. He began to love Phileas Fogg."

The guide was enthusiastic too. " 'I am a Parsee, and this woman is a Parsee.[3] Command me as you will,' " he said to Fogg.

The Parsee guide told the travelers more about the widow: She

---

[2] Despite Sir Francis's earlier protestations—"[The British government] takes particular care that the religious customs of the Indians should be respected" —it was, among other things, that government's attempts to abolish such abuses as suttee and child marriages that led to the bloody Indian Mutiny (Sepoy Rebellion), primarily in northern India, in 1857. Following this event, the crown (Queen Victoria, as empress of India) assumed rule of the country from the British East India Company. Britain "freed" India in 1947, ending 190 years of colonial rule.

[3] The Parsees are descendants of fire worshipers from Persia (now Iran), who came to India at the end of the tenth century. They make up the commercial class in India.

was a celebrated beauty of the Parsee race, the daughter of a wealthy Bombay merchant; after being left an orphan she had been married against her will to the old rajah of Bundelcund; and her name was Aouda. We also learn that Aouda had received a thoroughly English education in Bombay, and, "from her manners and intelligence, would be thought an European."

In other words, the beautiful Aouda was an Indian woman by birth only, and thus a perfect match for the obviously "purebred" Fogg. She was worthy of sharing a railroad car with Phileas Fogg and his kind, as she would be doing shortly—even a life.[4]

The would-be rescuers approached the pagoda of Pillaji, where the suttee was to take place at dawn the next day. After midnight, they attempted to breach a wall of the temple but were scared off by the guards.

Then Passepartout had an idea. He said to himself, " 'What folly! Why not, after all? It's a chance—perhaps the only one. . . .' " And then he slipped away without telling his master or the others where he was going or what he intended to do.

At dawn, the crowd began to stir. Fogg and his party, still without a plan, saw the rajah's corpse, his widow who was about to join him in death, and the funeral pyre, soaked with oil. A torch was brought, and the wood caught fire instantly.

Then, however, the supposedly dead rajah stood "like a spectre, took up his wife in his arms, and descended from the pyre in the midst of the clouds of smoke, which only heightened his ghostly appearance."

Fakirs, priests, and soldiers were seized with instant terror. They prostrated themselves on the ground, not daring to look at the rajah's return from the dead.

The rajah approached Fogg and Sir Francis and said, " 'Let us be off!' "

It was Passepartout, who had taken the place of the rajah.

---

[4] English author Rudyard Kipling, who was born in India in 1865, titled a poem "The White Man's Burden" to characterize how England viewed its obligations to its Indian colonials. (From the Indians' perspective, this slogan characterized English imperialism.)

With a still-drugged Aouda in tow, the travelers boarded the elephant, and were off at a brisk clip. However, a ball, fired from a rifle or revolver, passed through Phileas Fogg's hat, without doing any damage, in the midst of their great escape.

# In which *ENZA* leaves the world to us

It was the weekend of February 27–28, 1993, ten days after Bruno planted the hulls of the catamaran and grew fear in the crew and in himself too. If the superstitious believe bad things happen in threes on land, bad things were about to happen in twos to boats trying to sail around the world in under 80 days.

Besides our fall from grace on February 16, de Kersuason's *Charal* had hit a growler or something similar that day and was forced to retire. This weekend's double trouble would involve *ENZA*, sailed by Peter Blake and Robin Knox-Johnston, and—obviously—us.

On February 27, we received this telex:

TO ALL ABOARD COMMODORE
FROM THE DISCONSOLATE CREW OF ENZA
REGRET TO INFORM YOU WE WERE IN COLLISION
WITH AN UNKNOWN OBJECT LAST NIGHT AND

HAVE HOLED THE STARBOARD HULL. NOT SAFE
TO PROCEED AT SPEED SO RETURNING TO SOUTH
AFRICA FOR REPAIRS. WE ENJOYED OUR RACE
TOGETHER. PERHAPS ANOTHER TIME? GOOD
LUCK AND SAFE VOYAGE.

Then there was one, our *Commodore Explorer*, in the Jules
Verne Trophée Race. With the loss of our friends Robin
Knox-Johnston and Peter Blake on *ENZA*, the world
seemed a more forsaken place. Bruno telexed them back, as
best he could in English:

FROM COMMODORE EXPLORER CREW TO OUR
FRIENDS ON ENZA NEW ZEALAND.
    JUST RECEIVE YOUR MESSAGE. IT IS TO BAD
LUCK. BAD NEWS FOR THIS MORNING. WE
DECIDED TO SLOW DOWN LAST NIGHT, SO YOU
WILL PROBABLY BE VERY CLOSE FROM US. IF YOU
NEED HELP, WE LL BE ON THE FREQUENCIE RIGHT
NOW. WE LL REGRET YOUR FAIR SPIRIT IN THIS
INCREDIBLE PLANETE MATCH RACE AND HOPE
YOU LL BE BACK SOON AND SAFE. TAKE CARE
BRUNO/CAM/CHINOIS/MARC/JACQUES.

With her tail between her legs, it would take the cat *ENZA*
more than two weeks to reach Cape Town, South Africa.
    *ENZA*'s coskipper, Sir Robin Knox-Johnston, was the
first person to sail alone nonstop around the world. He
made his epic voyage from June 14, 1968, to April 22, 1969,
as a competitor in the London Sunday *Times* Golden Globe
Race. The race he won was a precursor of what around-the-
world voyaging under sail would become in our time: media sponsored, heavily hyped, a vehicle for national pride,
a competitive quest for ultimate ocean challenges.
    Knox-Johnston's story also shows how beautiful—how

sublime—a sail around the world can be—even, or especially, if you're alone. The story of another competitor in
that race, Donald Crowhurst, tells how appalling it can be.

Knox-Johnston was in some ways a product of George
Greenfield, a press agent who made another English sea
voyager, Francis Chichester, an international hero. In 1960,
Chichester won the inaugural *Observer* Singlehanded
Transatlantic Race (OSTAR), from Plymouth, England, to
New York, in a 39-footer, *Gipsy Moth III*, built especially for
the race. Chichester finished after 40 lonely days of sailing,
and his time trimmed 16 days off the solo record established in 1956. He would write a best-selling book about
his voyage.

Chichester's ultimate triumph came on May 28, 1967,
when he stepped ashore after completing a one-stop circumnavigation in his narrow 54-foot *Gipsy Moth IV*—a boat
he came to hate because of her infernal pitching. He was
sixty-five years old and physically infirm. Chichester was
met by a quarter of a million people, including Queen Elizabeth II, who knighted the world's oldest circumnavigator
on the spot. She used the same sword Queen Elizabeth I
had used to knight another famous English mariner and
another "Sir Francis"—Sir Francis Drake—in the sixteenth
century.[1]

---

[1] Drake sailed around the world, from 1577 to 1580, at Queen Elizabeth I's behest. His mission was ostensibly to disrupt Spanish ship-
ping, after relations between England and Spain deteriorated.
Drake's was the second voyage around the world; Portuguese explorer Ferdinand Magellan, sailing for Spain from 1519–1522, was
first, although Magellan died before completing the passage. Like
Magellan, Drake sailed west. Rounding South America, by the Strait
of Magellan, which took him 16 days to traverse, Drake sailed past
Chile and Peru, eventually landing near what is now San Francisco.
He called the area "new Albion," and claimed it for England. He
commanded five ships of which one, the *Golden Hind*, completed the
voyage. After the voyage, Sir Francis served as mayor of Plymouth

While the world welcomed Chichester as a hero of superhuman strength and will, he was, at the time, a frail old man who had taken on the mighty oceans and won. That added mightily to his stature.

Advanced age and ultimate accomplishment don't fully explain Great Britain's reaction to Chichester. In the post–World War II world, the sun had set at least somewhat on the British empire. The upstart America had flown the coop 200 years before and had come to the rescue of England in World War II. Even India—that symbol of British colonialism—had just been given its freedom after 190 years. The British—and the French as well—were behind the postwar United States in international political influence, technology, even in athletics. This may explain in part the energy with which British and French sailors took up sailing feats beginning in the 1960s.

Sailing is, in some ways, an interesting choice, as it is high tech and anachronistic at the same time. The earliest evidence of sailing dates back almost 6,000 years. A 133-foot sailing ship was found near the tomb of the pharaoh Cheops, who lived from 3,960 to 3,908 B.C.

The London Sunday *Times* had been a belated sponsor of Chichester's around-the-world voyage, and it sold a lot of extra newspapers when it published the old man's account of his adventure. The *Times* was eager for more. Robin Knox-Johnston, a merchant seaman, told George Greenfield of his interest in sailing *nonstop* around the world alone—a challenge Chichester had called "the Everest of the Sea."[2] Knox-Johnston also told Greenfield of his difficulty in securing funds. The press agent told him not to

---

and played an important role in England's defeat of the Spanish Armada in 1588.
[2] According to the formal definition of a "nonstop" circumnavigation, the voyage must be entirely "self-maintained." While a vessel may anchor, no supplies, water, medicine, replacement parts, et

worry, then contacted the Sunday *Times*. In doing some preliminary investigation, Murray Sayle, a Sunday *Times* reporter who had covered Chichester's feat, learned that dozens of others were contemplating such a voyage and had boats that were likely to do it faster than Knox-Johnston's 32-foot Colin Archer–type *Suhaili*, a slow if sturdy monohull.

"Why not a race?" suggested Ron Hall, Sayle's superior. Once the idea was proposed, the newspaper decided that if it were to bankroll anyone, it would be better to bet on more of a sure thing: someone like the colorful Australian dentist "Tahiti Bill" Howell, who was readying a large catamaran. The Sunday *Times* promptly forgot Robin Knox-Johnston, who seemed to be a tortoise among the more glamorous hares.

On March 17, 1968, the *Times* announced the contest. The paper put up a trophy, the Golden Globe, for the first to finish, along with a prize of £5,000 to go to the racer with the fastest time. Four days later, the first entry was received from a Donald Crowhurst, of England. Crowhurst's company, Electron Utilisation, which made a workable but not technically inspired radio direction finder that Crowhurst had designed, was about to fail. When he filed his entry, Crowhurst had no boat in which to sail and no money to buy one.

For months after announcing his intentions, Crowhurst tried to persuade the Cutty Sark Society, which owned *Gipsy Moth IV*, to loan it to him. The boat was about to be set in concrete at the National Maritime Museum in Greenwich, which replaced the Royal Observatory. Here the Greenwich, or Prime, Meridian, marked by a brass strip, is located.

---

cetera, may be brought aboard once it has departed. Nor can any outside help be accepted.

Someone commented that even concrete might not stop this boat from pitching. Crowhurst didn't agree; he wrote the society that *Gipsy Moth* "was the most suitable boat for the voyage in existence." How Crowhurst could make this assertion is strange, since Chichester was his hero. He had read all of Chichester's books, and the famous voyager had devoted page after page of his book *Gipsy Moth Circles the World* to hating this boat. However, not the least part of Crowhurst's identification with Chichester was the fact that since his voyages, everything Chichester touched had turned to gold.

Despite editorial support in the British boating magazines, the Cutty Sark Society gave Crowhurst a final and irrevocable no. Crowhurst turned elsewhere. A possessed and very persuasive man, he managed to convince Stanley Best, his backer in Electron Utilisation, to buy him a trimaran. This was after Best had announced he was pulling out of the business.

The boat Crowhurst ended up with was a modification of Arthur Piver's Victress design. Piver, you may recall, had died sailing *Nimble One*, a similar boat, on a qualification run for the 1968 OSTAR. That couldn't have been cheering news to Crowhurst.

Nevertheless, Crowhurst became as enthusiastic about the multihull as he had been about the monohull *Gipsy Moth*, although he had never sailed a multihull and was little more than a weekend sailor. He admitted to some concern about the multihull flipping over, as they are wont to do, then turning turtle in big seas and staying where it lay; but he was certain he could stop the trimaran from capsizing with an electronic sensing device that he said he would invent. Should the worst happen, he would invent a system to right the boat too. When Crowhurst started the race in his *Teignmouth Electron*, neither system had been invented.

Among the other sailors and boats in what ended up being a ten-boat affair was Nigel Tetley, sailing a Victress trimaran similar to Crowhurst's boat but comfortable enough that he and his wife had lived aboard it for years. Chay Blyth, a sergeant in the British Paratroopers who, with his captain, John Ridgway, had rowed across the Atlantic in 1966 in 92 days, was aboard the 30-foot cutter *Dytiscus*.[3] John Ridgway, now retired from the British Special Air Service, sailed the 30-foot sloop *English Rose*. Perhaps the most formidable entrant was Bernard Moitessier, a Frenchman who was already a legend among blue-water sailors. Moitessier had been planning such a voyage since 1967, and he announced that his interest in such a sail was spiritual, not competitive. Afraid that Moitessier might sail independent of the race and beat the winner, as Olivier de Kersauson later attempted to do in the 1993 Jules Verne Trophée Race, the Sunday *Times* dispatched Murray Sayle to France to persuade him to enter. Moitessier agreed for no other reason than that he liked the newspaperman's face.

Recognizing that the entrants' plans were progressing at various speeds, the *Times* allowed boats to start over a five-month period—between June 1 and October 31, 1968—and

---

[3] Chay Blyth never made it around the world in the Golden Globe Race; his boat, *Dytiscus*, ended up pitchpoling at the Cape of Good Hope. When his wife, Maureen, went to pick up the pieces, Blyth complained about the horrible downwind characteristics of his boat. She said, "Why not sail around the world the other way?" This was said in jest, because an east-to-west passage, as Magellan, Drake, and Slocum had done, is, to a large measure, into the strong westerly winds of Cape Horn and the Cape of Good Hope. Nevertheless Blyth accomplished a nonstop east-to-west circumnavigation of the world, in the 59-foot *British Steel*, in 1970–71. It took him 292 days, which, despite being "uphill," easily eclipsed the nonstop record of Robin Knox-Johnston, who traveled "downhill," or west to east.

to sail against the clock. The Golden Globe trophy, however, would go to the first to finish.

Two weeks before the earliest possible sailing date, Crowhurst had neither boat nor firm backing. Ridgway departed on the first day; Blyth on June 8; Knox-Johnston on June 14; Moitessier on August 21; Tetley on September 16; and Crowhurst on October 31, the last possible day. Neither Crowhurst nor his boat was ready.

The night before he had to depart, Crowhurst and his wife, Clare, rowed out to *Teignmouth Electron*, which had been built for him in haste and sailed only once. Despite the fact that there was a crew aboard her then, the maiden voyage had been a disaster. *Teignmouth Electron* would not sail any closer to the wind than 60 degrees, when 45 degrees is normal. On Crowhurst's last evening ashore, the boat was practically buried in unstowed gear. He and Clare did what they could and returned to their hotel at 2:00 A.M., exhausted and cranky. At last in bed, Crowhurst lay beside his wife and searched for the right words, say Nicholas Tomalin and Ron Hall in their extraordinary book *The Strange Last Voyage of Donald Crowhurst*, from which much of this account comes.[4] He wanted his wife to say, "Don't go. I need you to stay here." He was unable to say, "I'm afraid to go."

By the end of November 1968, Robin Knox-Johnston was leading the pack, but by this time the pack was smaller by half. Behind him were Tetley, Crowhurst, and Moitessier, although the position of the formidable Frenchman was anyone's guess, since he couldn't be persuaded to carry a radio. As the competitors dropped out, Crowhurst, the last to start and having a miserable time of it, began to think

---

[4] A fictionalized account of Crowhurst's voyage formed the basis of the recent bestselling novel *Outerbridge Reach*, by Robert Stone, published in 1992.

that he might win if he could just hold his boat together. When he heard that Knox-Johnston had passed New Zealand, this optimism was tempered. Wrote Crowhurst in his log: "He is certainly doing well. Good luck to him, the swine."

Knox-Johnston's troubles were many: His radio worked only now and then; his tiller broke; the self-steering rig broke and was eventually jettisoned; his boom-gooseneck required considerable repair. Yet this focused man, who both before and after the voyage was examined by a psychiatrist who found him "distressingly normal," was enjoying himself.

When his radio brought him news of the second manned Apollo space flight, from December 21 to 28, 1968, that made ten orbits around the moon, looking for a landing site, Knox-Johnston found the contrasts between what the astronauts were doing and what he was doing "appalling."[5]

As he wrote in his log: "It gave me food for thought. There they were, three men risking their lives to advance our knowledge, to expand the frontiers that have so far held us to this planet. The contrast between their magnificent effort and my own trip was appalling. I was doing absolutely nothing to advance scientific knowledge. I would not know how to. Nothing could be learned of human endurance from my experiences that could not be learned more quickly and accurately from tests under controlled conditions. . . .

"My mother, when asked for her opinion of the voyage, had replied that she considered it 'totally irresponsible,'

[5] In keeping with the Christmas season, the crewmen, Col. Frank Borman, Lt. Col. William A. Anders, and Capt. James A. Lovell, read aloud from the Book of Genesis. NASA broadcast their readings worldwide.

and on this Christmas Day, I began to think she was right. I was sailing around the world simply because I bloody well wanted to—and, I realized, I was thoroughly enjoying myself."

No psychiatrist would have found Donald Crowhurst "distressingly normal." The voyage was even worse than he had imagined. He was claustrophobic in his tiny cabin, "soaked, not wet," and deathly afraid that the boat would capsize in the Southern Ocean. Instead of being the hare of the contest, as he had hoped, his trimaran was a tortoise. He contacted his wife by radio in the hope that she might try to talk him out of pressing on; but Clare misunderstood what he wanted from her as she had on their last night together.

Crowhurst began to send fake radio messages. In November, he claimed a 243-mile run in 24 hours, a new world's record for small boats. And during the Christmas season when Knox-Johnston was enjoying such peace on earth, Crowhurst wired back: OFF BRAZIL AVERAGING 170 MILES DAILY STRONG SOUTHWEST TRADEWIND STOP BEST WISHES CHRISTMAS NEW YEAR TEIGNMOUTH. He was lying. Crowhurst was not in the trades that blow toward Brazil as a south*east* wind. He was still far to the north in the doldrums, or the "intertropical convergence zone," where the southeast trades of the southern hemisphere meet the northeast trades of the northern hemisphere, and his noon-to-noon run on this day was a scant 13 miles.

From faking messages, Crowhurst got the idea that he might fake the entire voyage without ever leaving the safety of the Atlantic. There were problems, however, with this ruse: (1) Faking the navigation would be a task for a mathematician; instead of using the declination of the sun to determine positions, he would have to assume positions and then compute the sun's altitude for a succession of *times* and places. (2) Weather conditions would have to be recorded in the log, and Crowhurst had no way to receive such reports from Australia and New Zealand, which were on the opposite side of the earth. (3) He might be seen by a passing ship where he was not supposed to be, or, conversely, he might not be seen by a passing ship in places where such sightings would be likely. (4) His radio transmissions would be picked up by marine operators in the wrong part of the world.

On January 17, 1969, Knox-Johnston rounded Cape Horn. "Yippee!!!" he wrote in his logbook. Moitessier was sighted off the Falkland Islands 18 days after Knox-Johnston. The eccentric Frenchman seemed a sure bet to pass him on the run northeast to England. Moitessier, however, was having a love affair with the Roaring Forties. He decided not to leave the Southern Ocean, and he continued sailing around the world for a second time. He wrote in his log: "I have no desire to return to Europe with all its false Gods. It is difficult to defend oneself against them—they eat your liver and suck your marrow and brutalize you in the end. . . . I am going where you can tie up a boat where you want to and the sun is free, and so is the air you breathe and the sea where you swim, and you can roast yourself on a coral reef." His wife, hearing that her husband was continuing around the world, commented that he must be temporarily insane.

Moitessier finally tied up his boat in Tahiti. He said then that "talking of records is stupid, an insult to the sea."[6]

Where Crowhurst was no one could be sure, since he

---

[6] Nevertheless, he owned several: He had been at sea alone for 301 days or 37,455 miles. Both the time and distance were records. The average speed of his 40-foot steel monohull ketch *Joshua*—named for Joshua Slocum, the world's first solo (but not nonstop) circumnavigator—was a credible 5.18 knots. Also, no other small vessel or single-hander had ever spent eight months or 29,000 miles in the Roar-

had maintained radio silence for three months, from January 19, when he'd reported that he was past New Zealand and heading for Cape Horn. Finally, on April 10, 1969, Crowhurst sent his public-relations man a cryptic wire that implied he had rounded the Horn and was heading home. When the newspapers computed his daily average, it proved to be 188.6 miles a day. Only one man was suspicious of Crowhurst's claims, his hero, Sir Francis Chichester, who told the race committee that he doubted this record-setting pace. Chichester had averaged 140 miles a day on his circumnavigation.[7]

Knox-Johnston completed his voyage on April 22, 1969, after 313 days at sea. He had sailed 30,123 nautical miles, for an average speed of four knots. His average day's run was 96.24 miles, so slow that the trimarans of Tetley and Crowhurst were expected to beat him. When Knox-Johnston finished, Crowhurst wired his congratulations on winning the trophy but reminded Knox-Johnston and the world that the real prize was for the fastest time. In Morse Code he tapped: "TICKLED AS TAR WITH TWO FIDS SUCCESS KNOX JOHNSTON BUT (SIC) KINDLY NOTE THAT RACEWINNER YET SUGGEST ACCURACY DEMANDS DISTINCTION BETWEEN GOLDEN GLOBE AND RACE."

Some 1,300 miles from the finish line, Nigel Tetley pushed his trimaran harder than he should have or would have had he not heard that Crowhurst was catching him. At this point, he had three records to his credit: the first multihull to round Cape Horn and, since he had crossed his outboard track, the first multihull to sail around the

---

ing Forties. (Moitessier would die in 1994, while I was writing this book.)

[7] To put what we were attempting to do into perspective, we would have to average 350 miles—or 210 more miles a day than Chichester —to sail around the world in under 80 days.

world by way of Cape Horn and the first to sail around the world solo.[8] The outboard hulls of Tetley's trimaran were leaking. Crowhurst had the same problem. In fact, he had landed in Río Salado, a hundred miles south of Buenos Aires, to repair his. This was another violation of the race rules.

On May 21, one of the outboard hulls broke off Tetley's Victress trimaran and stove in the main hull. He took to his lifeboat, and an hour or so after midnight watched the boat he and his wife had lived aboard for years sink. He got off a Mayday call and was picked up days later.

As England prepared for Crowhurst's triumphant return, he realized he could not pull it off. He stopped racing and filled his logbook with cryptic metaphysics involving God, time, and space. The last words he wrote were: "It is the end of my my game the truth has been revealed and it will be done as my family require me to do it. It is the time for your move to begin. I have not need to prolong the game It has been a good game that must be ended at the i will play this game when i choose I will resign the game 11 20 40 There is no reason for harmful."

On July 10, 1969, the Royal Mail vessel *Picardy*, some 1,800 miles from England, sighted a small yacht with a mizzensail set. The captain blasted his horn, but there was no response. A lifeboat was launched in the gentle sea, but no one was found aboard. There were dirty dishes in the sink, dismantled radio gear everywhere, and a soldering iron resting precariously on a tin, indicating that the yacht had not lost its crew overboard in rough seas. Also there

[8] Dr. David Lewis, a New Zealand physician, living in London, made the first circumnavigation in a multihull, a catamaran *Rehu Moana*, by way of the Strait of Magellan, from 1964 to '67. His passage began and ended in Plymouth, England. For most of it, he was accompanied by his wife and two daughters.

was a Navicator, the radio direction finder Crowhurst's defunct company manufactured.

The little boat was *Teignmouth Electron,* and her logs recorded Donald Crowhurst's voyage into insanity and, apparently, suicide.

As Chichester had done and Crowhurst had wished to do, Knox-Johnston wrote a best-selling book, *A World of My Own,* about his voyage. Like Chichester, Knox-Johnston was made Commander of the Order of the British Empire, or CBE, by Queen Elizabeth II. Now Knox-Johnston and *ENZA* were limping toward South Africa.

As promised, bad things were happening in twos to boats trying to sail around the world in under 80 days: Since the crash on February 16, 1993, we'd made tracks. On February 21, for example, *Commodore Explorer* was 500 miles due south of the Cape of Good Hope. This set a second record, from the English Channel to the Cape of Good Hope, in 21 days, 12 hours, 49 minutes. We had sailed 8,280 miles, or nearly one third of the way around the world. Up to this point, we'd averaged nearly 400 miles a day—again, not a bad day's run in a car. We were then three days ahead of an 80-day circumnavigation.

Bartolomeu Dias, from Portugal, was the first European to discover the Cape of Good Hope, in 1488. The first European to round the Cape of Good Hope and to sail to India was Vasco da Gama, also from Portugal, in 1497. It took da Gama 122 days to sail from Portugal to the Cape of Good Hope. That is 101 days longer than it took us to sail from France.

On the day we set this record, I saw a lonely seal swimming in the ocean. What's he doing here? I wondered.

That day, too, a huge flying fish landed on the net of *Commodore Explorer.* These guys prefer warm water, so what a flying fish was doing at 43 degrees south latitude, in 38-degree water, I didn't have a clue. Maybe he's running from the seal. But I'm not dwelling on that; mostly I was thinking, Dinner is served! I lunged for the fish, but I forgot I was tethered to the boat with my safety harness. It was just out of reach. Marc was convulsed by my floundering. I lunged a second time, and this time the boat leaned in such a way that the fish' rolled toward me. I'm at the head of the food chain, and this had to be this fish's worst nightmare. I grabbed him by the tail and went to whack him upside the head on a winch, but he slipped out of my hands and into the sea. He's gone—home free.

So much for my stint as king of the jungle. Later I found a second flying fish entwined in the net. "Dinner is served!" I announced to my shipmates after cooking *poisson volant* with onions and garlic in the "Flying Pig and Commodore Café on the Rive Gauche." It was probably imaginary, but I felt somewhat rejuvenated by eating unprocessed, unmechanized food.

Someplace beyond Cape Town, you pass over a dividing line at 20 degrees east longitude—you have to be very sensitive to notice it—and find yourself in the Indian Ocean. From the foot of Africa this ocean stretches nearly 6,200 miles (10,000 km) to the eastern edge of Australia. A rose by any name, the Indian Ocean looked no different from the Atlantic that we had just left behind.[9]

Within eight days of our crossing into the Indian Ocean,

---

[9] The Pacific Ocean, the largest, is 63,985,000 square miles; the Atlantic Ocean is next at 31,529,000 square miles, which is about half the size of the Pacific; and the Indian Ocean is the smallest at 28,357,000 square miles. Centuries before, the world was divided into "seven seas": the Atlantic, Indian, Pacific, Arctic, Mediterranean, Caribbean, and the Gulf of Mexico. Today, oceanographers tell us there are only three oceans or navigable seas: the Atlantic, Indian, and Pacific. The Arctic, Mediterranean, Caribbean, and Gulf of Mexico are merely part of the Atlantic and are considered "marginal seas." The marginal seas are separated from the Atlantic by straits: for example, the

India lay directly to our north. Interestingly, we were now at about the same east-west longitude as Fogg and Passepartout.

Up to this point, we had set our ship's clock ahead by a total of five hours to reflect the local time. This was at odds with Jean Passepartout, who obstinately refused to regulate his watch by the sun. " 'So much the worse for the sun, monsieur,' " he told Detective Fix at Suez. " 'The sun will be wrong, then!' " Passepartout made the same remark to Sir Francis Cromarty as their train entered the defiles of the Sutpour Mountains in India.

Time is normally changed, as described, every 15 degrees of longitude. At 42 degrees south latitude, where we were, a degree of longitude is about 44 nautical miles, or 51 statute miles. (At the equator a degree of longitude is 60.11 nautical miles or 69.17 statute miles.) Thus, every 660 nautical miles, or about every other day in a scalded cat like *Commodore Explorer*, there were only 23 hours in a day. Was I younger or older? I wondered as we chased the rising sun. No matter what the sun or clock said, I felt a good deal older than when I had left America on Thanksgiving night.

While I'd like to say keeping "ship's time" was perfectly orderly on *Commodore Explorer*, it wasn't. More than once, someone would report on deck for their 5:00 A.M. watch, fully dressed and more or less—usually less—ready to go, an hour early. "Bruno! *Quelle heure?*" would be the exasperated whine to our skipper and official timekeeper even if—or especially if—he was asleep.

South of 23¹/₂ degrees, the sun is always to your north, which seems odd, at first, to those of us who live in America or Europe, where the sun is always to the south. As I

---

Strait of Gibraltar separates the Mediterranean from the Atlantic, and the Straits of Florida separate the Gulf of Mexico from the Atlantic.

looked north toward the sun and toward India, I thought about Fogg and Passepartout. One hundred and twenty years after their fictitious voyage, we had a "horse race" going on—even if it was only in my mind's eye.

Given sufficient time, waves line up with the wind. However, some long storm-driven waves on the open ocean are resistant—quite resistant—to marching in lock-step. Sometime before February 28, 1993, a storm, likely near Antarctica, unleashed its fury, and its energy, in the form of a wave, came for us on Commodore Explorer thousands of miles away. It proved to be a sucker punch that nearly ended our voyage, as ENZA's had ended the day before.

Anatomy is destiny, as you've doubtless heard. Bruno said to me, "Eenie, meenie, minie, moe, you're the tallest, you go." Thus, I found myself in the middle of the trampoline on the last day of February, trying to hog-tie the bottom third of the mainsail, high above my head, after securing its third reef. The third reef brings it down to about storm-trysail size: a little sail to match the big wind that had been our companion since arriving in the Indian Ocean.[10]

In the boisterous wind, which was behind us, the boat was sailing along fairly smartly at about 19 knots. As I was doing this housekeeping, suddenly Marc, my watchmate, yelled at me in warning. Too late: a 45-foot wall of solid

[10] Later, we developed a better technique for the reefing of this over-sized mainsail. We'd drop the sail well below its reef height and tension the clew-reef line, at the back of the sail, without tensioning the halyard, which hoists it at the front. Then, I'd tie the accordioned folds of the sail at the reef points into a nice neat package around the boom. Lastly we would hoist the sail by the halyard. This left the bottom of the sail in a neater and tighter furl, which was cleaner aerodynamically. The wind worried the sail less. What sail was left was also flatter; this is desirable when it is windy. A flatter sail has less power, and thus the boat heels less.

green water broke aboard the boat, at 90 degrees from the other waves. A "rogue wave," sailors call this. I dove onto the trampoline and held on to it with my fingers and got smacked by a faceful of water. There was a huge cracking sound, which at first I thought was the 110-foot mast. For sailors, that is as if the sky is falling.

Marc said, "*Mon dieu!* That's big. What broke? Something must have broke!" Soon Jacques and Bruno came tumbling out of their starboard hull, which had received almost the full weight of the wave.

We slowed the boat down and hung over the starboard side. There were some shallow sixteen-inch cracks at the waterline, just aft of the main beam. A few minutes later, a second wave hit us in about the same place, from the same direction. While not as big as the first, it cracked the hull some more. Waves come in twos, and maybe it was the companion—the other side—of the first.

Was this the death knell? I worried, as did everyone else. Down below, however, in the starboard *dérive chambre*, which corresponded to the cracks in the hull, there wasn't much water. Immediately, Jacques and Chinois got to work on the cracks. The first step was to remove the paint there, which would prevent the Kevlar, carbon, and epoxy patch from adhering.

Jacques and Chinois did great work; it only took them eight hours to mend the boat with their "chemistry set." However, the voyage changed inexorably after that. Bruno never trusted the boat again. Also, he recognized clearly that if the boat really broke, he was broke. Financially ruined. Without *ENZA* and *Charal*, we walked alone; there was no competition anymore to push us. Or anyone to come to our rescue if we needed help.

On this disturbing last weekend in February, our safety net had been removed with the departure of *ENZA*. And we had suffered a body blow.

# In which Fogg and Passepartout find themselves under arrest in Calcutta

---

Aouda, still intoxicated by the drug she had been forced to inhale, slept in one of the howdahs (a covered seat) on the elephant. Sir Francis, who was familiar with the effects of hemp-fume intoxication, told Fogg and Passepartout that it wouldn't last long or be permanent. He was more concerned, however, about Aouda's fate. If she remained in India, she would " 'inevitably fall again into the hands of her executioners.' " Her safety depended on quitting this country. Fogg's response was noncommittal; he said that he would reflect on the matter. Gradually the effects of the drug began to ebb. Her fine eyes, Verne writes, "resumed all their soft Indian expression."

Then out of nowhere Verne presents an idealized standard of female beauty penned, he says, by the poet-king Ucaf Uddaul. While a nonsequitur, it is so extravagant and so wonderful, it is worth quoting: "Her shining tresses, divided in two parts, encircle the harmonious contour of her white and delicate cheeks, brilliant in their glow of freshness. Her ebony brows have the

The *Commodore Explorer*.
CREDIT: GIANNI GIANSANTI/SYGMA 281962

The crew working in the spray.
CREDIT: PASCAL DELLA ZUANA/SYGMA 282626

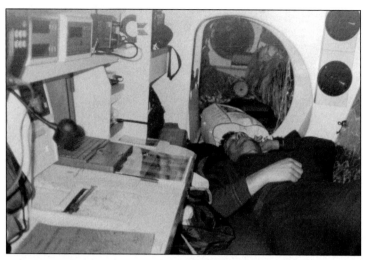

Bruno sleeping. Here's the navigation station,
including the Apple computer.
CREDIT: CAM LEWIS/SYGMA

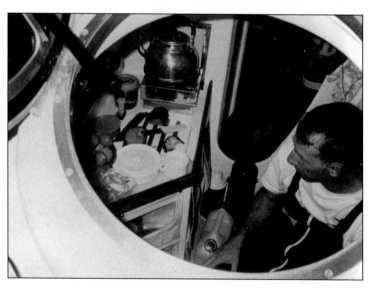

Keru, our friendly photographer, who sailed the first
six days with us to Cape Verde Islands.
CREDIT: CAM LEWIS/SYGMA

Steering at night
with a tired look
on my face.
CREDIT: CAM
LEWIS/SYGMA 285408

Chinois crouched under Casquette show galley.
CREDIT: CAM LEWIS/SYGMA 283049

Slow exposure showing the speed of the *Commodore Explorer*.
CREDIT: JACQUES VAPILLON

Driving against Cape Horn.
CREDIT: MARC VALLIN

*Commodore* upwind and in the spray.
CREDIT: GIANNI GIANSANTI/SYGMA 281962

Jacques lying on bowstriker.
CREDIT: THIERRY MARTINEZ AGENCE VANDYSTADT VOILE

Dwarfed
by a wave.

Reefing the *Commodore*.
CREDIT: GIANNI GIANSANTI / SYGMA

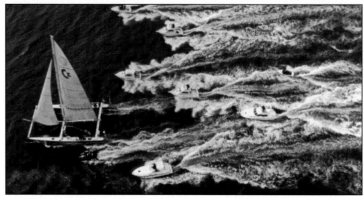

Surrounded by boats at the end of the journey.

Holding the flag at the finish.

Hugging Molly.

Hugging my father.

The crew of the *Commodore Explorer*.
L to R: Jacques, Chinois, Marc, Cam, Bruno.

form and charm of the bow of Kama, the god of love, and beneath her long silken lashes the purest reflections and a celestial
light swim, as the sacred lakes of Himalaya, in the black pupils of
her great clear eyes. Her teeth, fine, equal, and white, glitter
between her smiling lips like dewdrops in a passion-flower's half-
enveloped breast. Her delicately formed ears, her vermilion
hands, her little feet, curved and tender as the lotus-bud, glitter
with the brilliancy of the loveliest pearls of Ceylon, the most
dazzling diamonds of Golconda. Her narrow and supple waist,
which a hand may clasp around, sets forth the outline of her
rounded figure and the beauty of her bosom, where youth in its
flower displays the wealth of its treasures; and beneath the silken
folds of her tunic she seems to have been modelled in pure silver
by the godlike hand of Vicvàrcarma, the immortal sculptor."

It's poetry for poetry's sake, for after this ejaculation, Verne
tells us that's not Aouda. "It is enough to say, without applying
this poetical rhapsody to Aouda, that she was a charming woman,
in all the European acceptation of the phrase. She spoke English
with great purity, and the guide had not exaggerated in saying
that the young Parsee had been transformed by her bringing up."

Before boarding the train, Fogg paid the young Parsee guide
for his service. After what they had been through in rescuing
Aouda, Passepartout was stunned that his master paid him no
more than the agreed-upon sum. But then Fogg added, " 'Parsee,
you have been serviceable and devoted. I have paid for your
service, but not for your devotion. Would you like to have this
elephant? He is yours.' "

" 'Your honor is giving me a fortune!' " cried the guide.

" 'Take him, guide,' returned Fogg, 'and I shall still be your
debtor.' "

On the train, heading to Benares, Sir Francis told the rekindled
Aouda about the rescue, "dwelling upon the courage with which
Phileas Fogg had not hesitated to risk his life to save her and
recounting the happy sequel of the venture, the result of Passepartout's rash idea." Fogg said nothing, while the abashed Passe-

partout kept repeating, " 'It wasn't worth telling.' " Aouda thanked her rescuers more eloquently with her tears than her words.

Fogg's reflections about Aouda's fate reached a climax at this point. He told her that he would take her out of India to Hong Kong. She had, it seemed, a Parsee relative who was one of the principal merchants of Hong Kong, which was, according to Verne, "a wholly English city, though on an island on the Chinese coast."

At Benares on the Ganges, a holy river to the Hindus, the travelers bade farewell to Sir Francis, who was to join his regiment there.[1] Fogg, Passepartout, and now Aouda arrived at the train station in Calcutta on October 25. While the two days he had placed in the bank for a rainy day had been spent, Fogg was still precisely on schedule. However, as they were leaving the station to board the ship *Rangoon*, a steamer heading for Hong Kong, a policeman arrested both Fogg and Passepartout on unspecified charges. With Aouda following, they were taken to the police station, there to appear before Judge Obadiah, at half past eight.

Aouda said it was her fault that they'd been arrested, and they should leave her to her fate. Fogg thought it unlikely they had been arrested for stopping a suttee, however. " 'The complainants would not dare present themselves with such a charge,' " he said, as suttees were illegal in British-controlled India.

Verne describes Judge Obadiah as "a fat, round man." He was followed into the courtroom by a dutiful clerk, and they staged a comic routine. Judge Obadiah put his wig on, as is the English custom. " 'Heh! This is not my wig!' " he said.

" 'No, your worship. It is mine,' " said the clerk.

---

[1] Hinduism is the dominant religion in India. To Hindus, the Ganges River is the holiest place in the world—indeed some consider it a goddess. They bathe in it in mass immersions, since the river is said to bring purity, fertility, and wealth. Many Hindus also go there to die, believing it will lead to higher status in their next life.

" 'My dear Mr. Oysterpuff,' " said the judge, " 'how can a judge give a wise sentence in a clerk's wig?' "

Then three priests came in. The clerk began reading the charge against Phileas Fogg and his servant. They were accused of having violated " 'a place held consecrated by the Brahmin religion.' "

Fogg forthrightly admitted to the charge. Then he added, " 'I wish to hear these priests admit, in their turn, what they were going to do at the pagoda of Pillaji.' "

The judge was confused. " 'We are not talking of the pagoda of Pillaji, but of the pagoda of Malebar Hill, at Bombay.'

" 'And as proof . . . here are the desecrator's very shoes, which he left behind him,' " said the clerk.

" 'My shoes!' " cried Passepartout, which all but clinched the case.

This courtroom drama, we discover at this point, had been set in motion by Detective Fix. After overhearing Passepartout's confession to his master about the contretemps at Malebar Hill, when they first landed in India, Fix had consulted with the priests in Bombay, who told him about Passepartout's desecration. Fix lured them to Calcutta, with the promise of a "goodly sum in damages."

Due to the time lost in rescuing Aouda, Fix and his priests actually beat Fogg and Passepartout to Calcutta by two days. Fix, still without his cable of arrest from England, kept himself hidden at the back of the courtroom.

Judge Obadiah pronounced sentence in an ostentatious legal tongue: " 'I condemn the said Passepartout to imprisonment for fifteen days and a fine of three hundred pounds. . . . And inasmuch . . . as it is not proved that the act was not done by the connivance of the master with the servant, and as the master in any case must be held responsible for the acts of his paid servant, I condemn Phileas Fogg to a week's imprisonment and a fine of one hundred and fifty pounds.' " Detective Fix was exultant.

Fogg's imprisonment should allow sufficient time for the arrest warrant to arrive.

Fogg's wager appeared lost. However, as the clerk called the next case, Fogg rose and said, " 'I offer bail.' " The judge agreed they had the right. Bail would be £1,000 per prisoner. " 'I will pay it at once,' " said Fogg, removing fresh bank bills from his carpet-bag.

" 'Come!' " said Fogg to his servant.

" 'But let them at least give me back my shoes,' " said Passepartout. " 'Ah, these are pretty dear shoes! More than a thousand pounds apiece; besides, they pinch my feet.' "

Without a look back, Fogg gave up the bail and boarded the *Rangoon* with Passepartout and Aouda.

Fix was apoplectic; he even stamped his feet in frustration: " 'The rascal is off, after all! Two thousand pounds sacrificed! He's as prodigal as a thief! I'll follow him to the end of the world if necessary; but at the rate he is going on, the stolen money will soon be exhausted.' " Fogg had already spent £5,000, or about $15,000, since leaving London, "and the percentage of the sum recovered from the bank robber, promised to the detective, was rapidly diminishing."

# In which I plan my wedding on the way to Australia

It wasn't as advertised. After knocking out our two competitors, *ENZA New Zealand* and *Charal*, the Roaring Forties stopped their posturing. The days were clear, if cold. We'd typically wear hats and mittens. At night, a two-million-watt moon, which was growing larger by the day, and a sky full of stars caused the catamaran to glow in the dark. This made the sailing—indeed the living—easy.

So nice was it, we gave the kitty cat a little fluff and buff one day, as we streaked in the direction of Australia. It was a welcome break from tending to the catamaran's large and small failures and sundry mechanical insults, which ranged from the stove-in hull (potentially huge) to the diesel heater (large to me, small to the others) in the port hull. Being an American, burning fossil fuel seems an inalienable right, so I took it upon myself to keep it running. This was a tough job in an impossibly small space aft, behind the main beam.

Also, we lost our second and last man-overboard module or MOM. That could be a large problem if someone fell overboard, no problem if no one did. At this point, there wasn't much safety gear left on deck, however, which was troubling.

Multihulls are prone to capsizing, as described. Should this happen and should the boat turn upside down with crew in the cabins, there's no easy escape to fresh air. Thus, such boats have escape hatches on the sides of either hull. Should you be trapped inside when down turns to up, you can unlatch the hatch. Ours were about 18 inches by 22, and ahead of them were deflectors, to redirect the water away from them.

The escape hatch in our port hull leaked constantly, if lightly. On March 1, however, I was down in my galley. All of a sudden, the rubber gasket on the escape hatch blew, and water, flowing like a geyser, took aim at me. Within an instant, the floorboards in the cabin were floating.

I went on deck and said as calmly as I could, "Tack!" As we were on starboard tack, the port hull was the low hull, and it was pressed deep in the water. Once on port tack, the port hull was on the high side. This lessened the water pressure and the flow of water enough for us to seal the hatch with some siliconlike gook. That stopped the flood—it even stopped the leaking, at least for a time—but if *Commodore Explorer* turned over, it would have taken dynamite to loosen the escape hatch. Not good, I thought, but I decided to act like Scarlett O'Hara. "I'll worry about that tomorrow." Or when the time comes—if it comes.

As life turned uneventful, we availed ourselves of the opportunity to make tracks—to shred the planet. On one day in early March we did 420 nautical miles in 24 hours, or a 17.5-knot average. For me, it was just a wonderful time and place to pass through and absorb the vastness of our planet.

Marc and I were having a fine time on our watches, talking English, nattering away about life (Marc and his wife had had a baby son, Antoine, just before he left; Molly and I were going to have a child), airplanes (Marc is a helicopter pilot and I was a newly anointed airplane pilot), and birds.

On March 4, Marc and I shared the last apple, a Granny Smith. Marc is an eight-apple-a-day kind of guy, so you should've seen his face as he took the last bite. The expression on his face was sublime. He decided to savor the present rather than worry about the future without.

Although various species of albatross and petrels had been with us since we turned left in the South Atlantic, the arrival of the "Great Wanderer," as the albatross is described, welcomed us officially to the Southern Ocean. Albatross, or gooney birds, as they say in this part of the world, display a wingspan of up to 12 feet (3.7 meters). They truly live on the sea: they sleep on it, drink seawater, and subsist on small marine animals like squid. They only return to land to mate. Like some sailors I know. They are as elegant in the air as the frigatebird that had come to visit us when near the equator.

Sailors have a special affinity for, and at the same time dread of, the albatross, which is in some ways the "black cat" of the seas. The bird, it is thought, can capture a sailor's soul. It is considered a source of guilt, frustration, or a burden. In the poem "The Rime of the Ancient Mariner," written by Samuel Taylor Coleridge and published in 1798, a sailor, when in the Southern Ocean where we were, kills a friendly albatross with a crossbow for frivolous reasons. The voyage turns miserable after that as the wind ceased to blow. It is as if the ship is imprisoned in the doldrums with no chance of escape. Writes the poet in lines that have become immortal:

> Day after day, day after day,
> We stuck, nor breath nor motion;
> As idle as a painted ship
> Upon a painted ocean.
>
> Water, water, everywhere,
> And all the boards did shrink;
> Water, water, everywhere
> Nor any drop to drink.

The sailor, the ancient mariner, is condemned to life-in-death. He has an albatross around his neck, as that now familiar phrase has it. Coleridge writes:

> Instead of the Cross, the Albatross
> About my neck was hung.

Only after the ancient mariner repents of his sin is his ship allowed to return home. Further penance requires him to share the message that people must love and honor all God's creatures. It is this message he shares with a wedding guest just before the ceremony:

> He prayeth best, who loveth best
> All things both great and small;
> For the dear God who loveth us,
> He made and loveth all.

That is a message I applaud, too. As there are "no atheists in a foxhole," as the saying has it, I doubt there are many who sail around the world or venture out on the ocean. That is a lesson so eloquently advanced by Joshua Slocum, who made the first solo circumnavigation in 1895–98. You can't be struck by the beauty of nature without thinking about its Designer or Architect. At sea, there is too much beauty for this to be but a cosmic accident—a big bang.

Recall that Bruno has some affinity with this bird too. Indeed, in his book, he compares himself to an albatross. As this bird welcomed us to the Southern Ocean, Bruno promised it that we wouldn't leave any tangible evidence of our passing. For this reason, since leaving France, we had packed all our trash in the aft of either hull. "He prayeth best, who loveth best/All things both great and small. . . ."

Most of the time, however, as we sailed toward Australia, Bruno was in an "office funk"—tending to business but not finding much joy in the sailing—which was unfortunate, since sailing is one of his great joys.

After the rogue waves did their damage, Bruno talked by SSB radio to Peter Blake, on *ENZA*, about a place to make more permanent repairs to *Commodore Explorer*. They had plenty of time to talk, as it would take the damaged *ENZA* 16 days to reach port in Cape Town. Blake, from New Zealand, knew of an appropriate place on the South Island of New Zealand.

While Bruno was saying "repairs" to Blake, he was saying "reconnaissance mission" to us. At this point, Bruno came to the conclusion, I believe, that it was a lot cheaper to stop now. If the rig went over the side, it would cost him $250,000 to replace the mast and sails, and to ship the boat back to France. Bruno seemed to believe: We've already proven a point. We can do it. We've set all sorts of records. We have nothing to be embarrassed about if we stop now.

He was thinking about stopping while the rest of us were thinking about making time. At night, when the going got rough, we'd take down the spinnaker. Chinois, Marc, and I worried aloud that what with the permanent wave on the starboard side and no one out here to push us, this was going to turn into a fast delivery of the boat back to France. Save for Bruno, the crew seemed of the opinion: We're here, let's do it. Or: Damn the torpedoes. Full speed ahead!

At the same time Bruno was often in touch with Michel Horeau, our public-relations man, in France, basically dialing for dollars in the Southern Ocean. For days, Bruno agonized over the wording of a fund-raising appeal. He didn't want to appear to be begging. He wished to appeal tastefully to potential sponsors for financial support. The point Bruno wished to make, I think, was that this was really difficult on him. He wasn't having a lot of fun. And while we were doing well, he needed support—tangible support.

There was a vague promise of a $100,000 prize to anyone who broke the record from the Trophée Jules Verne Committee. However, since PMU, the French lottery organization, had pulled out after Florence Arthaud and Titouan Lamazou objected to their names being used in advertisements, the source of this money hadn't been established when the three multihulls departed France. Even if we were successful and even if the money was collected, that wouldn't go very far in paying off Bruno's debts.

I tried to encourage Bruno to come on deck—get out of the "office"—get some sunshine and fresh air. He spent tons of time down below, taking care of business.

The fruit of this labor was the Sector Watch sponsorship. I, however, didn't know about it until we returned to France, and Bruno's girlfriend deposited a bag full of watches that we were only too happy to wear. While the money was appreciated, it must have been the proverbial drop in the bucket.

If this project depressed him, Bruno spent a considerable amount of time on the Macintosh computer in his cabin drawing his next major project: a 123-foot Clipper Cat. It was his lifelong dream to build the boat someday and to race it around the world. He called the event "The Race," and he hoped to organize it too. The Race would be open to the top ten skippers in the world, as determined by a transatlantic race. Competitors would leave on the last day of 1999—the end of one millennium and the start of another—and follow the same course we were following.

How was the rest of the crew on *Commodore Explorer* faring as we sped toward Australia's Cape Leeuwin? Chinois was a man of steel. He never seemed to say much, never complained. He is happy, even when he's miserable and cold, which he was—all of us were—much of the time. Chinois, in particular, seemed to suffer from cold hands and cold feet. His heart, however, and his nature were unaffected.

I brought along Gore-Tex mittens and socks for the entire crew. Chinois was skeptical of these high-tech products. "No, no, I can't wear those," he said. Out of habit, he'd wear old beat-up gloves, which would get wet and then be worthless, but old customs die hard.

The French were skeptical of the Gore-Tex socks, I think, but by the time we'd finished, everyone had pretty happy feet—including Chinois, who after a while tried them. I don't think Chinois's clothes were as good as Marc's or mine. Marc had picked up on my shopping.

Jacques was still being Job, fine when he was on deck doing his job but difficult to separate from his bunk. He only had strength to sail and to eat and sleep. He cared little about personal hygiene. He rarely bathed or changed his clothes, which must have been hard on Bruno. Also, Jacques still had open sores from hives of unknown origin that he was forced to bandage. We took to calling him "Métro Man"—as the unwashed and unwanted are uncharitably described in France.

By telex Bruno consulted with Jean-Yves Chauve, a physician in France who advised us. He prescribed antibiotics for Jacques in very high doses.

As for me, I was sailing the boat with Marc and preparing that good freeze-dried food for my mates, the "baguette boys," as I had started to call them in honor of France's favorite bread.

Sometimes I'd fry bread or a huge pancake in a big frying pan. It was difficult to divide such things into five pieces, so often I'd cut them in half and cut the halves into thirds. Then, after each of us had had a piece, the sixth piece would be given to the winner of a trivia contest I conducted. I'd post the question of the day on a paper sign in the galley. There'd be questions like: How many home runs did Babe Ruth hit? Or who's Babe Ruth? Or what's a home run? Always, I won the bonus piece when it came to the subject of baseball. Or how tall is the Eiffel Tower? Bruno's answer was always the same: "Princess Stéphanie of Monaco"—a name-brand person in France and, apparently, a popular answer on French quiz shows. He only won the sixth piece once when I felt sorry for him and asked: Who is the worst-dressed princess in Monaco?

As we closed with Australia, I was incongruously planning my impending nuptials with Molly by telex and by fax. Molly and her roommate, Reese Brown, had finally cracked the code. They had figured out how to send telexes to me on *Commodore Explorer* by way of CompuServe. Before, she'd send her messages by fax to Michel Horeau in France. He'd retype them and then retransmit them to me. It was in this secondhand way that I had learned about the little "Camster"—our baby-to-be.

We chose May 22 as our wedding date at the New York Yacht Club station in Newport. She'd be four months pregant, but she didn't think her condition would be obvious.

For the ceremony Molly wanted to protect the guests with a tent, just in case the weather, which can be very perverse especially in Newport in May, was bad. Newport is on Aquidneck Island, stuck out in the Atlantic Ocean, and that typically makes May in Newport more winter than spring. I refused a tent, as I am willing to take a chance on the weather. Sailors do that all the time. Besides, I find a tent depressing: inward looking and isolated. Don't fence me in, is a motto I believe in. I wanted our wedding day to be wide open with endless possibilities and limitless horizons. I wanted our friends and Molly and me to be there for the world to see.

On February 28, Molly telexed me. One thing I found most interesting in this telex was that after being a two-some, we'd become three:

"Hello, Sweetness. Thank you for your faxes. They are so thoughtful and sensitive, they make me cry. We miss you so much. Everything is fine. I'm all tested and should get the results next week. I am thrilled that you are so excited too. I just cannot wait. We were by the ocean yesterday, and I told our little bundle of joy about his incredible father. We think and pray for you every day. . . ."

President Bill Clinton had been inaugurated almost two months after I left the U.S., and a week before I left France. I telexed Molly a month after his inauguration to find out how our new president was faring.

Molly began another telex with the words: "Are you sitting down? You may need a tranquilizer, so I hope the medicine kit is handy." She'd found the perfect diamond ring, she wrote. In this case, perfection costs $10,000. I faxed her back: "Got your telex. Tranquilizer wearing off. New car in jeopardy. Check stock market and call my accountant for tax angle. Will trade an old but trusty mountain bike for a deposit. How big is it? Can I skate on it?"

Nevertheless, money worries seemed far from my mind, at this point, while for Bruno as for Detective Fix, they occupied his every thought. "Buy it!" I cabled back. Compromise is key to any relationship. Molly got her ring; I didn't get the tent. Then we'd go over the guest list: the musts, maybes, and nevermores of life.

Molly was in Newport, in winter, and I was in a boat nearing Australia, in summer in top-down weather. We were almost at antipodal points—opposite ends of the earth—and yet we were planning our wedding, our lives together, by telex and by fax. Is this a great world or what? Actually, I enjoyed handling these domestic details. It was a welcome break from cooking, sailing, cleaning, sleeping, and hygiene—or lack thereof.

Not everything that bounced off the satellite, however, brought good news. By way of a telex from Peter Isler, sailing commentator for ESPN, who was at Cape Horn with the peripatetic Skip Novak doing a documentary on this area, I learned of the terrorist bombing of one of the Twin Towers of the World Trade Center in New York, on February 26. Six people died in the blast, more than a thousand were injured, and the costs of repair to the building and to businesses was $600 million. From my friend Steve Rosenberg I learned about the standoff between treasury agents and Branch Davidians, a religious cult, in Waco, Texas, beginning on February 28. From where I sat, this news seemed to be coming from another planet. Nevertheless, I worried about what waited for me ashore, as Molly and I were bringing another child onto this tumultuous planet.

On March 5, we were at 113 degrees east longitude—the same as Western Australia. There I'd sailed the 12-Meter World Championship in 1985 in the winds of war. "Godday, mites!" I said to myself, in my best "Strine" accent—the Australian answer to Cockney. For *Commodore Explorer* this would be a third major record; this one from the English Channel to Cape Leeuwin, Western Australia, in 33 days, 7 hours, and 48 minutes.

We were, however, at 49 degrees south longitude, about

840 miles south of the continent. This allowed us to clear comfortably Cape Leeuwin, at the southwest bulge of Australia; Southeast Cape on the Australian island of Tasmania; and South Cape on the south island of New Zealand— three land masses that push ever deeper into the south. Along with the Cape of Good Hope, off South Africa, and Cape Horn, off South America, these are the five great capes of southern voyaging—signposts that will lead you around the world.

On March 6, on the thirty-fourth day of sailing, I celebrated my thirty-sixth birthday. My shipmates didn't feel the day was worthy of special ceremony, so I threw myself a party, cooking a cake out of popcorn. We also enjoyed one of Kéruzoré's bottles of wine and a few beers. I'd brought along twelve cans of beer: four Foster's because Molly is the Foster's beer poster girl, four Budweisers, and four Smithwicks. There were telexes from home, from my sisters, father, stepmother, and many friends.

My father and stepmother telexed me from the family home in Sherborn, Massachusetts: "We follow your progress in our atlas, and you are getting into areas that are difficult to follow—that is, where the curve of the earth is hard to project on a flat piece of paper. Also, you are at the very bottom of the pages.

"At this very moment we are having an honest nor'easter with snow, so it is easy to get some idea of the elements you are battling. Even the dogs won't go out. The cross-country skiing has been terrific and with today's additions should continue. The Flower Show, of all things, is scheduled to open tonight in Boston, and if it does, should prove an interesting contrast inside and out." My stepmother likes to leave you laughing. She finished with a joke: "Groucho Marx says, 'You're only as old as the women you feel. . . .' "

Australia is either the world's smallest continent, or its

largest island. It is surrounded by the Indian Ocean on the west, and the Pacific on the east.[1] The country or continent is about the size of the United States. Australia is the only continent consisting of one nation, which is the sixth largest in the world. Its name comes from *terra australis incognita*, which is Latin meaning "unknown southern land." While Australia was the last continent to be inhabited by man and the last settled by Europeans, its name stems from confusion by early mapmakers on what constitutes Australia and what constitutes Antarctica.

The first European to see Australia was Abel Janszoon Tasman, a Dutch navigator. This was in 1642. Its East Coast, around the site of what would become Sydney, was explored by Lieutenant James Cook (later captain) on the *Endeavour*. Part of Cook's orders was to discover *terra australis incognita*. In 1770 Lieutenant Cook claimed the land for England.

In 1777, the first European settlement was established in Sydney. Convicts from Britain were among its first settlers. Today, the population of Australia is an estimated 16,800,000. That's like the population of New York in a country and continent the size of the United States.

I'd lived in Australia, and normally it takes about three days to drive across it. It took us on *Commodore Explorer* four days to sail from one end of Australia to the other. We were "driving" around the world, "on the road" like seagoing Jack Kerouacs.

---

[1] Where oceans begin and end is not an exact science, however. Many oceanographers consider that the western edge of the Pacific is at the Strait of Malacca, between the Malay Peninsula, and Sumatra, which is northwest of Australia. That would place all of Australia in the Pacific. In the next chapter of this book, Fogg, Passepartout, and now Aouda and Detective Fix will be sailing through the Strait of Malacca on the *Rangoon*, before stopping in Singapore and Hong Kong.

Between December 1869 and February 1870, the clipper ship *Patriarchal* sailed from London to Sydney, Australia, in 69 days. That record stood tall until 1975, when *Great Britain*, a yacht sailed by Mike Gilles, covered the distance in 67 days, 6 hours. We did it in 39 days.

Also worth mentioning: On the thirty-seventh day, on March 8, we passed what we considered the halfway point. Later, there would be arguments about what exactly was the halfway point. But I was in a hurry—we all were—and this one would do just fine.

At that moment, we were three days ahead of Fogg and Passepartout. Our average speed since leaving France more than a month ago was an astounding 16 knots.

# In which a gale causes Passepartout great anguish; Fix great delight

Fogg, Passepartout, and now Aouda left Calcutta on the *Rangoon*—a steamship belonging to the Peninsular and Oriental Company, a British firm—that plied the Chinese and Japanese Seas. They were heading for Hong Kong, 3,500 miles away. The voyage was expected to take from ten to twelve days.

The course they traveled was almost a perfect V, around much of "Southeast Asia," as the area has been called since World War II. This designation corresponded to Lord Louis Mountbatten's command during World War II, but it doesn't mean that there are many—indeed any—similarities among the various lands or particularly the people who live there.

By any name, Southeast Asia reaches from Burma to New Guinea, or from the Indian Ocean to the Pacific. The archipelago includes the 7,000 islands of the Philippines, the 3,000 islands in Indonesia, and the consequential islands of Sumatra, Java, and Borneo. The area has been described as looking like "scattered pieces from a jigsaw puzzle." Given the diversity of the islands and people, it might better be described as scattered pieces from different jigsaw puzzles.

On the mainland of Asia are Burma, the lengthy Malay Peninsula, Thailand, Cambodia, Laos, and Vietnam. The latter three countries were known as Indochina when Fogg would have made his voyage.

In Southeast Asia, East first met West. The impetus for the meeting was spices—the absolute "spice of life" in Europe at the time.

An empty spice rack is unlikely to send many into a frenzy today, or off on an 11,000-nautical-mile sea voyage; however, beginning in the thirteenth century, if not before, spices were viewed as status symbols. They were the ostrich feathers of the nineteenth century, the Perrier water or the Lexus of the twentieth. "Where wouldn't they go for pepper!" wrote Joseph Conrad, the novelist. "For a bag of pepper they would cut each other's throats without hesitation, and would forswear their souls. . . ." A clove, for example, could fetch a 2,000 percent profit in Europe.

In part, Christopher Columbus's four voyages were launched to discover a western route to the spices in the East. Columbus, an Italian, came to believe that Japan was 3,000 miles (4,800 km) *west* of Portugal, a distance within the range of existing ships and technology. He concluded the earth was considerably smaller than it is, and Europe and Asia were considerably larger than they are. These erroneous conclusions were based primarily on Ptolemy's eight-volume *The Geography*, written in the first century.

Columbus, sailing for Spain, landed in the Bahamas on October 12, 1492, at an island he named San Salvador. He called the local population "Indians." Columbus couldn't have been farther from the truth, as India and the Bahamas are practically at antipodal points. This misnomer "Indians" would continue to be applied to all indigenous peoples of North America, as well as Central and South America. Also, due to Columbus's confusion—he was the original "Wrong-Way" Corrigan—we distinguish the "East Indies" from the "West Indies."

On this voyage, Columbus established what may have been the first European settlement in the Western Hemisphere on Hispaniola, the island divided between Haiti and the Dominican Republic. When he reported back to King Ferdinand and Queen Isabella, of Spain, his royal patrons, he claimed he had reached islands just off the Asian coast. He brought back with him some gold and even six or seven "Indians."

When it came to colonial aspirations, Spain and Portugal were the major players in the late fifteenth and early sixteenth centuries. This period corresponded to the Renaissance elsewhere in Europe. The Portuguese were particularly ruthless. As St. Francis Xavier wrote about the Portuguese in the Moluccas, the only word they knew was *rapere*—to steal. They showed "an amazing capacity for inventing new tenses and participles."

After Columbus's first voyage, Spain and Portugal agreed to let Pope Alexander VI decide the two rival countries' claims to the "New World." The result was the Treaty of Tordesillas, signed in 1494. Spain was to get all territories in the "non-Christian world" to the *west* of a demarcation line some 100 leagues west of the Cape Verde Islands; Portugal was to get all territories to the east. Later, after King John II of Portugal complained, the line was moved another 270 leagues west. As a league is about three nautical miles, depending on the country, that alteration set the line at about 1,110 nautical miles west of the Cape Verde Islands—or at about 43 degrees west longitude. This gave to Spain the Caribbean Islands, the Bahamas, North, South, and Central America, and later the Pacific Ocean (which wouldn't be discovered until 1513, by Vasco Nuñez de Balboa, a Spanish conquistador). The westward shift, however, would allow Portugal to claim Brazil in 1500.

Columbus made a second voyage in 1493. This time, rather than the humble *Niña, Pinta*, and *Santa Maria*, he had 17 ships and 1,500 men. The size of the expedition reflected the great expectations of the crown. The 40 Spaniards he had left in Hispaniola had been killed, he discovered, and the colony destroyed.

In 1498, Vasco da Gama of Portugal sailed south and then east, rather than due west as Columbus had. Da Gama rounded the Cape of Good Hope and reached India. Asked what he wanted when he arrived in Calicut, on the southwestern coast, he said, "Christians and spices."

Da Gama's success for Portugal gave Spain renewed impetus to send Columbus west. Columbus would make two more voyages. On the third voyage, he reached the coast of South America— thereby becoming its "discoverer"—or perhaps more accurately its European discoverer. However, on the way home, he battled with a Spanish governor in Santa Domingo and was returned to Spain in chains. The captain of the ship that brought Columbus home to Spain was willing to remove the shackles, but Columbus insisted on wearing them when he appeared before the king and queen. The point he wished to make was that he had, in his agreement with his royal patrons, an exclusive right to this area. He was to be governor and viceroy of all lands he discovered and "admiral of the Ocean Sea."

Columbus died in 1506, two years after his fourth and final voyage. He still maintained that he had reached the East rather than the West. Whatever he believed, Columbus was the first European to "discover" and explore the "new world"—even if he refused to believe it was new. It was to prove a more important discovery than the place he had sought.

In 1521, Ferdinand Magellan, a Portuguese sailing for Spain, claimed what would be called the Philippines for his Spanish patrons. Magellan's voyage was to prove that the Spice Islands were on the Spanish side of the line, according to the Treaty of Tordesillas.[1]

Magellan was killed on Mactan Island in a local war, and Juan

---

[1] The Spice Islands, which comprise many islands and island groups in eastern Indonesia, are now called the Moluccas or Maluku.

Sebastian del Cano completed the circumnavigation—the world's first.

Leaving Calcutta, Fogg's party traveled south-southeast past the more than 200 Andaman Islands, the principal island group in the Bay of Bengal, belonging to India. The British established a settlement there in 1789. Like Australia, the islands served as a British penal colony, from 1858 to 1945.

Verne has little good to say about the Papuans who, he claims, live there. He writes, "The steamer passed along near the shores, but the savage Papuans, who are in the lowest scale of humanity, but are not, as has been asserted, cannibals, did not make their appearance."

Verne never visited this area; indeed, he traveled little. He did much of his research for his book *Around the World in Eighty Days* in libraries. The native population of the Andaman Islands are not Papuans but Andamanese. Until Europeans arrived in the middle of the nineteenth century, the Andamanese were a Stone-Age culture with no knowledge of agriculture, fire, or domestic animals. They were food gatherers, fishermen, and hunters.

Then the *Rangoon* passed through the Strait of Malacca, between the Malay Peninsula and Sumatra, considered by many oceanographers to be the end of the Indian Ocean and the beginning of the Pacific.

At the bottom of the Malay Peninsula—or the bottom of the V scribed by the *Rangoon*—is the island of Singapore. At 70 miles (110 km) north of the equator, this was as far south as Fogg and his party would get in their imaginary around-the-world voyage. The British purchased the island of Singapore in 1819, at the behest of Thomas Stamford Raffles, of the British East India Company. Singapore became a flourishing port and then a British Crown Colony in 1867. It is today an independent nation.

Next, the *Rangoon* would go north-northeast past what we now call Vietnam. In 1871, the year before Fogg and Passepartout might have commenced their fictitious voyage, the French colonized Indochina. Eventually France's Union of Indochina consisted of Cochin China (southern Vietnam), Annam (central Vietnam), Tonkin (northern Vietnam), Cambodia, and Laos.

The Union lasted until World War II, when Japan invaded Indochina. Resistance to Japanese rule was organized in Vietnam by Ho Chi Minh and his Viet Minh followers. In 1945, he declared Vietnam independent. Fearing Ho's communism, the United States supported the restoration of French rule. America's leaders believed wholly in the "domino theory"—once one country in a region fell to communism, all countries in that region would. They would knock each other over like dominoes, or so the theory went.

War broke out between the French and Vietnamese in 1947. In 1954 the French were defeated at Dien Bien Phu; at this point, the United States was providing 80 percent of the cost of the war effort. Following this defeat, Vietnam was divided into a North and a South Vietnam, along the seventeenth parallel, or latitude line. The government of North Vietnam was communist. The United States ended up supporting the government of South Vietnam. This embroiled the U.S. in the Vietnam War, which ended in a U.S. defeat in 1975. During the war, 58,000 Americans and two to three million Indochinese died. It cost the United States $150 billion. It also cost us our self-confidence—something that we have not fully regained twenty years after this awful war concluded.

In Hong Kong Aouda hoped to find her cousin Jejeeh, who might help her. Jejeeh, like Aouda, was a relative of Sir Jametsee Jeejeebhoy, who had made a fortune in the cotton business. Sir Jametsee, we learn, had been named a baronet by the English government, presumably for his success in business. Jejeeh was said to have been equally successful in Hong Kong.

Whether he would help her or not, Aouda didn't know. Fogg allayed her fears: "Everything would be mathematically arranged." Verne enjoyed his character's use of that word *mathematically*—first used by one of his doubting whist partners at the Reform Club. Verne writes parenthetically, "He used the very word."

At this, Aouda fastened on Fogg her wonderful eyes, as "clear as the sacred lakes of the Himalaya" (Verne again invokes the words of the "poet-king," Ucaf Uddaul), but "the intractable Fogg, as reserved as ever, did not seem at all inclined to throw himself into this lake." At least not yet.

In voice or in manner, Fogg was not demonstrative toward Aouda. However, the author tells us, "he seemed to be always on the watch that nothing should be wanting to Aouda's comfort." Aouda was puzzled by Fogg; however, she "always regarded him through the exalting medium of her gratitude." From Passepartout, she learned about the wager, to travel around the world in 80 days. This made her smile.

The *Rangoon*, Verne says, was built of iron and weighed 1,770 tons. She had engines of 400 horsepower. The steam engine, which powered the Industrial Revolution as well as the *Rangoon*, dates back to 1698. The principle of a steam engine is that when water turns to steam, its volume expands at least 1,600 times. When generated in an enclosed space, it can be harnessed to do work. For example, steam can push a piston in one direction (in a single-acting reciprocating steam engine) and push it in the opposite direction (in a double-acting reciprocating steam engine). The back-and-forth motion of the piston can be changed to circular motion by means of a crankshaft and a connecting rod. In time, this circular motion would turn a paddle wheel on a ship and later a screw propeller.

The first steamboat operated in France in 1783 on the Saone River. In 1790, John Fitch established the first steamboat for passengers, between Trenton, New Jersey, and Philadelphia. Molly Fitch, my fiancée then and now my wife, is a direct descendant of John Fitch.[2]

[2] Rudolf Diesel was awarded a patent for a diesel engine, which burned oil rather than coal, in 1892. In 1910 a diesel engine was first used on the *Vulcanus*, a Dutch tanker. By 1930, the diesel would sound the death knell for sail on commercial ships used by industrial nations.

Many vessels of this era, the fictitious *Rangoon* included, used both coal-burning engines and sails. When the wind was fair they used sails to augment their steam engines. When it wasn't, they furled the sails.

Also aboard the *Rangoon* was Detective Fix, who recognized that Hong Kong would be the last British Crown Colony on which Fogg would likely set foot. If, prior to arriving at Hong Kong, the *Rangoon* would stop in Singapore, a British Crown Colony, too, for more coal, Fix recognized this would only be a brief stop. In Hong Kong Fogg's party would have a longer wait. Here, a simple warrant of arrest would suffice. Anywhere else, Fix would need an extradition warrant—a considerable complication.

Since boarding the *Rangoon* in Calcutta, Fix had not made his presence known to Passepartout, whom he had befriended first in Suez and then on the *Mongolia*, traveling from Suez to Bombay. Nevertheless, he had kept a close watch on Fogg's traveling party and was particularly confused by the presence of Aouda. In the Calcutta courtroom, he had hidden himself in the background. Now he had decided that it was time to question Passepartout.

Fix encountered the French servant as he was "promenading up the forward part of the steamer." Passepartout was nonplussed by the meeting. " 'Why, I left you at Bombay, and here you are, on the way to Hong Kong! Are you going around the world too?' " he said.

Fix allowed that he was not. His plan, he said, was to stay in Hong Kong. He offered to buy Passepartout a glass of gin. This the thirsty Frenchman gladly accepted. In the course of this first drink, Passepartout explained to Fix what Aouda was doing there. How they'd saved her from the suttee.

While an innocent, Passepartout was struck by the fact that Fix kept turning up in their lives. After all, while aboard the *Mongolia*, he had announced Bombay as his destination. Then it occurred to Passepartout: "He's a spy sent to keep us in view." He was an agent of the gentlemen of the Reform Club. The Frenchman decided to "chaff Fix, when he had the chance, with mysterious allusions, which, however, need not betray his real suspicions."

On Thursday, October 31, 1872, the *Rangoon* anchored in Singapore. She was a half day early, or ahead of schedule. Fogg duly noted this in his journal. This left Fogg six days, to reach Hong Kong, some 1,300 miles away. There Fogg and his party would catch the steamer for Yokohama, Japan, which would depart on November 6.

Departing Singapore, the weather turned contrary. As the wind was from the southwest and the *Rangoon* was heading northeast, the captain was nevertheless able to hoist all sails. Verne tells us that "under the double action of steam and sail, the vessel made rapid progress along the coast of Anam [central Vietnam] and Cochin China [southern Vietnam]."[3]

At times, however, the *Rangoon* had to shorten sail, "owing to its defective construction." This drove Passepartout wild; however, it didn't seem to worry Fogg at all. Noting Passepartout's impatience, Detective Fix asked him, " 'You are in a great hurry, then, . . . to reach Hong Kong?'

" 'A very great hurry!' " agreed Passepartout.

" 'Mr. Fogg, I suppose, is anxious to catch the steamer for Yokohama?'

" 'Terribly anxious.'

" 'You believe in this journey around the world, then?'

" 'Absolutely. Don't you, Mr. Fix?'

" 'I? I don't believe a word of it.' "

Then Passepartout, who had vowed to " 'chaff Fix, when he had the chance, with mysterious allusions,' " says, " 'You're a sly dog!' " and then winked at him. This knowing wink troubled the detective. He wondered if the Frenchmen had guessed his true intentions. He decided it was time to deal unambiguously with Passepartout.

If Passepartout could have willed the steamer forward, he

---

[3] The translator spells Annam with one *n*.

would have. One day, while he was leaning on a rail near the engine room, and observing the engine, the steamer pitched, throwing its screw propeller out of the water. The steam came hissing out of the valves, which made Passepartout apoplectic. He exclaimed, " 'The valves are not sufficiently charged! We are not going. Oh, these English! If this was an American craft, we should blow up, perhaps, but we should at all events go faster!' "

The wind, however, swung northwest and blew a gale. The *Rangoon* struck all her sails, but even "the rigging proved too much," writes Verne. The captain speculated that they would reach Hong Kong at least 20 hours late and perhaps later if the storm didn't abate. Twenty hours means Fogg would miss the steamer for Japan—his bet would be lost.

Each of the three protagonists had a different reaction to the storm. Detective Fix, for example, was overjoyed. "Each delay filled him with hope, for it became more and more probable that Fogg would be obliged to remain some days at Hong Kong; and now the heavens themselves became his allies, with the gusts and squalls. It mattered not that they made him sea-sick—he made no account of his inconvenience; and whilst his body was writhing under their effects, his spirit bounded with hopeful exultation."

As for Passepartout? "The storm exasperated him, the gale made him furious, and he longed to lash the obstinate sea into obedience." So much anguish did Detective Fix see in Passepartout, one would have thought the £20,000 wager was to come from Passepartout's pocket, not Fogg's.

What of Phileas Fogg? "This man of nerve manifested neither impatience nor annoyance; it seemed as if the storm were a part of his programme, and had been foreseen. Aouda was amazed to find him as calm as he had been from the first time she saw him."

Hong Kong was finally sighted at 5:00 A.M. on November 6. The *Rangoon* was 24 hours behind schedule, and doubtless the *Carnatic*, the boat Fogg hoped to take to Japan, had sailed. The next steamer would leave for there in a week.

# In which we sail
# under the
# aurora australis

---

On our thirty-eighth day at sea, on March 10, 1993, the living was still easy.

Auckland, New Zealand, lay 1,500 miles to the northeast. At half that distance was the bottom, or south side, of the South Island of New Zealand. This was a two-day run in an apparently healthy *Commodore Explorer* if Bruno opted to bail out, as he'd been threatening to do. Bruno, you will recall, had been in radio contact with Peter Blake on the broken *ENZA*, asking about a sheltered place—a snug harbor—on the South Island to repair our boat. *Commodore Explorer* had been damaged by a rogue wave about two weeks before.

From my perspective and the crew's, so far, so good. We'd suffered an insult, a body blow, but we weren't broken yet. Once you stop in a voyage like this, you may never start again. It's called "inertia," which is anathema to adventurers. It is the fundamental difference between a house and a boat. If at first blush that seems an unlikely comparison, consider the words of Arthur Ransome, the author, who once wrote, "Houses are but badly built boats, so firmly aground that you cannot think of moving them. They are definitely inferior things, belonging to the vegetable, not the animal, world, rooted and stationary, incapable of gay transition."

Still, between New Zealand and Cape Horn, a distance of 3,950 nautical miles, there is almost no place to run, no place to hide. Also, with the wind almost inexorably and relentlessly behind you, it is no easy matter to turn back into it. Here, in the Roaring Forties and Howling Fifties, it can be said: the earth is more flat than round—and many a good boat and capable crew has sailed off the edge. For around-the-world sailors, this is truly a no-man's land. Discretion or valor is one of the toughest calls a skipper has to make, so I understood—at least a little—how difficult the decision was that Bruno was weighing. Perhaps he'd gained a modicum of confidence in the repairs to the starboard hull, because New Zealand seemed too distant to make that dreaded left-hand turn to run for the barn.

I placed a bet with Chinois—dinner for two at the restaurant of the winner's choice—on when we'd pass Cape Horn. I chose March 22, at 1200 hours, which was 11 days away. Chinois opted for March 23, at midnight.

This day we passed near Macquarie Island, a veritable speck in the Pacific Ocean that belongs to Australia, but without seeing it. This disappointed me. It's strange that when you live surrounded by dirt, you long for a view of the water; when you live surrounded by water, you long for a peek at dirt. Above my galley I kept a postcard of heli-skiing in the Monashees—a fine use for dirt.

Near Macquarie Island the ocean shoals from a depth of 12,000 feet to 300 feet. Called the Macquarie Ridge and the Campbell Plateau, it extends from New Zealand south to

Antarctica, as if a seawall. As a result of this abrupt transition, or shoaling, you can experience huge seas and even riptides. Bruno said that his kid brother Loïck got knocked down here seven times in the previous Vendée Globe Race, nonstop alone around the world. He'd sailed close by the island in hopes of seeing dirt and perhaps penguins. I guess when you're sailing solo, it gets lonely out here. However, he hadn't considered the precipitous shoaling and was lucky to escape with only a loss of dignity.

This day Bruno decided he needed a haircut. He wanted a flattop like the exotic female rock star Grace Jones. "I'll cut your hair," I told him. I got the scissors from the sail-repair kit. If I butcher the job, I thought, he'll have at least six weeks to recover. Plenty of time. As the old saw goes: The difference between a good and bad haircut is one week.

Bruno came out on deck with a newspaper we'd brought from France when we departed 39 days before. That was about as fresh as formal news got on *Commodore Explorer*. As he read his newspaper, looking like a most proper French burgher, I snipped away at his mane. It actually turned out fairly well. After that, Bruno would sit at his navigation station—there was only sitting headroom there —and rub his head against the cabin roof. He trained his Grace-Jones 'do to stay flat by rubbing it against the headliner.

I wanted to fax Molly after cooking supper, but we were sailing in a satellite, and thus communications, void and had been for a couple of days.

In the midst of this blackout, one telex found us, however. It was in English but it was unsigned. Bruno called me over to his starboard hull to help translate it. It was a poem, entitled "The Quitter," written by the Canadian poet Robert Service. I can remember memorizing his poems, including this one, in school. The version sent to us read:

> When you're lost in the Wild, and you're scared as a
>   child,
> And Death looks you bang in the eye,
> And you're sore as a boil, it's according to Hoyle
> To cock your revolver and . . . die.
> But the Code of a Man says: "Fight all you can,"
> And self-dissolution is barred.
> In hunger and woe, oh, it's easy to blow . . .
> It's the hell-served-for-breakfast that's hard.
>
> "You're sick of the game!" Well, now, that's a shame.
> You're young and you're brave and you're bright.
> "You've had a raw deal!" I know—but don't squeal,
> Buck up, do your damnedest, and fight.
> It's the plugging away that will win you the day,
> So don't be a piker, old pard!
> Just draw on your grit; it's so easy to quit:
> It's the keeping-your-chin-up that's hard.

Neither Bruno nor I had any idea who had sent this to us. We didn't know how they'd learned that Bruno was suffering from a crisis of confidence in the boat and the voyage. All we could figure was that it must have been something Michel Horeau, our press liaison in Paris, had passed to the media. We didn't even know how they'd gotten our telex number. However, the timing and anonymity of the message seemed to settle—at least a little—Bruno's troubled mind. His chin, if not up, was at least not headed down. And we were still heading east, toward the rising sun, not north for the "barn."

The telex released a floodgate of such messages to us that were endlessly interesting. A few came from a homeless man that Bruno had befriended in 1987, while waiting for his brother Stéphane to finish windsurfing alone across the Atlantic. The Peyron family is famous in France, and Stéphane's feat was in all the newspapers. The homeless guy had traveled from Paris to le Pouliguen (Bruno's home) with his dog and shopping cart to welcome Stéphane home. This was a distance of 400 kilometers (248 miles)—given his means, this must have been some adventure.

Bruno gave him some food, some money, and some friendship—after all, they were, in some important ways, kindred souls. Somehow, this guy figured out how to send telexes to us on *Commodore Explorer* and found the money to do it. These telexes, in particular, made Bruno happy.

From such telexes we got the overwhelming sense we weren't alone out there. With ship-to-shore radio, fax, telex, and weather faxes—however episodic—that characterize voyaging at the end of this century, what a difference, I thought, from the circumnavigation of Joshua Slocum in 1895–98 or the polar explorations of Peary, Scott, Amundsen, and Shackleton at the beginning of this century when radio was in its infancy. We almost never "walked" alone; they almost always did.

Our alcohol situation was growing critical. Recall that as we crossed the equator, a month ago, I'd first sounded the alarm. We were using this cooking fuel at a much higher rate than I'd figured on. This day I asked the crew to boil only as much water as they needed. I also asked them, if they were called on deck, not to leave the stove on. Finally, I wrote a fax to the stove manufacturer inquiring about the possibility of burning alternate fuels. We had diesel and a little gasoline. I wondered if there was some combination of these two fuels that would allow me to cook food, without cooking the boat and its inhabitants.

Later, I discovered Bruno had never sent the fax.

Whether he thought such outside assistance would violate the rules or spirit of the race or whether he thought I was nuts to consider mixing gas and diesel, I don't know. It might have been both of these things.

Late that night I lay on my back on the trampoline and peered transfixed at the sky. Marc was driving, from the starboard cockpit, with the cat ambling downwind at an easy 15 knots. The night was dry. It was easy to pretend that I was on a hammock, anchored in space to two stars, and swinging gently between them. Above me were huge swirls of light: greens and reds, pinks and blues. The evening sky was positively aglow. Luminous. The sky seemed a kaleidoscope with pleated curtains of twinkling light.

In the southern hemisphere, where we were, I watched what is called the "aurora australis," or southern lights. Back north, it is called the "aurora borealis" or northern lights. I was voicing my appreciation to Marc. From my mind to my mouth, nonstop and unabridged; I'm like Passepartout that way. Marc, while interested, was less awestruck. He'd been intrigued by birds at one point in his life and had gone trekking in Greenland to study them. While there, he'd seen cosmic displays of this magnitude before. Been there, done that.

I wondered aloud if I should wake up Bruno, Chinois, and Jacques, who were off-watch and presumably asleep. At that moment, I sensed more than saw Bruno. He was peering at the sky through the *casquette* of his cabin. I asked him if he'd ever seen anything like this before. Never like this, he said, his voice full of wonder.

Men—at least those I hang around with—are uncomfortable with wonder. Typically, the conversation moves from wonder to why at catamaran speeds. Bruno and I speculated about the causes of auroras. Scientists say they are caused by massive electrical discharges. The interaction involves solar winds (ionized gas flaming into space from the corona of the sun) and the magnetic force of the earth. The discharged current, in the form of energized electrons, is channeled toward the earth's north and south magnetic poles by the earth's magnetic field, as a compass needle points to magnetic north. This happens at altitudes of 60 to 200 miles.

These ionized electrons collide with upper atmospheric atoms and molecules and excite them too. These over-stimulated electrons are rendered briefly luminous, like a television screen. The dominant green light comes from energized oxygen atoms, which sustain life on this tiny planet —perhaps the only one in the universe that supports life. The crimson comes from energized nitrogen molecules.

With the phenomenon being concentrated very near to the magnetic poles, the farther north or south you are, the better is the display. We were then at 52 degrees south latitude: a decent seat. Also, the closer you are to the south or north magnetic pole, the better is the viewing. We were then about 1,150 nautical miles away from the south magnetic pole, which, as of 1975, was on the Antarctic coast, at 66 degrees south latitude, 139 degrees east longitude, or due south of Adelaide, Australia. This is why you can see the aurora australis in the middle latitudes in Australia and New Zealand but not very often in middle latitudes in South Africa or South America. It is also why you can see the aurora borealis in middle latitudes in America (the location of the north magnetic pole, again as of 1975, was 76 degrees north latitude, 100 degrees west longitude, or in Bathurst Island in Canada's Northwest Territories) but not very often in the middle latitudes of Europe.

It is also known that aurora activity increases in March and September, when the sun seems to cross the equator, in its northerly and southerly meander. Although why this is so isn't clear. This was March 11: prime time. Also, I've since learned that auroral displays are strongest when sunspot activity is greatest. Increased sunspot activity tends to degrade radio communications, which we'd been experiencing. The cause could have been sunspots. Of course, it could have been a loose connection too. Bruno, however, would accuse me of accidentally reprogramming the computer that received telexes.

The next day, we passed 1,440 miles due north of Antarctica's Ross Sea and Ice Shelf—the world's largest body of floating ice. It is a place central to Antarctic explorers, exploration, and scientists.

While the continent of Antarctica, which we were rounding, is roughly circular in shape, the Ross Sea and Ice Shelf is a Texas-size fissure that is 700 miles closer to the South Pole—the prize of geography and exploration in the beginning of this century, as the moon was the prize in the middle of the century. A sign of the times, perhaps, I don't know what the prize is at the end of our century. Perhaps it is "virtual reality"—sanitized exploration from the safety of a computer screen.

The Ross Sea and Ice Shelf, an arm of the Pacific Ocean off Antarctica, was the landing site for such famous Antarctic explorers as Captain Robert Falcon Scott, of England, who tried to reach the South Pole in 1902; Sir Ernest Shackleton, of England, who in 1908 got within 98 miles of the South Pole and later tried to cross the continent; Roald Amundsen, of Norway, who in 1911 reached the South Pole; and the same Captain Scott, who stood at the South Pole one thin month after Amundsen and died of starvation, the cold, and a broken heart, I'm certain, on the return trip with his men. These men were the prime movers in Antarctica at the start of this century. They were like astronauts in the sixties or sport figures—heaven help us—in the nineties.

While many nations—Argentina, Australia, Chile, France, New Zealand, Norway, and the United Kingdom—

claim parts of Antarctica resulting from early sightings and landings of countrymen, the United States and Russia recognize no territorial claims. Nevertheless, for me, there is something of a family compound here: Little America, on the eastern edge of the Ross Ice Shelf, near the Bay of Whales. Here Admiral Byrd established his headquarters in 1929. He put his base camps in this area during the five expeditions he would lead to Antarctica. Farther to the east is Marie Byrd Land, named for his wife.

Shackleton, Amundsen, Scott, and Byrd are the big four of Antarctic exploration—indeed exploration generally. They ushered in what has been called the "heroic age." In words and in deeds, they blazed the trail that all modern-day adventurers follow. Yet, they are all but forgotten in the faded pages of history.

I thought about these men as our wakes crossed south of New Zealand, separated by as many as 91 years. They'd been heading south to Antarctica, to the worst weather on earth. We were heading east, toward the rising sun and, at the same time, around Antarctica. They were explorers, "standing where man has never stood before," to use the cliché. It's harder to find such places anymore, so we are more adventurers than explorers. For example, on *Commodore Explorer*, four Frenchmen and one American were racing fictitious characters from an 1873 novel of a famous French author around the world. This was the theme of our voyage. Were the purposes of these famous Antarctic explorers more noble? The truth is, I don't know. They just got here first.

Nevertheless, modern adventurers and those interested in adventure should pay homage to these men, as we are all children of Shackleton, Amundsen, Byrd, and Scott. Before coming on this voyage, I had read their books thoroughly. Indeed, I'd brought Sir Ernest Shackleton's *South* with me on this voyage. Shackleton's second expedition, to cross Antarctica by way of the South Pole, as described in this book, was an unqualified failure: Shackleton never landed a man on Antarctica and, indeed, he only spied land once. He also watched his ship *Endurance*—"by endurance we conquer" was the Shackleton family motto—being crushed by the ice.[1] However, Shackleton mined more gold in failure—and all of his expeditions could be characterized as failures—than the rest did in success. No one was a better leader of men and no one ever survived a greater adventure. Also, no one ever wrote more eloquently about it.

I learned about leadership from Shackleton, the ultimate man of action; food and organization from Amundsen, the ultimate organizational man; the harnessing of high technology from Byrd; and purity of heart and purpose from Scott.

These men, further, taught us about survival, about strength, the resiliency of the human body and spirit, and the eye-bewitching beauty of hostile climates. They also turned starvation, deprivation, eating dogs and horses, dehydration, snow-blindness, exhaustion, frozen feet and hands, and hypothermia into virtues. If you can't find something salutary in those things, you'll never understand adventuring.

"He lived like a mighty rushing wind," wrote Hugh Robert Mill about Ernest Shackleton. A better life description, I can't imagine.

---

[1] Vivian Fuchs, a British geologist, essentially made this trans-Antarctic passage in 1957–58, as part of the International Geophysical Year (IGY). He traveled across Filchner Ice Shelf, at the Weddell Sea, past the South Pole, to McMurdo Sound, at the Ross Sea, in 99 days. He used dogs and snow tractors and aircraft for support. Fuchs, was knighted for his accomplishment.

# In which Detective Fix drugs Passepartout in a Hong Kong opium den

On November 6, 1872, Fogg and his party had apparently missed the boat, the *Carnatic*, in Hong Kong. The next steamer wouldn't leave for Yokohama, Japan, for a week.

However, as a pilot boarded the *Rangoon*, to take it into Hong Kong, Fogg asked him when the next steamer would leave for Yokohama. At high tide, tomorrow morning, was the pilot's reply. To Fogg's question What is the name of the boat? the pilot replied: " 'The *Carnatic*.'

" 'Ought she not have gone yesterday?' Fogg asked.

" 'Yes, sir; but they had to repair one of her boilers, and so her departure was postponed till to-morrow.' "

Fogg was now 24 hours, or one day, behind schedule 35 days after departing London. However, the freighter *General Grant*, which crossed the Pacific from Yokohama to San Francisco, wouldn't leave until the *Carnatic* arrived there. This was because *Carnatic* fed passengers to the *General Grant*. Fogg felt sure that the lost day could be regained on the 22-day crossing of the Pacific.

He left Aouda and Passepartout in the Club Hotel in Hong Kong. Then he went in search of Aouda's cousin Jejeeh, at the Exchange. There he learned Jejeeh had left Hong Kong two years before, having retired after amassing a fortune. He now lived in Holland. When Fogg returned and told her what he'd learned, Aouda asked, " 'What ought I to do, Mr. Fogg?'

" 'It is very simple. . . . Go on to Europe.'

" 'But I cannot intrude—'

" 'You do not intrude, nor do you in the least embarrass my project. Passepartout!' " At this, Fogg sent his servant to the *Carnatic* to engage three cabins.

"Hong Kong," Verne writes, "is an island which came into the possession of the English by the treaty of Nankin[g], after the war of 1842; and the colonizing genius of the English has created upon it an important city and an excellent port. The island is situated at the mouth of the Canton River, and is separated by about sixty miles from the Portuguese town of Macao, on the opposite coast. Hong Kong had beaten Macao in the struggle for the Chinese trade, and now the greater part of the transportation of Chinese goods finds its depôt at the former place. Docks, hospitals, wharves, a Gothic cathedral, a government house, macadamized streets, give to Hong Kong the appearance of a town in Kent or Surrey transferred by some strange magic to the antipodes."

Upon reaching the quay, where the *Carnatic* was to embark, Passepartout ran into Detective Fix, who seemed very agitated. " 'This is bad . . . for the gentlemen of the Reform Club,' " muttered Passepartout with an ironic smile. Rather than worrying about the gentlemen of the Reform Club, Fix was in a rage himself because the warrant for the arrest of Phileas Fogg hadn't arrived from London. And this was the last British port.

Passepartout purchased his three tickets and learned that rather than leaving tomorrow morning, the *Carnatic* would sail this evening. " 'That will suit my master all the better,' " he said to Fix.

At this point, Detective Fix invited Passepartout into a tavern on the quay that caught his eye. Rather than just a tavern where liquor is dispersed, "Fix and Passepartout saw that they were in a smoking-house, haunted by those wretched, cadaverous, idiotic creatures, to whom the English merchants sell every year the miserable drug called opium, to the amount of one million four hundred thousand pounds—thousands devoted to one of the most despicable vices which afflict humanity! The Chinese government has in vain attempted to deal with the evil by stringent laws. [The drug] passed gradually from the rich, to whom it was at first exclusively reserved, to the lower classes, and then its ravages could not be arrested. Opium is smoked everywhere, at all times, by men and women, in the Celestial Empire. . . . A great smoker can smoke as many as eight pipes a day; but he dies in five years."

Verne in his description of Hong Kong writes about "the colonizing genius of the English." Perhaps in many ways this was true, but consider how the British came to rule Hong Kong. They gained Hong Kong by winning the first "Opium War."

China objected to the importation of opium, an illegal drug, by British merchants. As Verne indicates, it was a remarkably profitable trade, however. Britain won the first Opium War in 1839–42, which contested this matter, and for reparations, as specified in the Treaty of Nanking and the Treaty of Bogue, it ceded Hong Kong to the British. It further opened several ports, including Shanghai, to the British. Also, British citizens were to be tried in British courts in China in a doctrine known as "extraterritoriality." In due time other nations of the West were granted similar privileges.

Fighting China in the second Opium War were the combined forces of Britain and France, who were triumphant. China, however, refused to sign the Treaty of Tientsin, in 1858. The result was that Peking was captured. Finally, in 1860, China accepted the treaty. Among other things, the importation of opium was legalized. More ports were opened, and Christian missionaries were allowed into the country. Obviously, there was a need for them with such a serious drug problem.

At the tavern Passepartout and Fix ordered two bottles of port, to which the Frenchmen did justice. As Passepartout was getting ready to leave, to apprise his master of the change in schedule, Detective Fix grabbed his arm and said, " 'I want to have a serious talk with you.' " Fix asked Passepartout if he knew who he really was. Passepartout said that Fix was an agent of the gentlemen of the Reform Club, sent to " 'interrupt my master's journey.' " Fix disabused him of that notion. " 'I am a police detective; sent out here by the London office.' " Then he showed Passepartout his commission—its genuineness "could not be doubted."

Fix explained patiently, " 'Mr. Fogg's wager is only a pretext, of which you and the gentlemen of the Reform are dupes.' " The motive, he said, was the robbery of the Bank of England that had occurred on September 28. Passepartout is having none of that, however. " 'What nonsense,' " fairly shouted Passepartout, striking his fist on the table. " 'My master is the most honorable of men!' "

Fix made his case: " 'How can you tell? You know scarcely anything about him. You went into his service the day he came away; and he came away on a foolish pretext, without trunks, and carrying a large amount in bank-notes. And yet you are bold enough to assert that he is an honest man!' "

Then Fix threatened Passepartout: " 'Would you like to be arrested as his accomplice?' " As if suffering a blow, Passepartout supported his head with his hands. Weakly he asked, " 'Well, what do you want of me?' " Fix wanted Passepartout to detain his master in Hong Kong, until the warrant arrived. He even offered to share the £2,000 reward with the Frenchman.

Passepartout stammered, " 'Mr. Fix . . . even should what you say be true—if my master is really the robber you are seeking for —which I deny—I have been, am, in his service; I have seen his generosity and goodness; and I will never betray him—not for all the gold in the world. I come from a village where they don't eat that kind of bread!' "

However, after that eruption, Passepartout oddly enough joined Detective Fix in another friendly drink. The Frenchman felt himself "yielding more and more to the effects of the liquor." In more modern crime dramas, the detective would have slipped Passepartout a "Mickey Finn"—a drink adulterated with a drug, like chloral hydrate. Here, however, Fix grabbed a full opium pipe that just happened to be on their table, like chocolate mints on the pillows of the finest hotels. He passed it to Passepartout, who placed it in his mouth, lit it, and drew several puffs. In that instant, Passepartout joined the "wretched, cadaverous, idiotic creatures," to use Verne's description. The action was completely out of character. In or out of character, Passepartout passed out at the table.

" 'At last!' said Fix. 'Mr. Fogg will not be informed of the time of the *Carnatic*'s departure; and, if he is, he will have to go without this cursed Frenchman!' "

Phileas Fogg was aware that night that his servant hadn't returned to his hotel room, but "did not disturb himself with the matter." Nor did Passepartout show up the next morning. A palanquin, a man-pulled vehicle, took Fogg and Aouda to the dock. There Fogg learned that the *Carnatic* had sailed the night before. Verne says, "No sign of disappointment appeared on his face, and he merely remarked to Aouda, 'It is an accident, madam; nothing more.' "

At this point, Detective Fix, lurking in the shadows, decided to introduce himself to Fogg. " 'Were you not, like me, sir, a passenger by the *Rangoon*, which arrived yesterday?' " Fogg said he was. Fix continued that he'd hoped to meet Fogg's servant here. " 'Do you know where he is, sir?' " anxiously asked Aouda. " 'What!' " said Fix, feigning ignorance. " 'Is he not with you?' "

As the conversation continued, Fogg commented that the next scheduled boat was to leave in a week. Fix was for a moment overjoyed, at least privately, as the warrant would surely arrive in that time. Then Fogg said, " 'But there are other vessels besides the *Carnatic*. . . .' "

Fogg offered his arm to Aouda, and the two of them strolled the docks looking for another vessel that might take them to Yokohama. This consumed three hours, with Detective Fix following like a lost puppy.

Finally a sailor approached them and asked: " 'Is your honour looking for a boat?' " Fogg allowed that he was. He would pay £100 a day and an additional reward of £200 if his party reached Yokohama in time. Fogg said he must get to Yokohama by November 14, to catch the steamer to San Francisco.

The sailor was, he said, the owner of a small, if fleet, pilot boat. Fogg asked Aouda if she would be frightened to make the passage in such a diminutive vessel. " 'Not with you, Mr. Fogg,' " was her answer. The sailor, however, declined the offer. " 'I could not risk myself, my men, or my little boat of scarcely twenty tons on so long a voyage at this time of year. Besides, we could not reach Yokohama in time, for it is sixteen hundred and sixty miles from Hong Kong.'

" 'Only sixteen hundred,' " said the punctilious Fogg, correcting him. The pilot thought for a moment. " 'But . . . it might be arranged another way. . . . By going to Nagasaki, at the extreme south of Japan, or even to Shanghai, which is only eight hundred miles from here. In going to Shanghai we should not be forced to sail wide of the Chinese coast, which would be a great advantage, as the currents run northward, and would aid us.' "

Fogg didn't understand the logic. " 'Pilot, I must take the American steamer at Yokohama, and not at Shanghai or Nagasaki.' "

Then the captain, John Bunsby, of the *Tankadere*, explained, " 'The San Francisco steamer does not start from Yokohama. It puts in at Yokohama and Nagasaki but it starts from Shanghai.' " The boat, he said, will leave Shanghai on November 11, at seven in the evening. " 'We have, therefore, four days before us, that is ninety-six hours; and in that time, if we had good luck and a south-west wind, and the sea was calm, we could make those eight hundred miles to Shanghai.' "

The bargain was struck. They would leave on the *Tankadere* in an hour. Fogg even invited Fix to accompany them.

However, Aouda worried about the missing Passepartout. She and Fogg went off to the police station and the French consulate. Fogg left money to aid in the search effort. Then they packed their bags and joined Captain Bunsby, his crew of four "hardy mariners," and Fix on the two-masted *Tankadere*. The author describes the *Tankadere* "as a neat little craft of twenty tons, as gracefully built as if she were a racing yacht." Indeed, the boat had won several prizes in pilot-boat races.

The *Tankadere* departed on November 7. The accommodations were "confined but neat." Fogg apologized to Fix for having " 'nothing better to offer you.' " The detective was mortified by having profited from the kindness of his quarry. Detective Fix said to himself, " 'Though rascal as he is, he is a polite one!' "

The voyage between Hong Kong and Shanghai is 800 miles, to the north-northeast. This, however, was not a propitious time of the year to be making the passage. Fogg, for the first time, showed some impatience: " 'I do not need, pilot . . . to advise you to use all possible speed.'

" 'Trust me, your honour,' " said Captain Bunsby. " 'We are carrying all the sail the wind will let us.' "

He assured Fogg they would reach Shanghai in time. To that end, Verne writes in a chapter that shows his knowledge and love of sailing, "the crew set to work in good earnest, inspired by the reward to be gained. There was not a sheet which was not tightened, not a sail which was not vigorously hoisted; not a lurch could be charged to the man at the helm. They worked as desperately as if they were contesting the Royal Yacht regatta."

At dusk on November 8, "The sun had set . . . in a red mist, in the midst of the phosphorescent scintillations of the ocean." As November 8 was giving way to November 9, the *Tankadere* entered the Formosa Strait, which separates the island of Formosa, where Taiwan is, from mainland China. After crossing the Tropic of Cancer there—at 23½ degrees, the summer sun's highest position in the northern sky—the barometer slipped ominously. This was despite the propitious red sky at night, supposedly a "sailor's delight."

Captain Bunsby asked for a private audience with Phileas Fogg. A typhoon was coming, he warned.[1] " 'Is the wind north or south?' " Fogg asked. When told it would be coming from the south, Fogg said, " 'Glad it's a typhoon from the south, for it will carry us forward.' " Captain Bunsby was stunned. " 'Oh, if you take it that way, I've nothing more to say.' "

As the storm hit, on the thirty-eighth day of Fogg's trip, the captain asked his passengers to go below, for their safety. They refused, as it was too stuffy in the small cabin. All sails were struck, save for a storm jib—but a wisp of a sail.

Then Verne grows overwrought in his description of the *Tankadere* fighting the typhoon: "With but its bit of sail, the *Tankadere* was lifted like a feather by a wind an idea of whose violence can scarcely be given. To compare her speed to four times that of a locomotive going on full steam would be below the truth."

The speed of the fastest locomotives in 1872 was 80 mph. Verne has the *Tankadere* going 320 mph. And that is "below the truth."

Verne continues: "The boat scudded thus northward during the whole day, borne on by monstrous waves, preserving always,

[1] Typhoons and hurricanes are different names for the same phenomenon. Large and violent storms with sustained winds of at least 75 mph (120 km/h) are called hurricanes in the Atlantic and the eastern Pacific, i.e., the oceans that surround North and South America. *Hurricane* comes from the West Indian word *huracán*, meaning "big wind." Similar storms in the western Pacific, the area Fogg and his party were currently traversing, are called typhoons, from the Chinese word *taifun*, meaning "great wind." The typhoon and hurricane season is from July to November. The typhoon that struck the *Tankadere* arrived on November 9. The South China Sea, where the pilot's boat was, is famous for typhoons.

fortunately, a speed equal to theirs. Twenty times she seemed almost to be submerged by these mountains of water which rose behind her; but the adroit management of the pilot saved her. The passengers were often bathed in spray, but they submitted to it philosophically. Fix cursed it, no doubt; but Aouda, with her eyes fastened upon her protector, whose coolness amazed her, showed herself worthy of him, and bravely weathered the storm. As for Phileas Fogg, it seemed just as if the typhoon were a part of his programme."

Toward evening the wind hauled around to the northwest and increased in violence. As Shanghai was to the northeast, the boat was practically facing off with the wind. The seas now struck the boat with unabated violence. Each leap forward was followed by a retort—a return blow—from the waves. Captain Bunsby said to Fogg, "'I think, your honour, that we should do well to make for one of the ports on the coast.'"

Fogg said, "'I think so too.'"

To Captain Bunsby's question, which one? Fogg answered, "'I know of but one. . . . Shanghai!'"

# In which
# sound and fury
# signify nothing

---

If, on the thirty-eighth day since leaving London, Fogg and his party were battling a typhoon on the *Tankadere* on November 9, 1872, on our fortieth day since leaving France, March 12, 1993, we crossed the international date line. This set another record. No sailboat had ever sailed halfway around the world, as measured by longitude, in less time. This man-made line at 180 degrees is scribed about 120 nautical miles to the east of New Zealand. An international agreement in 1884 decided that the day *ends* just east of this line and *begins* just west of it. Thus, between ending and beginning, 24 hours separate the time zones on either side of the date line.[1] When cross-

---

[1] As described, there are 12 time zones to the east of the Greenwich Meridian, or Prime Meridian, each representing 15 degrees, which is one hour difference. They are labeled −1 to −12. There are 12 time zones to the west of Greenwich, each representing one hour difference. They are labeled +1 to +12. The +12 zone and the −12 zone meet

ing it, those heading west to east toward the rising sun—as we were—repeat a day. Those heading east to west toward the setting sun lose a day.

While the international date line tends to straddle the 180-degree longitude line, where it passes over certain island groups, such as the Fiji Islands, it makes a jog. Imagine how confusing it would be to have it Sunday in Lauthala in the Fiji Islands and Monday in Vanua Levu, also in the Fiji Islands and only 25 miles away. In the Fiji islands, the date line is shifted to the east some 200 nautical miles to make it the same day throughout the island group.

Whatever the date line demanded, Bruno, I don't believe, would have chosen to repeat this day. He let out a groan as I visited him in his electronic lair in the starboard hull, which was also his "home office," and his and Jacques's home sweet home. (At this point in the journey, half of an 80-day circumnavigation, it might better be described as home *sweat* home for unambiguous reasons.) Bruno's neck and back were "killing him," he said.

Normally, in a small boat the navigator faces forward or back. Thus when the boat pitches—rises and falls to meet the endless waves—the navigator's head bobs forward and back. This is the way heads were designed to bob. The diminutive navigator's station on *Commodore Explorer*, however, was situated so Bruno sat sideways. Therefore his head bobbed from side to side, as the boat pitched. Also, there was so little headroom down below that his head scraped the headliner even when seated. After 40 days of having his head bounce off the headliner, and bob from side to side, Bruno's back and neck were shot. This was exacerbated by the fact that he couldn't put his feet

---

at the international date line, which is directly opposite the Greenwich Meridian. The −12 and +12 designation represents a difference of 24 hours, or one day.

squarely underneath him, as gear was piled under his navigator's station. In essence, Bruno navigated in the fetal position.

Stretching exercises and aspirin took care of the symptoms, in time. While we couldn't correct the athwartships' orientation of the navigator's station, we moved supplies from his and Jacques's starboard hull to our port hull, to give Bruno more room. The first 50 days of food had been stored in the port hull. The last 43 days were stored in their starboard hull. At this point, 40 days into the voyage, our side was practically empty; their side remained full to bursting.

Passing by Antarctica's Ross Sea and Ice Shelf, which was due south of us for a full 800 nautical miles, would span three days, from March 11 to March 14. This is, as described, the world's largest body of floating ice. Here I got my first whiff of land since we had left Kéruzoré at the Cape Verde Islands on February 6, the sixth day. This day, March 14, the wind was from the south, off Antarctica, and it held the rich aroma of dirt. As the sea has a sweet, distinctive smell, so, too, does land—particularly when you've been deprived of it for more than a month. Like a siren song, it spoke to me of home. Later, I figured that it could have been penguin poop that I found so evocative.

Wonder of wonders, the wind off Antarctica, a place that can be characterized as "endless winter," was also warm. It was a pleasant break from the smells of *Commodore Explorer:* onions, garlic, and sweaty, moldering bodies.

As summer was giving way to fall on the calendar in the southern hemisphere, it was winter where we were in the Howling Fifties, and no one seemed enthusiastic about baring all and bathing. As there was no heat in our hull, the best anyone could manage was a hurried swipe with a baby wipe.

As Richard Henry Dana, Jr., wrote in his classic book *Two*

*Years Before the Mast,* which I took with me on the voyage: "Not a razor, nor a brush, nor a drop of water, except the rain and the spray, had come near us all the time. . . . Who would strip and wash himself in salt water on deck, in the snow and ice, with the thermometer at zero?"

Dana was describing a passage in 1836 through these very waters. He was then a young student at Harvard College who had taken a break from his studies and spent two years at sea to regain his health. Rather than sail in a private cabin, which his father, a poet, essayist, and editor of the *North American Review,* could well afford, Dana elected to sail "before the mast," with the ordinary seaman. He twice rounded Cape Horn—or "doubled it," as seamen describe rounding the cape in both directions.[2]

No one could fault Chinois for neglecting his personal hygiene, however, as *Commodore Explorer* streaked toward Cape Horn. From belowdecks, as I cooked a meal, I glanced at him now and again as he thoroughly brushed his teeth. After he'd finished, he used his toothbrush to brush his theatrical mustache. "That's the last time I borrow your toothbrush!" I shouted up to him.

On March 15, the forty-third day, we were 2,000 miles due south of Polynesia. Bruno began joking—at least I believe he was joking—about aborting the voyage and heading north for Polynesia. He said that we should go there,

---

[2] Dana was most taken by San Juan Capistrano in what we now call "southern California." He described it as "the only romantic spot on the coast." He wrote, "The rocks were as large as those of Nahant [between Boston and Marblehead on the North Shore] or Newport, but, to my eye, more grand and broken. Besides, there was a grandeur in everything around, which gave a solemnity to the scene, a silence and solitariness which affected every part! Not a human being but ourselves for miles, and no sound heard but the pulsations of the great Pacific!" Dana Point and Dana Cove, near San Juan Capistrano, were named for him.

turn *Commodore Explorer* into a charter boat, and have some fun.

Now that we were well beyond the south island of New Zealand, Polynesia became the next safe haven in his mind. The ambivalence he apparently felt for the voyage—or perhaps it was the financial ruin that he sensed waited for him back home in France—never wandered far from his mind. Bruno was like the melancholy prince of Denmark:

> To be, or not to be: that is the question:
> Whether 'tis nobler in the mind to suffer
> The slings and arrows of outrageous fortune,
> Or to take arms against a sea of troubles.

Bruno is mý friend, and I sympathized hugely with him as he agonized whether to press on or bail out—"To be, or not to be." If the chemical Band-Aid Jacques and Chinois had fashioned on the starboard hull failed, he was ruined. There might even be loss of life. Similarly, if the mast failed, he was ruined. Again, there might even be loss of life.

However, there were four other crew members aboard *Commodore Explorer* who were risking their lives—perhaps not their financial lives—and had been toiling 12- to 20-hour days for 43 days, at this point, to make this work. We were currently ahead of the record—ahead of Fogg—and more than halfway around the earth. Was quitting the best thing for us? Every time Bruno talked about bailing out, it was like a kick in the gut to me. Or even lower.

Likely, Bruno considered all of this as we hurried past New Zealand and then Polynesia. While he threatened to make those dreaded left-hand turns—there would be another as we passed Rio de Janeiro—he never made one.

We had burned a considerable amount of videotape by this point; some of it, I felt, was quite dramatic. Bruno began to focus his attentions on getting the videotape ashore and then back to France as we passed Cape Horn. He felt confident that once potential sponsors saw the adventure we were living, they'd be more likely to help us. He asked me to wrap the videotape carefully for the transfer.

What worried me, however, was that Bruno seemed to be pinning all his hopes for financial rescue on the videotapes. What would happen, I wondered, if we couldn't make the hand-off? Or worse, what would happen if we could, and no one in France cared about where we were and what we were doing? Maybe Bruno knew how successful Michel Horeau had been in telling our story in France, but I didn't.

Peter Isler and Gary Jobson, ESPN's sailing commentators, were at Cape Horn at the same time, filming a program on this part of the world, aboard Skip Novak's *Pelagic*. I know all of them well, so I began corresponding with them by telex and by fax, about the possibility of their picking up our tapes at Cape Horn. It was in the course of one of these transmissions that I learned that Isler's wife, J.J., was pregnant back home in San Diego. She was about as far along as my Molly was.

This way, I also learned the disquieting news about the bombing of one of the Twin Towers at the World Trade Center in New York. With a wife and baby on the way, that news brought more distress than it otherwise might have during my lone-wolf days.

ESPN's filming was wrapping up, however, and Peter and Gary doubted that they would still be there when we arrived. Skip had another charter. So, Bruno began making other arrangements. First, he hoped his brother Stéphane would be able to pick up the tapes. Stéphane, who had actually windsurfed around Cape Horn, and Bruno had done this for their brother Loïck in the 1989 Vendée Globe Challenge Race. They had chartered a little sailboat, taken it out to Cape Horn, met Loïck, and picked up his video-tapes. That sounds much easier than it was, as Cape Horn is the focus of the worst weather on earth. They broached, nearly capsized, and ripped sails.

Stéphane was unable to do it, so Bruno turned to Eugène Rigduel, a Frenchman who has considerable experience in this part of the world. On Bruno's ticket, Eugène arrived in Puerto Williams, in Chile, where he made arrangements with the Chilean military to send out a helicopter to re-trieve our tapes.

The weather was changing dramatically from one day to the next as we closed on Cape Horn. If on March 13, the winds were warm off Antarctica, the next day, Jacques and Chinois had sleet and hail on a dreary-overcast watch. The water at 55 or 56 degrees south latitude was just slightly above freezing, as was the air. You dressed for skiing in the rain, and still the damp penetrated to your very marrow. As seamen used to say, "There's no difference between summer and winter at the Horn beyond [the amount of] daylight."

I suffered—apparently alone—in the port hull without heat. It fell to me, the American, to try to fix the heater in our cabin, which had been doing a death rattle since we'd arrived in the south. The lack of heat, as I've mentioned, didn't seem to affect Marc and Chinois, or at least not enough to get them to help me in repairing the heater. Bruno and Jacques had more than enough heat in their tropical paradise on the starboard side. Indeed, Bruno would only allow Jacques to cook himself to about me-dium rare before he turned the thing off. From time to time, when I was good, I'd be permitted to go over to Bruno and Jacques's starboard hull for a snooze. I consid-ered this a Miami Beach vacation.

Not only was it freezing in our cabin, in the high forties or low fifties, the low temperatures caused the air to condense, which dripped here, there, and everywhere, but mostly on my bunk. Marc and Chinois, who were on opposite watches, were "hot-bunking" it in the forward bunk, which was relatively dry except for the occasional wave that would find its way down through the hatch. Such was the luck of the draw. I felt like Pigpen in *Peanuts,* who lives with a dust cloud over his head, except my cloud leaked cold water.

I'd sponge water from the bunk as best I could before climbing into it, but those moments of finishing a cold, clammy watch at 5:00 A.M. and climbing into a cold, clammy—indeed, water-soaked—berth had to be the nadir of the voyage. The nadir of my life. Oh, lost, I felt. Most of the time I slept in my one suit of foul-weather gear, but it was moist, too, from rain and spray on the outside and sweat on the inside.

It wasn't just condensation, however, that made life belowdecks on *Commodore Explorer* so unbearable. The boat leaked relentlessly through the laminate aft. First I tried to plug the holes—what seemed to be the remnants of old fittings. When that didn't stem the tide, I drilled holes in the bulkhead to try to redirect the water away from my bunk. It was a little deep-sea plumbing. Later, back in France, when the boat was pulled from the water, we found cracks around the rudder bearings, from when we had hit something. They might have been caused by our collision with an unknown object on February 23. While I didn't know it then, this was letting the water in.

There were also leaks from the Dorade vents, into the forward cabins. When you closed the vents, to stop the leaking, the boat sweated. There were also leaks through the *casquettes*, whose reason for being was to keep water from going down the hatches. There were leaks from the two escape hatches in the hulls, even though we'd sealed the one in our cabin. While the silicon seal was sufficient, I was sure, to keep us from ever getting out to fresh air should the boat go over, water eventually found its way in again. Also, with the cold, water condensed around any screw heads or bolts. Back in France, Molly had covered many, but not all, of these fittings with a neoprenelike material to prevent condensation from forming on them.

The biggest problem, however, was the amount of sea- and rainwater each man brought down, stuck to his foul-weather gear. There was no way to stay dry on deck, as the bow wave often came a-calling with the good fellowship of a fire hose.

As "Minister of the Interior," I cleaned up our half of the boat every day, dumped the trash aft, cooked three squares, and worried about the health and well-being of the crew. With that portfolio, I tried to get the guys to participate in a sponge, or chamois, patrol to wipe the water out of the boat, but couldn't get them to participate with much enthusiasm.

I tried to train these guys to lift the floorboards every day and take out a little bit of water, but could only get them to do it reluctantly.

As I wrote in my log about 10 days before Cape Horn, "Living like a spring Eskimo back aft. The igloo's melting and everything's wet."

I'd been working on the heater since we arrived in the Southern Ocean, off Cape Town. The heater was in a tiny compartment under the back beam. It was connected to a five-gallon diesel tank, which was behind the beam. To fix it, you would crawl back there, and there would be diesel fuel, which leaked, and water, which leaked, sloshing around. You'd start the repair by bailing and then sponging the area, but diesel is a noxious fuel, as anyone who has followed a city bus can tell you. Also, it was dark down there, so you'd wear a headlight like a coal miner. It was cold, too, and there were sharp edges and fittings that would poke you as the boat lurched along. Basically, fixing the heater required an icy trip to Hell.

I'm not an intuitive mechanic: I didn't grow up with motorcycles moldering in the backyard—I had horses rather than motorbikes, a rowboat rather than an outboard. But if something breaks, I'll try to figure it out. What angered me was that Chinois was supposed to be in charge of all this mechanical stuff; however, the lack of heat didn't daunt him. It didn't bother Bruno, either, because his cabin was often too toasty in his estimation.

I got the heater running five or six times. The primary problem was that seawater would come back into it through the exhaust. The exhaust pipe was in a loop that was supposed to prevent the water from reaching the heater, but it didn't work. First, the seawater backed up and fried the wick. I fashioned a new one out of asbestos insulation that I also stuffed around the exhaust to try to keep the water from getting back in. Then I used a little solder for the wires that controlled a thermostat. That worked for several days, but eventually, there would be five more trips back aft to Hell, to try to get the heater running again. The French crew seemed amused by my efforts: the American fighting for the right to burn fossil fuel. "Isn't that why you guys fought Saddam Hussein?" one of them asked me.

Finally, I got angry at Bruno and insisted that he telex the manufacturer of the heater. While we had two of these things, there were no spare parts, save for an extra glow plug, no manual, and certainly no wiring diagram, which I desperately needed. The heater had an electric thermostat that seemed to turn it off long before it made sufficient heat. Like my stillborn telex about burning alternative fuels in my cooking stove, I don't know if Bruno bothered to send this telex to the heater manufacturer.

As we closed on Cape Horn, I asked Marc if he'd mind if

I went to work on the heater, during our watch, when nothing much was going on. We were on port tack, so I told him if he needed me, just pound on the deck with a winch handle. I'm down there in the diesel fuel and seawater, which is burning my skin and turning my stomach. I'm swearing so loudly that Marc can hear me. I can hear him laughing at me too. Finally, I think I've fixed the thing. As I try to light it, there's a puff of black, oily smoke. I'm afraid the thing's on fire, and will burn down the boat thousands of miles from any help. So I grab the heater, which is unbolted, and scramble over the sleeping Chinois and bolt out of the hatch, followed quickly by Chinois, who is coughing and gagging and believes that the boat is on fire.

Marc sees my face covered in soot, with the heater in my hand, and starts to laugh. "Well, I think I've finally screwed the pooch," I say. Indeed, I had. The heater never worked again. I consoled myself by recalling the deprivations that Scott, Shackleton, Amundsen, and Byrd had suffered.

In some important ways sailors are blind, since they can't see the wind. So to make up for the fact that sailors are "blind," they must use their other senses better. Sometimes their other senses can fool them, however.

As noted, the 86-foot *Commodore Explorer* weighed 21,280 pounds or 9.5 displacement or long tons. For every boat length it traveled, it had to push 21,280 pounds of water out of the way. At 14 knots—sufficient speed to sail around the world in under 80 days—it traveled one boat length, or 86 feet, in under four seconds. At 20 knots it traveled those 86 feet in under three seconds. The point of this is that pushing all of that water out of the way made for a tremendous racket when belowdecks.

The sound was unlike anything I'd ever heard. I tried to describe it in a telex home: "Get a cassette recorder. Rent a soft-top Corvette, preferably one with a loud exhaust system. Go into a car wash. Then rip Velcro open and shut rapidly as you gun the engine at the same time as the brushes try to erase the paint. Go home and play the tape back at maximum volume and let me know if it's noisy or not."

Monohulls, which travel half as fast, or even less, don't make near the noise of a multihull, even though they push more water out of the way.

Imagine trying to sleep in a car wash, and you'll have an idea how difficult life was on *Commodore Explorer*. Only 20-hour workdays, seven days a week, made sleep possible if not plentiful. Sometimes I'd wear foam earplugs, and sometimes I'd try to block out the noise belowdecks with music. One day, I played a CD of Vivaldi's "Four Seasons" for four hours on the speakers in our port hull. His "Winter" movement, I thought, seemed particularly appropriate to my mood. Four hours of Vivaldi proved to be a lifetime for Chinois. "NO—MORE—VIVALDI!" he told me.

In time, you could tell how fast we were going by the noise belowdecks. It got so you didn't need to look at the knot meter—we had a repeater in our hull that would give boat speed. It was similar when you were on deck: you could tell a great deal about the boat and the conditions by the noise it made.

There was no engine on *Commodore Explorer*; however, we had a diesel-fuel-burning generator to charge the batteries for electric power. (There was also a small gas-powered backup generator.) We didn't need to run this noisy-smelly generator very often, as two propellerlike devices, which spun in the wind, provided almost all the charge that the batteries required.

The propellers were situated off each hull behind the back beam. They were fairly quiet until the wind came forward and blew above 30 or 35 knots. Then, the noise was positively deafening. Almost everyone has heard a bathroom fan that has gone slightly awry. Multiply that by a thousand.

When that occurred, when the noise got overwhelming, someone would have to go back there and lasso the blades. After they were hog-tied, things would quiet down.

The propellers were mounted dangerously low on two too-short sections made from Windsurfer masts. Because of their low height, you almost never went aft, where the blades were, unless you absolutely had to, and never at night. That, however, was the toilet of choice. The heavy-weather alternative was a bucket, which no one relished.

When *Commodore Explorer* was back at the Multiplast boatyard soon after the voyage ended, a tempest hit. One of the blades broke off and penetrated the carbon-fiber hull. If Chinois, who is about five feet seven, had been struck by the blade spinning in 35 knots of wind, it might have cut off his head. If I had been struck, it might have cut off my head at the waist. A couple of times Jacques had gone back there when he was really tired—almost walking in his sleep—and I'd yelled at him to be careful.

Before we left France, I'd painted the blades with a fluo-rescent-orange paint to make them more apparent. When the blades started whining in protest, they also give off a harmonic, which was even less palatable. Sometimes I wondered if my high-visibility paint job had thrown the blades out of kilter.

As we neared Cape Horn, Marc, my watchmate, who was driving, sensed the boat was overpowered. It was night, and the wind was ripping along—well above 35 knots—yet we had the big reaching headsail up and a full main. The reacher is 2,005 square feet (185 sq m), the un-reefed main is 3,240 square feet (221 sq m). This repre-sented a veritable cloud of sail. Marc formulated this plan to shorten sail, so as to slow the boat down: "Put the staysail up; take the reacher down; put the Solent up [a Number 3, 100-percent headsail]; take the staysail down, put a reef in the main, bag the sails, and pull them to the high side. Then everything should be fine," he said.

*Commodore Explorer* used no roller-reefing devices. Marc, who was in charge of the sails, believes sails with hanks are far more dependable. Also, roller-reefing devices create more windage and require more weight aloft. Nevertheless, what we had was unquestionably a whole lot more work. To change a hanked headsail, for example, you had to drag the replacement sail in its bag forward, if it wasn't already there. The sail, made of space-age Spectra, weighed more than a quarter ton with its bag full of water, which it invariably was. Dragging it across the heaving "waterbed" —the trampoline—as geysers burst forth here and there and the bow wave took aim at you was tough and dangerous work. Also you never went forward without your harness and without being tethered to a safety line. A slip off this boat, and you were likely but a memory. However, like a dog tethered to a clothesline, this limited your range of motion.

Then while you were at the bow, the bottom hank or two on the current, or "old," headsail, as sailors say, had to be unclipped and the "new" sail hanked onto the bottom of the headstay and its sheets run aft on both sides—that's a long stroll aft. The old sail was lowered and unclipped, and then the new sail was hoisted by the halyard. Next, the old sail had to be folded and rebagged and hauled to the high side. Bagging a wet sail is like getting a size-16 body into a size-6 dress. That represents an easy half hour of time and a difficult half hour of work.

Compare that to roller-reefing, such as was used on the recently departed *ENZA*. Roller-reefing is akin to a horizontal window shade. To make a headsail smaller or to strike it entirely, it is merely rolled up. That can usually be done from the safety of the cockpit and usually without waking up the off-watch. To make it larger, it is unrolled. This is five minutes of work at the most.

The maneuver Marc suggested would require all hands on deck. So before waking Jacques and Chinois, who desperately needed their rest, I went to the starboard hull to wake Bruno and to tell him what Marc proposed: "Put the staysail up; take the reacher down; put the Solent up; take the staysail down; put a reef in the main; bag the sails; and bring them to the high side." Bruno said with a yawn, "What does he think this is, the America's Cup?" Marc sailed in the 1986–87 America's Cup trials aboard *French Kiss*.

Bruno stuck his head out of the hatch and listened and looked for a moment to get a sense of the boat. "Lasso the wind vanes," he ordered. I did that—carefully. Immediately, peace returned to the "land." We never touched a sail; didn't need to. It was all "sound and fury, signifying nothing." Jacques and Chinois slept on.

# In which Fogg, Passepartout, and now Fix begin pulling on the same oar

---

The typhoon that Fogg, Aouda, and Fix found themselves in during the passage from Hong Kong to Shanghai blew itself out the next morning, on November 10, 1872. "The tempest had been as brief as terrific," writes Verne. By dawn the next day, November 11, the *Tankadere* was 100 miles from Shanghai. Fogg had to be there that evening by seven to catch the steamer for Yokohama. However, when that time came, they were still three miles from Shanghai. Then, the American boat, the *General Grant*, appeared. " 'Confound her!' " said Captain Bunsby, of the *Tankadere*. His reward of £200 seemed lost by only a few short miles or minutes.

" 'Signal her!' " Fogg ordered. The flag was run up to half-mast —a signal of distress. Then the cannon aboard the *Tankadere* was fired. Verne leaves Fogg, Aouda, and Fix here for a bit of dramatic tension.

Next, we find ourselves on the *Carnatic*, the steamer, bound for Yokohama, Japan, that Fogg and Aouda and presumably Passepartout, left drugged in Hong Kong, had missed. However, we learn that on the second day at sea, November 8, a cabin door had opened and out had come a passenger "with a half-stupefied eye, staggering gait, and disordered hair." It was the missing Frenchman, much the worse for wear.

Apparently, after Fix left the opium den, Passepartout was carried by two waiters to a bed reserved for smokers. Even in his richly colored dreams one thought held firm: "The *Carnatic!* the *Carnatic!*" He woke up within three hours and staggered down to the dock, from which the steamer was about to depart. He crossed the plank to the *Carnatic* and then fell unconscious on the deck. Having a ticket, indeed three, he was deposited unceremoniously in a cabin. After he awoke, Passepartout learned from a purser that he was on the *Carnatic*, heading for Yokohama, and that there was no Phileas Fogg or Aouda aboard the boat.

Passepartout realized that he had never told his master about the early departure of the *Carnatic*, so it was his fault that they had missed the boat, and Fogg, presumably, had lost the bet. He had likely been arrested, too, by Detective Fix. "Ah, if Fix ever came within his reach," Passepartout thought, "what a settling of accounts there would be." The mere idea caused him to pull at his hair. The Frenchman had other problems, however: while he had a ticket for the *Carnatic*, which entitled him to all meals, he had "not so much as a penny." What would he do when he reached Japan?

The *Carnatic* arrived in Yokohama, the port for Tokyo, at dawn on November 13, 1872. On the western edge of Tokyo Bay, the port had first been opened to foreigners in 1859, thirteen years before Passepartout's arrival. It would be closed again to foreign trade in 1899.

While Passepartout ate a hearty breakfast, before departing the *Carnatic*, he didn't eat anything else the entire first day. He fed his eyes on the people and the customs. He noticed that "the military profession is as much respected in Japan as it is despised in China." He also noticed the women, "whom he thought not especially handsome—who took little steps with their little feet . . . and who displayed tight-looking eyes, flat chests, teeth fashionably blackened, and gowns crossed with silken scarves."

Passepartout was famished the next morning. He considered selling his beloved watch, but concluded he'd rather starve first. Then he decided that he might "sing for his supper." However, he realized he was too well dressed to be a busker, so he went to trade his garments "for clothes more in harmony with the project."

Passepartout traded his European clothes, which were very much in demand, for an old Japanese coat, and "a sort of one-sided turban, faded with long use." He also received in change a few pieces of silver to stuff in his pocket. The silver he immediately traded for a small meal at a teahouse of modest appearance.

Before making his singing debut, however, he decided to visit the docks. He was truly eager to leave this country. There he spied a placard for an "acrobatic Japanese troupe." Their big attraction, the placard proclaimed in English, was "long noses!" The troupe, the placard said, was soon to depart for the United States. " 'The United States!' " exclaimed Passepartout. " 'That's just what I want.' " It was as if he couldn't stop his round-the-world momentum.

Passepartout followed a man dressed as a clown to the Japanese quarter, where he introduced himself to the "Honourable William Batulcar," the proprietor of the circus and an American. Passepartout offered himself as his servant, but Batulcar had no need for one, as he already had two. Then Batulcar had an idea. " 'You are a Frenchman, aren't you?' " Passepartout, while dressed in mostly Japanese garb, admits he is. " 'Then you ought to know how to make grimaces?' " the American asked. Passepartout was puzzled by this question. " 'Why, we Frenchmen know how to make grimaces, it is true—but not any better than the Americans do.' " Batulcar admitted the truth in that statement, but said he was interested in signing Passepartout on as a clown.

He noticed that Passepartout was strong, and asked if he could sing. Passepartout said he could. Then Batulcar asked if Passepartout could "'sing standing on your head, with a top spinning on your left foot, and a sabre balanced on your right?'"

Passepartout replied, "'Humph! I think so,' recalling the exercises of his younger days." He was hired by Batulcar; his first performance was to be that very afternoon.

Passepartout participated in the performance of the Long Noses, a show, Verne instructs us, "to which Europe is as yet a stranger." It likely still is.

Here, the cast was attired in fashion from the Middle Ages. On their shoulders, however, were wings, but "what especially distinguished them was the long noses, which were fastened to their faces, and the uses which they made of them. The noses were made of bamboo, and were five, six, and even ten feet long, some straight, others curved, some ribboned, and some having imitation warts upon them. It was upon these appendages, fixed tightly on their real noses, that they performed their gymnastic exercises."

Finally, the last scene, a human pyramid, was announced with fanfare. Passepartout was one of several clowns designated to form the base of the pyramid; however, rather than standing on shoulders, each succeeding layer of humanity would stand on noses. Some fifty people were involved. Eventually the human pyramid reached "to the very cornices of the theater."

It was all very impressive; however, suddenly one of the "lower noses" vanished from the pyramid, which collapsed like a house of cards. There were bodies and noses sprawled every which way. It was amazing that no one was impaled on a proboscis. It was Passepartout who had broken ranks, when he saw his master in the crowd. "'Ah, my master! my master!'" he cried.

Here Verne describes how Fogg and Aouda happened to be part of the audience. The pair, as well as Detective Fix, had been successful in flagging down the Yokohama steamer, the *General Grant*. Fogg had rewarded Captain Bunsby the price stipulated, £200, plus an additional £550. Arriving in Yokohama, Fogg had searched in vain for Passepartout at the French and English embassies. Fogg and Aouda had come to the theater, Verne tells us, out of "chance, or perhaps a kind of presentiment."

Aouda informed Passepartout that a Mr. Fix had accompanied them. Verne writes that "Passepartout did not change countenance on hearing this name. He thought that the time had not yet arrived to divulge to his master what had taken place between the detective and himself; and in the account he gave of his absence, he simply excused himself for having been overtaken by drunkenness, in smoking opium at a tavern in Hong Kong."

Fogg listened coldly to the narrative of his servant. However, he gave him money for "clothing more in harmony with his position." That evening, the party boarded the *General Grant,* a large paddle-wheel steamer, of two thousand five hundred tons. Verne, ever a fan of technology, can't resist describing how she worked: "The massive walking-beam rose and fell above the deck; at one end a piston-rod worked up and down; and at the other was a connecting-rod which, in changing the rectilinear motion to a circular one, was directly connected with the shafts of the paddles."

Also, we learn the *General Grant* had three masts for sails, giving a substantial assist to the steam engine. The boat should "average twelve miles an hour," and cross the Pacific in 21 days. Fogg then noted in his logbook, he should reach San Francisco by December 2, New York by the 11th, and London on December 20— several hours ahead of schedule for an eighty-day circling of the world.

Verne writes: "On the ninth day after leaving Yokohama, Phileas Fogg had traversed exactly one half of the terrestrial globe. The *General Grant* passed, on the 23rd of November, the one hundred and eightieth meridian, and was at the very antipodes of London. Mr. Fogg had, it is true, exhausted fifty-two of the eighty days in which he was to complete the tour and there were only twenty-eight left. But, though he was only half-way by the difference of meridians, he had really gone over two-thirds of the whole journey; for he had been obliged to make long circuits from London to Aden, from Aden to Bombay, from Calcutta to Singapore, and from Singapore to Yokohama. Could he have followed without deviation the fiftieth parallel, which is that of London, the whole distance would only have been about twelve thousand miles; whereas he would be forced, by the irregular methods of locomotion, to traverse twenty-six thousand, of which he had, on the twenty-third of November, accomplished seventeen thousand five hundred. . . ."

Verne is wrong here, because the earth is 16,062 statute miles or 13,967 nautical miles around at the fiftieth parallel, and Fogg's voyage would be closer to 24,000 statute miles (21,000 nautical miles) than 26,000 as Verne describes it.[1]

In our circumnavigation of 27,000 nautical miles, we passed the one hundred and eightieth meridian, or international date line, on the fortieth day, as described in the previous chapter. Nevertheless, while Fogg's passage was by now practically a straight line of about 7,940 nautical miles (as I figure it) or 9,130 statute miles, using the dependable steamships, and American railroads, which were second to none, our passage from the international date line was 10,500 nautical miles. Not only was our distance about 2,560 nautical miles farther, but from the date line onward, we could expect the worst conditions. Indeed, Cape Horn could be expected to extract a toll. Once in the Atlantic, we could expect headwinds, and no winds in the doldrums. Nevertheless, we had a three-day lead on Fogg at this point. Was it enough? I wondered.

Verne addresses Passepartout's family watch in this chapter too: "It happened also on the twenty-third of November, that Passepartout made a joyful discovery. It will be remembered that the obstinate fellow had insisted on keeping his famous family watch at London time, and on regarding that of the countries he had passed through as quite false and unreliable. Now, on this

[1] See Appendix.

day, though he had not changed the hands, he found that his watch exactly agreed with the ship's chronometers. . . .

"Passepartout was ignorant that, if the face of his watch had been divided into twenty-four hours . . . he would have no reason for exultation; for the hands of his watch would then, instead of as now indicating nine o'clock in the morning, indicate nine o'clock in the evening, that is the twenty-first hour after midnight —precisely the difference between London time and that of the one hundred and eightieth meridian."

Unbeknownst to Passepartout, Detective Fix was on the *General Grant* too. Finally, he had his arrest warrant, but it was useless, as the alleged felon Phileas Fogg was no longer on British soil— indeed any soil at all. Fix decided to follow him, until he returned to England, which Fogg seemed bent on doing. Fix worried, however, that there would be little money left for his reward, as Fogg had already spent, by his calculation, more than £5,000.

Fix hoped to avoid meeting Passepartout on the *General Grant*. However, when the Frenchman saw him he gave him "a perfect volley of blows, which proved the great superiority of French over English pugilistic skill," wrote Verne chauvinistically.

When Passepartout was finished, Fix told him that while in the past he had done everything in his power to delay Fogg, now that he seemed intent on reaching England he would do everything in his power to facilitate the voyage. " 'Are we friends?' asked the detective.

" 'Friends? No . . . but allies perhaps. At the least sign of treason, however, I'll twist your neck for you,' " warned Passepartout.

It seemed as if Fogg, Passepartout, and now Fix were pulling on the same oar. However, while their common destination was the British Isles, Fogg and Passepartout's hope was that the journey would end at the Reform Club, Fix's at the reformatory.

# In which a private hurricane meets us at Cape Horn

---

Cape Horn, the gatekeeper for around-the-world sailors, is located in the Drake Passage on Horn Island—the southern tip of South America—at 55 degrees 57 minutes south latitude. It is part of Tierra del Fuego and belongs to Chile. (Argentina also has part of Tierra del Fuego.) Cape Horn was named by Willem Schouten, a Dutch navigator, who in 1616 was the first European to sail around it. Schouten was born in Hoorn, in the Netherlands.

If Schouten was the first European to round it, Sir Francis Drake, of England, was likely the first to see it in 1578 in his around-the-world voyage. Drake, who made the world's second circumnavigation, opted for the Strait of Magellan, discovered in 1520 by Ferdinand Magellan, of Portugal, whose expedition made the world's first circumnavigation. After passing through the Strait of Magellan,

Drake was blown south, where he may have seen Cape Horn.

Cape Horn's distance from the equator, 3,360 nautical miles, and proximity to the Antarctic Circle, 630 nautical miles, is one reason why the weather here is so contrary.[1] There are other reasons.

Put your finger over the end of a hose, and the water explodes out of the smaller opening. Between Cape Horn, at the bottom of South America, and the Antarctica Peninsula is the Drake Passage, a distance of only 420 nautical miles. Through this narrow opening the wind and the weather roar out, like water from a constricted hose.

Besides the squeezing of the weather systems between Cape Horn and the Antarctic Peninsula, the Andes Mountains, which form the backbone of South America, start at Cape Horn. Here, they show a mean height of 6,600 feet (2000 m). The wind comes rip-roaring down those 6,600 foot peaks to sea level like an avalanche.

My friend Peter Stalkus, the captain of a ship that supplies the United States and New Zealand bases in Antarctica, whom I consulted with before I left, told me unambiguously: be out of there by Valentine's Day. It was now more than a month later. Stalkus was down there when we were, and I tried to telex his ship, the *Green Wave*, for ice information as well as to receive friendly words from home, but without success.

In autumn, between Antarctica and Cape Horn, a new low-pressure system comes roaring forth, west to east, about every 36 hours. Unstable low-pressure systems make for foul weather no matter where in the world you are. In the southern hemisphere, the winds around the lows move *clockwise*. This is the complete opposite of winds around lows in the northern hemisphere, which move *counterclock-*

---

[1] The Antarctic Circle is at 66 degrees 30 minutes south latitude.

*wise*. Indeed, everything, even the direction the toilet flushes is reversed between the northern hemisphere and the southern.

Therefore, in the southern hemisphere you want to be on the north side of the center of the low when heading to the east, toward the rising sun. With the clockwise flow around the low, the wind is likely to stay behind you if you are north of the center. Keeping the wind behind you is particularly important on a delicate multihull. In fact, up to this time, save for when the escape hatch blew, we hadn't tacked *Commodore Explorer*. On the south side of the low, it is likely to be on your nose, when heading east.

At the same time that you want to stay on the north side of the lows, you need to head south. Cape Horn lies at 55 degrees 57 minutes south latitude. Recall that the farther south you go, the distance around the world is shorter, as the circle you're traversing is smaller. So, in essence, you want to sail south to shorten the distance but stay north of the lows. It was a twisty road, which Bruno navigated magnificently. He spent 15 hours a day poring over weather faxes that bounced off satellites and found their way to *Commodore Explorer*.

Between March 15 and March 25, the most difficult period of the voyage, Bruno took us north and south to keep the wind behind us but almost always toward the goal: Cape Horn.

Always, too, he looked behind him, watching the weather that would likely spell the difference between success and failure on the voyage. For Bruno, it must have been like watching an eighteen-wheeler drive too fast and too close behind you in the family car on the interstate. Make a mistake, and you might end up a hood ornament on a Diamond Rio. Make a mistake in this part of the world, and you might end up a ghost of Cape Horn. There are thousands of them. This is the primary graveyard—the killing field—of the Pacific.

We had some huge days, like March 17–18, when we did 420 miles, when the wind was behind us and manageable, but we had some minuscule days, such as March 18–19, when we notched only 130 miles, with the wind forward of the beam and the seas absolutely ferocious. It wasn't that we couldn't sail fast, we just couldn't do so without destroying the boat. These two days, following one another, showed how variable the weather was down here.

The catamaran laboring in these seas caused me to speculate on the nature of "cats." There are many types of "cats," I wrote in a telex home: "Lions, fat cats, cool cats, Cat Stevens, Siamese, cheetahs, Pumas, Felix, Tony the Tiger, Toms, Pink Panthers, Persians, and Black Cats. Well what we've got here is a damn pound cat. Tough-rough hissin' and screechin' like an alley cat."

With the "pound cat" this bad with the wind forward of the beam, what would she be like, I wondered, with the wind on the nose? We could expect headwinds on the push to the finish up the Atlantic. The likelihood of headwinds was why it seemed so important that we be comfortably ahead of Fogg when we stuck our nose into the Atlantic. The Atlantic, our first and last ocean, begins at Cape Horn.

If we only notched 130 miles in the 24-hour period of March 18–19, it was little better the next two days. We did 170 nautical miles on March 19–20, and 240 miles on March 20–21.[2] That was 540 miles in three days, when we needed to average 1,008 miles in that period. Our three-day lead on Fogg carried to this point was now a one-day lead. And

[2] March 20 was the first day of spring in the northern hemisphere, where we were heading, fall in the southern hemisphere, where we were.

Cape Horn—likely the most unfriendly spot on earth—was not even near. It was, on March 21, still 1,560 miles away.

March 22 was the day I had chosen in the pool for our passage of Cape Horn. We were still at least four days away. No free lunch for you, pal, I thought as I prepared a freeze-dried fare for my shipmates. Or for Chinois, who had opted for March 23.

With the three-day cycle of stormy low-pressure systems, Bruno's fear was that we'd be rounding Cape Horn in the company of one of them. As we approached the Horn, however, the forecast was benign: light winds from the southwest, at 8 to 12 knots. It seemed as if we were sailing into an anticyclone (a gentle high-pressure system) and an anticlimax. Forecasts lie, as I've said.

At 2:00 A.M. on March 24, Marc and I relieved Jacques and Chinois. *Commodore Explorer* sailed under a full main with the Solent up. The boat was doing 20 knots with occasional sprints to 25. At this point, the boat was under control—if just barely. The wind was from the west and behind us.

Marc and I decided it was time to take the Solent down, and put the smaller staysail up. Also, it was time to take a reef in the main. This was done, but the boat was still doing 20 knots now with sprints as high as 28. Obviously, the wind was increasing as we decreased sail area. If we didn't stay ahead of it, we might crash. So we put a second reef in the main, but, again, there was no change in the boat's speed. Then a third reef was taken, and the staysail was struck. Yet there was no change. It was as if we had sailed off the edge of the earth and were falling through space. In free fall, there was nothing we could do to arrest our speed. It reminded me of the seventeenth day—the day when Bruno had planted the hulls and nearly pitchpoled the boat.

At this point, our course was such that we were clearing

Cape Horn, if just barely. If the wind stayed in the same place or went clockwise, to the northwest, we'd be fine. If it went counterclockwise, to the southwest or south, we'd be fighting off a lee shore—and this is likely the worst lee shore on earth. Sailing is a game of angles, and, at this point, a meager 5-degree wind shift might spell the difference between success and failure—even, life and death. This day the game was beginning to seem like Russian roulette.

Bruno was on the radio trying desperately to reach Chilean officials, to find out from where this low was coming and whether it was passing to the north or south of us. A phantom low, it wasn't on any of the weather maps. However, Bruno doesn't speak much Spanish, and the Chileans didn't speak any French. The conversation might have been funny, if the subject weren't so serious. With Bruno working on his computers and radio in his electronic lair, Marc and I again joked that he was writing his last will and testament. This was gallows humor, believe me.

As if to distract ourselves, Marc and I chatted in a full-blown shout—which you had to do to be heard over the cacophony on deck, caused by the wind shrieking in the rigging and the chaos of the seas. Without a doubt, we were in the "Howling Fifties." Marc described the waves as "huge and not happy." Again, there are no atheists in foxholes or, likely, on small boats sailing around the world. I believe the sea has many moods, too, and so Marc's words made me chuckle. These were "not happy seas." At least they made Marc and me unhappy.

Behind us the wind was blowing the tops off the waves; at times there was so much water being blown into the boat that it was like trying to breathe in a steambath. As in a steambath, you couldn't see much, either, mainly eerie outlines. The seas were stirred to an angry froth with whitecaps everywhere. The waves were now 40 feet, and they seemed to be reaching out for us like the grim reaper. Seaweed was blowing from the waves and into the cockpit, like slimy projectiles.

When I was driving, the wind ripped at my foul-weather gear and pasted it to my back. While there was a small seat behind the wheel, it was too small for me and too uncomfortable to use. Thus, the boat had to be steered standing up. Normally, this wasn't a problem; however, this early morning in March the wind seemed intent on bending me over the wheel. I used my arms to push my body away from the wheel. At the same time, I had to use my arms and hands to steer. It gave my steering a jerky, unsteady motion that was never more inappropriate than at that moment.

There is almost no land anywhere on earth in this latitude band and, save for the Macquarie Ridge and the Campbell Plateau, south of New Zealand, very few shoals. With neither land nor much shallow water, the waves proceed around the earth with little or nothing to stand in their way, or to knock them down to size. They are often huge, arrogant, and "not happy," as Marc might say. The Roaring Forties and Howling Fifties are places of perpetual motion. High energy.

To add to our troubles, another shoal, the continental shelf, arises near Cape Horn. The sea floor rises from 2,500 feet to 100 feet. Here, the seas lose some of their horizontal punch. Then they grow confused and rise up. As we crossed the continental shelf, the seas changed from 40 to 60 footers and showed no pattern that you could discern.

Still the wind continued to build. It was blowing 55 knots at this point. As the wind increased, the barometer, which measures air pressure, fell precipitously. What became clear at this point was that a low-pressure system had spun off from somewhere, likely Antarctica, and it was headed for us on *Commodore Explorer*.

At 5:00 A.M., Jacques and Chinois relieved us. I went below to try to sleep, but could only manage a fitful hour of it. The noise belowdecks was otherworldly.

Unable to sleep, I dressed and went on deck, and *Commodore Explorer* was bare of sails. Even then, her 102-foot wing mast, which towered 110 feet above the water, presented a sizable 238 square feet (22 sq. m.) of what amounted to sail area. Only if the mast should fall or should the sailboat turn on its side or upside down could that area be hidden from the wind. Not appropriate solutions. While I couldn't "compare her speed to four times that of a locomotive going on full steam," as Verne breathlessly described the *Tankadere* in her typhoon, we were now doing 25 knots without sails. This is unquestionably something of a sailing sound barrier.

In sailing, the wind is both your friend and foe. Some days you love it; some days you want more of it—particularly when the clock is ticking, the winds are light, and you're going nowhere fast—and some days, like this one, you want none of it. On a day such as this the wind is unambiguously your enemy—a child that's gone bad. It seemed bent upon murder and mayhem, and who got caught up in it, it didn't care.

No one could take long tricks at the wheel. Marc, my watchmate, was soon driving again. Then Bruno called for a "taxi" and hustled across the trampoline. Asked, "How's it going?" Marc—Mr. Transatlantic Record Holder—said, "I'm getting the hang of it." Despite Marc's "machismo," it was obvious that one mistake, one wave that wasn't traversed just right, and he'd lose it. Then where we'd go, no one knew.

You can pray at the altar for salvation, "make wild vomits into the black night," as Richard Henry Dana, Jr., described his very first night at sea, or get back to work. I chose the latter. I went back to the port hull to cook breakfast. This day we'd need all the fuel we could get. I started making pancakes—stacks and stacks of them. Besides, by being belowdecks, I didn't have to look at the chaos of weather, which made it slightly more palatable. At this point, however, Bruno stuck his head down in my galley and said, "Hey, Lewie, what do you think about parking this beast?"

In a monohull this is accomplished by turning the boat head to wind. This is an orientation a monohull will maintain like a weathervane. At the same time, a storm jib might be backed, or trimmed, to the upwind side. This makes the boat want to turn downwind. A storm trysail (a small loose-footed mainsail designed to be used when the conditions are appalling) is often flown to give the boat some forward drive. Lastly, the wheel is lashed to windward, turning the boat back into the wind.

The idea is that somewhere in this dynamic tension the boat will sail at from 40 to 60 degrees to the wind at a speed of a couple of knots. At the same time it will slide sideways at about the same speed. The boat doesn't have to be constantly steered and should ride relatively easily—or at least that's the theory. Some monohulls do this better than others, and some monohulls won't do this at all.

No one, as far as we knew, had ever tried this in a multihull of this size. Marc and Chinois had been across the Atlantic on this boat several times, including both times she set the transatlantic record. And Bruno is considered the "best big-cat sailor on the planet—period," according to *Seahorse* magazine. Jacques has sailed tens of thousands of miles with Bruno. My guess is that these guys had sailed close to half a million miles in these oversized, overstimulated multihulls. Compared to theirs, my multihull accomplishments were meager. So I went along for the ride. Besides, when in France do what the French do.

Bruno's plan was to get the sails off the front of the boat.

If we could move the weight aft and to windward, the bows would be less likely to bury, as they had on the seventeenth day. So in 60 and 65 knots of wind, we crawled forward. Most of the time, there was too much wind and horizontally blowing water to stand. Then we took the two soaking-wet headsails, one at a time, off the bow and dragged them over the main beam. While in ordinary times, the main beam seemed little more than a speed bump, this day it seemed like a foothill in the Andes. It took four men to move one sail. Each sail was then tied to the back beam, on the weather side, behind the helmsman.

Another sail was tied to the back beam on the leeward side, so I was dispatched across the trampoline to the low side to retrieve it, to get its weight to the high side. I was belayed like a mountain climber on a dangerous traverse. Once there, we had to winch the sail to the high side, so great was the weight, wind, and incline.

Next Bruno wanted to pull both dagger boards out of the water with halyards. Without dagger boards, he reasoned, the catamaran would slide sideways—dissipating much of the violence of the wind and seas. His plan was to use the headsail halyards to pull up the dagger boards, so they were completely out of the water. Who should do this was decided in a most democratic fashion: Bruno went, "Eenie, meenie, minie, moe, you're the American, you go." (I'd heard those words before in February when a "volunteer" was needed to tie off the reef. A rogue wave caught me in the act. It was this wave that cracked the starboard hull.)

So from the port side, the windward side, I crawled forward again, this time to the martingale on the bow. Here a halyard was shackled. It was slow going, because I had to move three feet, unclip my safety harness, clip it to another staunch fitting, move three feet, and go through the process again. For me, it was like pushing a boulder uphill. At the same time, I was being belayed from the cockpit in case my safety harness broke—they have been known to do that.

This was a 2:1 halyard, to make it easier for the short-handed crew to raise sails. As a result, the halyard was, in essence, two pieces of line—rather than the usual one—and at the bottom was an oversized Harken block. It was now blowing a steady 65 knots, and I was concerned that the windage from this doubled halyard would blow me off my feet—even off the boat. The potential to turn into a human kite was considerable. So first I tied a safety rope around the halyard so I could let go if I started to levitate without losing the halyard.

By this time, it was raining, too, and the spray from the bow wave was finding me on the bow. It was like working underwater, and I couldn't see which side of the headstay the halyard was on. I even had to hold my breath from time to time, as there was no air near me to breathe. Carefully and very slowly I took the halyard to the leeward side and started working my way aft. Even without a stitch of sail, the boat was pitched steeply—just from the wing mast in the wind—and a river on the low side was moving at a speed of 25 knots: the speed of the boat. It even had rapids. The white-water river seemed determined to wash me from *Commodore Explorer*. If I fell from the boat, clearly I was dead, because with no sails up and no engine, there was no way this boat could turn back to find me. Aside from that, the water was little above freezing. In water this cold, you might live an hour or two before hypothermia claimed you. Recall our man-overboard modules (MOM) were lost half a world away.

Finally, I secured the line to the top of the dagger board. With the halyard, we hoisted the leeward dagger board out of the water. It was then I noticed that the halyard was twisted around the headstay, but to me that seemed a small matter at this point. With a second halyard, the windward dagger board was more easily raised. I returned to the cockpit and secured my safety line, which would keep me tethered to the boat, near to Marc and Bruno's safety line.

The moment of truth had arrived. Marc said to Bruno, "Tell me when you want me to turn the boat." At that point, I removed my knife from the pocket of my foul-weather gear and opened the blade. Marc looked forward —never back; it would be Bruno's call. Bruno looked aft, studying the waves. Like a spectator at a tennis match I was looking both ways but kept my mouth firmly shut. Finally Bruno said, *"Maintenant!"* and Marc turned the helm of the 86-foot-long, 45-foot-wide catamaran hard to port and into the wind and waves. Catamarans don't have the same affinity for turning into the wind and stopping as do monohulls. They tend to go backward almost as fast as they go forward. *Commodore Explorer* had gone that way at a frightening clip of speed when we tried to turn into the wind to drop Kéruzoré off at the Cape Verde Islands. If this boat started backward, I thought, the rudders on the back of each hull would break in an instant. Also, what would happen when we faced off with what by now had become our demons, the wind and waves—would they turn us over? I worried.

"She's holding!" I said with an explosion of breath. "She's holding!" Then Marc and Bruno, working together, turned the helm hard to port and then lashed the wheel to hold us closer into the wind. We all started breathing again. I closed my knife and put it back in my pocket. Only then did I notice that Marc and Bruno were doing the same thing. Each of us had been afraid the catamaran would go over, as we turned into the wind and waves, and we'd be trapped by our safety lines under the trampoline and under the water. With our knives we could cut the safety lines and, perhaps, not drown.

One man stayed on the windward side under the *casquette* to keep a lookout. The rest of us retired to our respective cabins. We donned our survival suits, which provide flotation as well as protection from the elements. This made us look inflated to 25 psi like the Pillsbury Doughboy or the Michelin Man. Then we waited.

In our port cabin, we prepared for a capsize. I took all the glass—all the Tabasco bottles, all the mustard jars—and the aggressive knives, and packed them away. This way they wouldn't maim or murder one of us if our world turned upside down. Marc and Chinois located all the survival gear: the EPIRB, flares, life jackets, and hand-held VHF radio.

For the entire day, the wind remained above 60 knots. This was an awful neighborhood in which to be living in this part of the world in this type of boat. There was one gust that registered 85 on the anemometer. According to the Beaufort scale of wind forces, 64–71 knots of wind is "hurricane" strength. From time to time, I glanced at the escape hatch that had been glued shut after its seal blew. If the boat went over, I wondered, how would we get out to fresh air? I kept my thoughts to myself, however. There were end caps over the two big beams, to keep the water out of them, should we capsize. During the storm, one of them blew off. I worried that if the boat went over, our flotation would be sorely compromised.

With the dagger boards up, the boat aimed for the "beach," or toward the rugged coast of Chile, but mostly it sideslipped toward Cape Horn Island. I prayed it would miss it.

As a precaution, Bruno got on the SSB to France. He told Michel Horeau, comfortably ensconced in his barge on the Seine, which doubled as his office, that we were in some trouble. We were in a lot of wind, but we were safe up to this point. Nevertheless, the situation wasn't pretty. He told Horeau that the barometer had dropped like a stone, and worse, none of this was advertised. Bruno just wanted Horeau to know where we were and that we could be in trouble.

From Michel Horeau, the press learned of our plight—which was his job—but so did Molly in Jamestown, Rhode Island, and my father in Boston.

Then we waited. With little else to do, I turned on the video camera. If we were lucky, I would record my cabin mates, Chinois and Marc—both of whom looked like they'd seen the dark side of the moon—at the pivotal moment in this voyage, likely the pivotal moment in their lives. If we were unlucky, someone might have a "snuff film."

As the camera ran, I asked Chinois if he was having fun. He responded in his deep and throaty voice: "NOT—AT—ALL!" Moments later a wave smashed the hull and knocked me off my perch. In the video, you can see the camera jump several feet as I went sprawling.

Meanwhile, in the other hull, Jacques was worried about the halyard that I'd mistakenly wrapped around the head-stay. In a heroic bit of seamanship, he went to remedy this. When he took the halyard off the leeward dagger board, the dagger board dropped down three feet and bit into the ocean. Then *Commodore Explorer* got hit by a couple of 60-foot waves that broke aboard, and the boat just shuddered. A steady diet of these, and she would likely be reduced to carbon-fiber dust. An oil slick.

The windage on the halyard was terrible as Jacques slowly moved against the river on the leeward side and toward the headstay. Slowly and painfully he unwrapped it and then brought it aft.

It was clip, crawl three feet, unclip, reclip, and crawl. And so on. He, too, played Sisyphus. It took him three hours to fix my mistake. It was worse watching him than doing it myself; I was worried about him the entire time. While losing the halyard would have been a nuisance—this boat had a history of being forced out of races because of lost halyards—losing Jacques would have been a tragedy. He made it, however. It was, to be sure, Jacques's shining hour—the moment he returned from the dead. Jacques's grand gesture spoke volumes that all of us were pulling hard for home, like Fogg, Passepartout, and even Detective Fix. With two thirds of the world behind us, the crew of *Commodore Explorer* seemed to be taking "arms against a sea of troubles."

At the end of this day, the longest of my life, the winds started to diminish. By 3:00 A.M. on March 25, the wind had dropped to 45 knots, which felt like a calm day at the beach. While we still had occasional gusts to 60, we put up the storm jib and started sailing again. Bruno was anxious to reach Cape Horn in daylight for the videotape exchange. At 1000, local time, Cape Horn was 50 miles away. At 1400 hours, we sailed within two miles of Cape Horn. There we posed in front of that famous rock that we'd worked so hard to reach.

While there, I filled up a five-liter jerrycan of Cape Horn water. I thought it might be worth something someday—like snake oil. I also thought perhaps the acorn hadn't fallen far from the tree. Marc did the same thing.

The dividing line between the Pacific and Atlantic oceans is a line drawn from Cape Horn to the South Shetland Islands off the tip of Antarctica. We crossed that line and started sailing up the Atlantic Ocean for home.

It was the fifty-third day of the voyage, and, for the first time, we were but even with Fogg and his party. The day of the storm, March 24 to March 25, we'd only made about 170 miles—half of what was needed. Being even with Fogg was worse than it sounds, since the Atlantic promised headwinds, and no winds in the doldrums.

For Bruno there was more bad news: the Chilean officials wouldn't allow the helicopter that Eugène had enlisted to take off to retrieve our videotape and still film. In it, too, were video love letters from Marc to Michelle, his wife, and to Antoine, their new son, and from me to Molly and our baby-to-be. The officials said helicopters couldn't take off when the wind was above 50 knots.

Bruno, who had put all his fund-raising "eggs" in the videotape "basket," argued strenuously that it wasn't blowing above 50 knots, and at that point it wasn't. At least where we were. He might as well have been spitting into the wind, however, for all it got him.

# In which
# Passepartout is captured
# by Indians in the
# Wild, Wild West

At 7:00 A.M. on December 3, 1872, Fogg, Aouda,
and Passepartout stepped ashore in San Francisco. The city is
described through Passepartout's eyes: "The wide streets, the low,
evenly ranged houses, the Anglo-Saxon Gothic churches, the
great docks, the palatial wooden and brick warehouses, the numerous conveyances, omnibuses, horse-cars, and upon the side-
walks, not only Americans and Europeans, but Chinese and Indians. Passepartout was surprised at all he saw. San Francisco was
no longer the legendary city of 1849—a city of banditti, assas-
sins, and incendiaries, who had flocked hither in crowds in pursuit of plunder; a paradise of outlaws, where they gambled with
gold-dust, a revolver in one hand and a bowie-knife in the other:
it was now a great commercial emporium." Further, San Francisco
was not "the Californian capital," as Verne described it.

Passepartout, who had heard of attacks on trains by Sioux and
Pawnees in the American West, asked his master if it might be
appropriate to purchase " 'some dozens of Enfield rifles and Colt's

revolvers.' " While Fogg doubted they would be necessary, he told his servant to do as he pleased. Passepartout purchased a half dozen "six-barrelled revolvers," Verne writes.

Fogg and Aouda ventured out on the streets of San Francisco, ostensibly to get Fogg's passport visaed. There they happened upon Detective Fix, who, of course, they knew from the *Tankadere*. Fix asked to join them on their stroll. The three of them found themselves in a political rally on the streets of San Francisco that quickly turned into a political riot. Both Fogg and Fix were "roughly hustled in their attempts to protect their fair companion," Aouda. A brawny man with a red beard, flushed faced, and sizable shoulders, apparently a leader of one of the factions, seemed intent on striking Fogg. Fix rushed in and received it in his stead. " 'Yankee!' " fairly shouted Phileas Fogg. " 'Englishman!' " returned the ruffian. " 'We will meet again!' " " 'What is your name?' " demanded the American. Fogg told him and asked for his name. " 'Colonel Stamp Proctor' " was the reply.

Afterward, Fogg promised Fix he would come back to America and settle the score. " 'It would not be right for an Englishman to permit himself to be treated in that way, without retaliating.' " Later, we learn that the rally and riot were for no more exalted and no less incongruous office than that of justice of the peace.

Fogg and his party boarded a train that left at 6:00 P.M. on December 3. The station was in Oakland, across San Francisco Bay. Verne doesn't say how Fogg's party got to Oakland, but as this was long before the San Francisco–Oakland Bay Bridge was completed in 1936, to accommodate the automobile, they would likely have boarded a ferry, probably a Horace Carpentier ferry. Carpentier established ferry service between San Francisco and Oakland in 1852. He was well positioned when Oakland became the terminus in 1869 for the transcontinental railroad.

If the "unforeseen" didn't raise its head, they could expect to be in New York in seven days. A steamer, which Fogg needed to catch, would cross the Atlantic, starting on December 11.

If they had attempted this "3,786-mile cross-country journey" but three years before, it would have taken at least six months, Verne notes. However, on May 10, 1869, the tracks of the Central Pacific Railroad, building east from Oakland, met the tracks of the Union Pacific Railroad, building west from Omaha, Nebraska. The last railroad stake was driven at Promontory Point, Utah, on the north side of the Great Salt Lake. From Omaha to New York travelers had a choice of five main lines.

The period between the American Civil War and World War I, or between 1865 and 1916, was the golden age of railroad construction in this country. In those 50 years, the railroad network increased from 35,000 miles (56,000 km) to 254,000 miles (406,400 km) as no other form of transportation arose to challenge the railroad. To put this into perspective: by 1890, one third of the world's railroad tracks were in the United States. After World War I came the automobile.

America was now spanned from sea to shining sea. Verne warns us, however, that the territory between "Omaha and the Pacific . . . is still infested by Indians and wild beasts, and a large tract which the Mormons, after they were driven from Illinois in 1845, began to colonize."

The train traveled slowly at 20 miles an hour. One hour after departure from the Oakland station, it began to snow, Verne says. Twenty miles from Oakland, the train would have been in Martinez, which is at sea level on the Carquinez Strait. With due respect to Verne, it must have been a rare day in December, because it almost never snows there.

By midnight, the train passed Sacramento; by seven, on the morning of December 4, the train entered the Sierra Nevada mountains. At nine o'clock, the train entered Nevada through the Carson Valley, and at midday it reached Reno. This day the train was stopped for three hours waiting for a "troop of ten or twelve thousand head of buffalo," to clear the tracks. At nine o'clock that evening, the train penetrated Utah. Next it passed north of the Great Salt Lake. The translator, but not the author, describes the Great Salt Lake as being "three miles eight hundred feet above the sea." That would be 16,640 feet, which is 2,145 feet higher

than Mount Whitney in the Sierra Nevada Range in California—
the highest mountain in the lower 48 states. Actually the Great
Salt Lake is 4,390 feet above sea level.[1]

Before arriving in Ogden, Utah, the train reached Promontory
Point, where, as described, the Union Pacific and Central Pacific
railroads had joined hands three years before. On a six-hour lay-
over in Ogden, on December 5, Fogg, Aouda, and Passepartout
visited Salt Lake City. There Passepartout was perplexed by the
Mormon practice of polygamy. Writes Verne, "His common
sense pitied, above all, the husband. It seemed to him a terrible
thing to have to guide so many wives at once across the vicissi-
tudes of life and to conduct them, as it were, in a body to the
Mormon paradise, with the prospect of seeing them in the company of the glorious Smith, who doubtless was the chief ornament of that delightful place, to all eternity.[2] He imagined—perhaps he was mistaken—the fair ones of Salt Lake City cast rather
alarming glances on his person. Happily, his stay there was but
brief."

On the evening of December 6, the train entered the Wyo-
ming Territory. The following morning, it stopped at Green
River. Aouda noticed several passengers using the stop to breathe
fresh air. Among them, she was shocked to see, was the evil
Colonel Stamp Proctor, who had "so grossly insulted Phileas
Fogg at the San Francisco meeting." Aouda, we learn for the first

[1] The French edition reads: *"Trois mille huit cents pieds au-dessus du niveau de la
mer."* *Mille* means "thousand" as well as "mile."

[2] Joseph Smith founded the Mormon church, or the Church of Jesus Christ
of Latter-day Saints, in 1830 in Fayette, New York. With a small group of
followers, Smith settled in Kirtland, Ohio, and Jackson County, Missouri.
Eventually, the church moved to Nauvoo, Illinois. When rumors about polygamy spread, Smith was murdered by an armed mob in 1844. He was
replaced by Brigham Young. Two years later, Young led a march to the
Great Salt Basin in Utah. Eventually Young was named the first territorial
governor of Utah. The United States government challenged the church on
its tenet of polygamy. Polygamy as well as unfounded reports of a rebellion
against the U.S. government nearly led to a war. Laws against polygamy
were passed in 1862 and 1882. The church officially ended the practice in
1890.

time, "was attached to the man [Fogg] who, however coldly, gave her daily evidences of the most absolute devotion." She characterized her feelings as "gratitude," but Verne tells us it "was really more than that."

As Fogg slept, Aouda communicated her fears about Colonel Proctor to Passepartout and Detective Fix. Both men volunteered to defend Fogg. This caused Passepartout to soften in his feelings toward the detective. " 'Would you really fight for him?' " asked Passepartout.

Detective Fix said with a determined will, " 'I would do anything to get him back, living, to Europe.' "

However, Aouda recognized that Fogg would not allow another to fight his battles. He must be distracted. Passepartout stated that one of Fogg's major diversions was whist, the card game he indefatigably played with the gentlemen of the Reform Club. When Fogg awoke, Fix suggested a game of whist. Fogg demurred, thinking they had neither the correct number of players nor cards. Then Aouda volunteered to play. "I understand whist. It is part of an English education." Cards were purchased from the steward, and they played three-handed whist using a "dummy" as the fourth. Aouda played well enough that she "even received some compliments . . . from Fogg." (Beauty and whist too. Could Fogg have found a more perfect soulmate?)

The train reached the Rocky Mountains on December 7. At Medicine Bow, Wyoming, the train was stopped by a red signal. Passepartout, who was not playing whist, was dispatched to find out why the train had made this unanticipated stop. In the group that crowded around the conductor, engineer, and signalman was Colonel Stamp Proctor, who was conspicuous by "his insolent manner." The signalman told them, " 'No! You can't pass! The bridge at Medicine Bow is shaky, and would not bear the weight of the train.' " This would necessitate a six-hour delay, as the passengers must walk 10 or 15 miles over a plain covered with snow to pass the swollen river. On the opposite side, they would be met by another train, dispatched from Omaha.

As he was returning to the train to tell his master the dispir-
iting news, Passepartout encountered the engineer, a "true Yankee," named Forster, who announced, with that famous "Yankee
ingenuity," " 'Gentlemen, perhaps there is a way, after all, to get
over.' " Forster's grandiose plan was for the train to attain its
highest possible speed and then, in essence, leap the river. Apparently, in Verne's mind, when it comes to discretion and valor,
Americans lean toward the latter. The group was quite taken with
the engineer's plan, but none more so than the blustering Colonel
Proctor. Passepartout, however, felt the plan "a little too American." Besides, by now he'd figured out a slight variation on this
theme, which, to him, seemed far more prudent. When he tried
to present it, however, he was shouted down, mostly by Colonel
Proctor, who asked, " 'Are you afraid?' "

" 'I afraid!' " responded Passepartout. Then he said to himself,
"Very well; I will show these people that a Frenchman can be as
American as they!" Nevertheless, he continued to mull over his
idea. It varied from the original but a little; that was, to have the
passengers walk over the bridge *first* and then, when they were
safely across, have the train make its leap without them. At least
they wouldn't be forced to go down with the "ship." Besides, the
train would be that much lighter.

The train was backed up a mile to get a running start. By the
time it reached the bridge it was going 100 mph. "It hardly bore
upon the rails at all," wrote Verne. "And they passed over! It was
like a flash. . . . But scarcely had the train passed the river,
when the bridge, completely ruined, fell with a crash into the
rapids of Medicine Bow."

Verne's science is in error here. The weight of a body doesn't
vary with speed. The train going 100 mph horizontally weighs
no more or less than the same train standing still.[3]

Good or bad science, the whist game continued unabated. As

[3] The mass or weight of the body doesn't change; neither does the accelera-
tion due to gravity. The operative word here is *horizontal*. Evil Kneivel can

Phileas Fogg was about to play a spade, a voice behind him said, " 'I should play a diamond.' " It was Colonel Proctor. Fogg and Proctor recognized one another at once. " 'You don't understand anything about whist,' " said Proctor.

" 'Perhaps I do, as well as another,' " said Fogg, who stood to meet the challenge. At this point, Detective Fix tried to intercede, but Fogg wouldn't allow it. " 'This affair is mine and mine only. . . .' " he said. Colonel Proctor proposed a duel. While Fogg was most amenable to that, he attempted to postpone it, so as not to interfere with his tour of the world. " 'Will you appoint a meeting for six months hence?' "

" 'Why not ten years hence?' " said the bullying American. Fogg and Colonel Proctor went to the last car on the train. They were accompanied by Detective Fix, Passepartout, and a conductor. The conductor politely asked the other passengers to clear out, " 'as two gentlemen [have] an affair of honour to settle.' " There were only a dozen of them, and they left willingly. When the train whistle sounded, they were to begin firing. However, before this happened, "Cries of terror proceeded from the interior of the train."

The train was under attack by a band of Sioux. Fogg and Colonel Proctor joined the fight. The Sioux first attacked the engine and stunned the engineer and his stoker with blows rather than bullets from their muskets. A Sioux chief tried to halt the train, but not knowing how to work the valves he brought the engine up to full throttle. Aouda, we learn, behaved "courageously from the first. She defended herself, like a true heroine, with a revolver, which she shot through the broken windows whenever a savage made his appearance. Twenty Sioux had fallen mortally wounded to the ground, and the wheels crushed those who fell upon the rails as if they had been worms."

The conductor, who was fighting beside Fogg, told him that

---

jump cars on his motorcycle because there is a *vertical* component to his ramp.

the train had to be stopped within five minutes. At Fort Kearney, the next station, there was a garrison of soldiers who would surely help them. There was no law and order beyond that. "It shall be stopped," promised Fogg, about to rush from the car. However, Passepartout beat him to it.

Verne describes Passepartout's heroic passage: "The brave fellow . . . opening a door unperceived by the Indians, succeeded in slipping under the car; and while the struggle continued, and the balls whizzed across each other over his head, he made use of his old acrobatic experience, and with amazing agility worked his way under the cars, holding on to the chains, aiding himself by the brakes and edges of the sashes, creeping from one car to another with marvelous skill, and thus gaining the forward end of the train." Finally, Passepartout was able to uncouple the train from the engine.

Using the brakes, the Frenchman stopped the train "less than a hundred feet from the Kearney station." There the soldiers helped the passengers defeat the Sioux. When order was restored, it was determined that several passengers were missing, among them Passepartout, whose bravery had surely saved them all.

While Detective Fix was slightly wounded, Fogg and Aouda were unharmed. One of the "most seriously hurt" was Colonel Stamp Proctor, writes Verne. "A ball had entered his groin."

As the injured were being attended to, Phileas Fogg, risking his entire wager, volunteered to go in search of his servant. " 'I will find him, living or dead,' " he said quietly to Aouda. That grand gesture brought tears to her eyes.

While it took some persuading, Fogg was able to get help from thirty soldiers at the fort. Even the doubting Detective Fix volunteered to go, but Fogg preferred that he stay with Aouda. Fogg promised the soldiers a $5,000 reward if they were successful in saving Passepartout and the other missing passengers. Before departing, Fogg handed Aouda his precious carpetbag with what remained of his £20,000.

As Fogg departed into the Nebraska winter weather, the two remaining protagonists, Aouda and Detective Fix, drew very different conclusions about the character of Phileas Fogg. Aouda, Verne writes, thought "of the simple and noble generosity, the tranquil courage of Phileas Fogg. He had sacrificed his fortune, and was now risking his life, all without hesitation, from duty, in silence."

Fix's thoughts were more complex, more hard boiled: " 'I have been an idiot,' " he said to himself. " '. . . He has gone, and won't come back! But how is it that I, Fix, who have in my pocket a warrant for his arrest, have been so fascinated by him? Decidedly, I am nothing but an ass!' "

In the midst of these thoughts, the wayward locomotive returned. The engine had eventually run out of steam and coasted to a halt. In time, the engineer and stoker, who were not dead but merely unconscious, woke up, and fired the boiler. They returned backward and recoupled the engine to the remainder of the train. This being America, immediately they announced their intention to depart. Aouda asked them to wait for " 'the prisoners—our unfortunate fellow-travellers—'

" 'I cannot interrupt the trip. We are already three hours behind time,' " said the conductor. The next train, Aouda learned, wouldn't leave before tomorrow evening. " 'But then it will be too late! We must wait.' " Despite her pleas, the train pulled out without Aouda and Detective Fix and, of course, Fogg and Passepartout. Fogg's wager seemed surely lost.

That day, as Aouda and Fix waited, a snowstorm raged. Nevertheless, Aouda kept going to the end of the platform trying to pierce the snow, in hopes of seeing Fogg, Passepartout, and the others. Early that evening, it stopped snowing but turned frigid, as is often winter's one-two punch on the prairie. Throughout the night, Aouda remained awake; she left the station from time to time to peer into the dark plain. Fix did not sleep either. At one point a man approached him. They had brief words, but Fix curtailed the conversation by shaking his head no.

# In which
# we're chased by
# pirates and party
# with mermaids

After Cape Horn, which we rounded on March 25, 1993, our fifty-third day at sea, there was a sense aboard *Commodore Explorer*—for the crew if perhaps not the skipper—that we were going to make it. Maybe we weren't going to break the fictitious 80-day record of Phileas Fogg, but certainly the record of Titouan Lamazou, who in the course of the 1989–90 Vendée Globe Race had sailed *Ecureuil d'Aquitaine II* around the world in 109 days, 8 hours, and 48 minutes.

It's a small world, as the saying has it, and never more so than when another French sailor takes aim at the world. Until March 12, 1993, or two weeks before we passed Cape Horn, that record stood a good chance of being eclipsed in the 1992–93 edition of this race. As it happened, Alain Gautier, sailing on *Bagages Superior*, would finish on March 12 and would miss breaking Lamazou's record by less than one day.

While not breaking the record, Gautier won the race, and so some 120,000 spectators cheered his return to France's les Sables d'Olonne. Only in France. As mentioned, American Mike Plant was heading there in October 1992, for the start of this race when he disappeared at sea after the keel of his boat fell off. During the race, a second sailor, Nigel Burgess, a British yacht broker, was found afloat but dead in his survival suit with a deep gash in his head. His boat, named *Nigel Burgess Yachtbrokers*, was found afloat too. Burgess had sent a distress call saying his boat was taking on water in a storm that savaged the fleet shortly after the start.

This storm caused Bruno's brother Loïck to drop out after his hull on *Fujicolor* delaminated. Further, another French sailor, Philippe Poupon, had to turn back in this storm when the keel bolts, which join the keel to the hull, on his ketch *Fleury Michon* began to loosen. He rejoined the race and fought back. Poupon was within 300 miles of catching the leader, Gautier, when one of his two masts broke. He limped home to finish third.

When we passed Cape Horn, 20,000 nautical miles were behind us, with 7,000 more to go—at least as the crow flies. While it may not wish to, a crow can fly into the wind. Wishing or not, a sailboat can't. The closest it can sail is about 45 degrees to the wind. So to get to a point upwind, a sailboat must tack. This zigzag course, also known as beating, resembles the path of your laced shoelace. It is a cruel sailing geometry that can even double the distance you have to sail.

Bruno reckoned we had 9,000 miles to go at this point with some beating figured in. To break the fictitious 80-day record, we would need to average 14 knots. However, in the Atlantic at this time of year, any number of traps and blockades await a boat heading in a northeasterly direction, as we were. We'd have to be very lucky *and* very good to average 14 knots. The passage northeast across the Atlantic, which would reach from 56 degrees south latitude to 48 degrees north latitude, was likely the most tactically demanding part of the voyage.

We would sail from winterlike weather where we were in the deep south, to autumnlike weather at the Tropic of Capricorn, to summer on either side of the equator, to spring from the Tropic of Cancer to France. It was like Vivaldi's "Four Seasons"—a composition that I played so often, Chinois almost jumped ship. I found it to be a perfect musical rendition of the voyage, however—a theme song.

In theory, the winds at this time of year work this way: The prevailing westerlies blow between 30 and 60 degrees in either hemisphere. It is these westerly winds that blow with some consistency across North America, Europe, and Asia—indeed over the most populated areas on earth.

Next, when we were off the coast of Brazil, we should encounter the southeast trades that would be favorable. When in them, we should be able to gallop this duo-hulled boat across the planet. The southeast trades run this time of year from about 30 degrees south latitude to about 10 degrees south or even to the equator. Trade winds, which blow from the east, contrary to the prevailing westerlies, show a consistency in direction and in velocity.

Next, however, we'd have to cross the doldrums, the breathless area, on the north side of the equator. Historically, the doldrums were thought of as a fairly wide band on either side of the equator. However, satellites have shown the doldrums, more properly called the "intertropical convergence zone," is a much narrower band, a few degrees north of the equator. As described, here the southeast trades of the southern hemisphere meet the northeast trades of the northern hemisphere and tend to blow one another out.

From the equator to about the Tropic of Cancer, at $23^1/2$ degrees north latitude, we'd have the aforementioned northeast trades, which would be unfavorable. We'd have to beat upwind—a good description, because it's analogous to beating your head against a wall. It was also something we had not done up to this point. Beating is the soft underbelly of a multihull. Such two- or three-hulled boats have little affinity for sailing upwind.

That's what the book on meteorology says; reality can be very different, depending on how settled or unsettled is the weather. Thus, Bruno spent many hours at the computer screen leading us northeast toward France through high-pressure systems and low-pressure systems that were like an opponent's queen on a chessboard: ambidextrous and dangerous. The themes of this work were to avoid headwinds, avoid light winds, and avoid heavy winds and big seas that might break the boat. Bruno would receive weather faxes on the Sat-C system about four times a day. He had the computer capability of placing the weather patterns over our route. It was both an art and a science, and Bruno played it masterfully.

I felt supremely confident after Cape Horn. Marc, however, cautioned me against such hubris. In essence, he said, "Don't count your chickens before they're hatched." Marc said that getting out of the south means getting north of the Falkland Islands, which lie 350 nautical miles east northeast of Cape Horn. However, after the Horn, the wind died to about 35 knots, which, following the private hurricane we'd experienced, seemed like tradewind sailing south of the equator.

It took us one day to get due south of the Falkland Islands and two more days to pass them on a gradual left-hand turn to the north. Bruno gave the islands a wide berth, as he didn't wish to get caught in their windless lee. He gave South America a wide berth, too, but for opposite reasons. He wanted to avoid the blasts of wind that can charge down from the Andes, which as you go north get as high as 22,835 feet—the highest point in the western hemisphere—and can wreak havoc on a boat, particularly a delicate multihull.

However, by going well east of the Falklands, we had headwinds and then no winds. It was slow going, but it gave us time to recover after the Cape Horn storm and to appreciate the birds that congregated from Burdwood Bank, due east of Cape Horn, to the Falklands. It seemed like a convention for terns and albatross. These birds seemed so comfortable here, so thoroughly adapted to this rigorous, elemental, ever-changing environment. Compared to them, we were strangers in a strange land—wary and never quite comfortable. We were forever expecting the 102-foot wing mast to topple, someone to fall overboard, or the 86-foot carbon fiber hulls to strike something and turn to dust. We were in a boat that defied nature; these birds seem hardly noticed by it. "The Falklands must be Birdland," I wrote in my journal.

While there are more than 200 islands in the Falkland group, we never saw one. A relative lack of islands is a characteristic of the Atlantic Ocean. The Pacific seems positively pockmarked with islands, a veritable adolescent of an ocean, while the Atlantic has but few. They include the Falkland Islands, where we were, the South Georgia Islands, where Shackleton landed and later died, the Cape Verde Islands, where Kéruzoré, our photographer, was set adrift, St. Helena, Tristan da Cunha, the Azores, the Madeira Islands, the Canaries, Bermuda, the British Isles, Greenland, Iceland, Svalbard, and the West Indies Ascension.

Then again, we had never seen any islands in the Pacific, either, until we reached Cape Horn, where we'd posed like the most shameless tourists. Before that, the only other land we'd seen was the Cape Verde Islands.

The warning I had sounded about our consumption of alcohol when we crossed the equator on the ninth day, was now a reality. We were practically out of this cooking fuel. We tried eating freeze-dried food rehydrated in cold water, but it had the consistency of volcanic ash.

If I didn't do something soon, I figured, these guys would starve. So I took the alcohol stove from the starboard hull and brought it on deck to the port hull, placing it under the *casquette* to protect it from the wind.

The stove used a fuel cell—a spongelike device that absorbs alcohol. It would soak up about a liter of alcohol and burn for five or six hours. Left with insufficient alcohol, I took one of these cells and loaded it with diesel fuel and a little gas, a shot-glass full, to get it burning. In Mexico, where I had traveled as a youth for the Laser Pan American Championship, I'd seen diesel-fuel cut with gasoline used in smudge pots to mark roadside accidents. Apparently, the gas gets the diesel fuel hot enough to burn. Then I lit the thing, and it went puff! (Kids, don't try this at home! Remember, I'm a highly trained professional.)

It did work, however, although it caused black soot to fly everywhere, even down the hatch and into the port cabin, that part of the duplex where Marc, Chinois, and I lived. It also blackened my body, including my face.

I started calling it my "third-world barbecue," which is, I'm sure, politically incorrect. After a few tries, I persuaded Bruno to let me move the "barbecue" to a platform aft, where the life raft lived. I drilled some holes in the platform and tied the stove to it with Kevlar twine, which essentially won't burn. Twice a day, I'd boil a large quantity of water on my barbecue. Then we'd keep it hot in thermoses.

Bruno made it famous in some telexes he wrote back to

France. He wrote: "[We're on] the fastest third-world bar-becue flying raft! Why? Because the Minister of Interior [c'est moi] has continued his experiments. Obstinate, after he nearly set the port hull on fire, Cam eventually man-aged to install his horror show in the life-raft support aft. All I can tell you is if the Argos system that is tracking us ceases to work, take a satellite photo of the area, follow the black smoke, and under it, you'll find the exhilarated cook, proud of his accomplishments. He's delusional. He thinks he's a New York City hot-dog vendor, but if he is, he's selling them off a boat that's going 27 knots."

In that telex of Bruno's, celebrating my third-world bar-becue, he talked about pollution. This was not surprising, as my "hot-dog cart" was likely the major source of it in this remarkably pristine piece of the world. Bruno wrote, "Keeping all the nonbiodegradable trash on board is a small price to pay in regard to the purity of the air and water we saw in the south. Our trash will come back to France with the boat, and, perhaps, we'll put it up for auc-tion. As I promised the albatross when we reached the For-ties, their realm, we have hardly touched their territory and, maybe, we'll have the privilege to return someday.

" 'For a more blue world' might be an appropriate motto for future *Explorer* programs. Obviously, we would love to return to explore the last untouched places and hopefully to find it little the worse for wear. Riding this trash wagon seems a small price to pay for the privilege to live on this beautiful blue planet.

"Talking about the planet, we can safely say, 'It is round!' "

On March 29, *Commodore Explorer* covered only 150 miles in 22 hours—close to our worst performance since depart-ing Ouessant on January 31. A high-pressure system was anchored 300 miles to the northwest of us, near the Golfo de San Jorge in Argentina. Again, the winds in the southern hemisphere are opposite to those in the northern hemisphere, so the wind moves counterclockwise around a high. By being east of it, we expected the wind to be behind us; however, we didn't expect the wind to die, which it did. We were "as idle as a painted ship/Upon a painted ocean," to invoke the immortal words of Samuel Taylor Coleridge. Meanwhile, the clock was going tick-tock.

The center of this high-pressure system was expected to move northeast, to St. Helena Island, a thousand miles off the coast of Africa, by April 1. A British colony, St. Helena is where Napoleon I was exiled for the second and final time, in 1815. He remained there until 1821, when he died.

While St. Helena and Napoleon are important to the French, our interest wasn't historical. Rather, it was tactical. As the high-pressure system headed northeast toward St. Helena, and we headed north, we needed to pass in front of it. If we lost the race, we'd end up to the west of the high and get headwinds, what with its counterclockwise flow. That contrary wall of wind might well prevent us from reaching France in time.

Bruno sent a telex to France on March 30 that reflected his ambivalent mood toward the voyage that he'd been unable to shake. First it summarized the breaks and hurts the boat and crew had suffered so far. They seem, said Bruno, "rather minor in regard to the route and extreme conditions."

Then he summarized our accomplishments to date:

- "Beat our competitors and the records of the clipper ships on the main navigational routes.[1]
- ". . . Round(ed) the three capes including the Horn."

[1] The records set by *Commodore Explorer* up to this point included: 1) English Channel to equator: 8 days, 19 hours, and 26 minutes; 2) English Channel to Cape of Good Hope (South Africa): 21 days, 12

Then he offered what amounted to a meditation: "It might be wise to stop dreaming here and forget about the world tour in 80 days, which today seems pretty hard to achieve. But since the Horn has decided to let us pass, the only thing to do is to go as far as we can. The equator would be fine, the Azores would be better, France would be magic.

"Contrary to what one might think, the passage up the Atlantic may be very delicate and will likely be very hard on the gear. It will be difficult to avoid all contrary winds. After the question: Horn or not Horn? the question is: equator or not equator? St. Helena will decide. Verdict at the end of the week." Once again Bruno was sounding like the melancholy Prince of Denmark: "To be or not to be . . ."

On April 1, a day to be marked like the Ides of March, I sent Molly this telex: "Sunny trade-wind conditions with boat speed around 30 knots. Lots of spray and warm air flying by. Last night we were chased by a pirate gunboat for three hours. Shots exchanged, but we were able to hoist big blue (spinnaker) and blew 'em off. No injuries and have reported incident to international maritime authorities.

"Escorted by thousands of seabirds, whales, and por-

---

hours, and 48 minutes; 3) English Channel to Cape Leeuwin (Australia): 33 days, 7 hours, and 48 minutes; 4) Cape of Good Hope to Cape Leeuwin: 11 days and 9 hours; 5) Cape of Good Hope to Southeast Cape (Tasmania): 15 days and 3 hours; 6) English Channel to Southeast Cape: 36 days, 15 hours, and 48 minutes; 7) nonstop halfway around the world under sail (180-degree meridian): 40 days; 8) Cape Leeuwin to Southeast Cape: 3 days and 8 hours; 9) Southeast Cape to Southwest Cape (Stewart Island, New Zealand): 2 days, 4 hours, and 40 minutes; 10) Cape Leeuwin to Southwest Cape: 5 days, 12 hours, and 40 minutes; 11) Cape of Good Hope to Southwest Cape: 17 days, 7 hours, and 40 minutes; and 12) Southwest Cape to Cape Horn: 14 days, 10 hours, and 14 minutes.

poises all morning to city of Lost Atlantis where we found King Neptune frolicking with thousands of beautiful mermaids in a magic world of crystal and gold. Plotted position for return visit as we only had time for a mahi-mahi burger, fries, and cold beer—I drank three. Now have five mermaids with us to Azores; smell a bit fishy, but they say we'll get used to it. They love flying fish and are showing me new catch-and-cook techniques. Have been averaging over 600 miles a day since Horn and expect to arrive in France around April 12.

"Cheers Cam and smiling Commodore Crew"

Molly went running to *Sailing World* magazine, a *New York Times* magazine in Newport. She told them about our being chased by pirates and how we were on track for a 71-day circumnavigation. Sean McNeill, an editor there, was skeptical and asked to see the date of the telex. It was April 1.

Molly faxed me back that day with local news. She ended it with the line: "Just returned from the doctor, and we're having twins!"

Nevertheless, my telex had a certain life of its own. It was published tongue-firmly-in-cheek in the Patagonia catalog—a company for which I work. In 1994, I received a telephone call from an Australian filmmaker making a movie about piracy. He seemed disappointed when I told him it was an April Fool's hoax.

# In which Fogg, Passepartout, Aouda, and Fix sail across America's frozen heartland

Aouda and Detective Fix spent a restless night at the Fort Kearney station. The next morning, gunshots were heard. The soldiers rushed out of the fort, and Aouda and Fix hurried from the train station. There was Phileas Fogg marching at the head of an orderly band. The missing passengers, including Passepartout, were all present, as were the soldiers.

We learn the captives gained their safety this way: Passepartout and his fellow passengers struggled with their Sioux captors. The Frenchman felled three with his fists. At that moment, Phileas Fogg and his soldiers arrived. The Indians, as Columbus first called them, were routed.

Aouda, Verne writes, "took her protector's hand and pressed it in her own, too much moved to speak."

Passepartout asked about the train. " 'Gone,' " said Fix.

" 'And when does the next train pass here?' " Fogg wondered.

" 'Not till this evening.' "

" 'Ah!' " replied Phileas Fogg, which was as forceful an exclamation as he would voice.

It was time for an accounting. Fogg, we discover, needed to make up eight hours to have any chance—and it was a slim chance—of boarding the Liverpool steamer, which was scheduled to depart New York at nine o'clock on the evening on December 11.

Detective Fix, of all people, had a plan. The mode of transportation could be " 'a sledge [sled] with sails' "—a sort of iceboat. The mysterious man who had approached Fix the previous evening had proposed such an idea.

That man, whose name was Mudge, was at this very minute pacing up and down nervously in front of the station. Fogg went out to meet him. Verne writes, "There Mr. Fogg examined a curious vehicle, a kind of frame on two long beams, a little raised in front like the runner of a sledge and upon which there was room for five or six persons. A high mast was fixed on the frame, held firmly by metallic lashings, to which was attached a large brigantine sail. This mast held an iron stay upon which to hoist a jib-sail. Behind, a sort of rudder served to guide the vehicle. It was, in short, a sledge rigged like a sloop. During the winter, when the trains are blocked up by the snow, these sledges make extremely rapid journeys across the frozen plains from one station to another. . . . With the wind behind them, they slip over the surface of the prairies with a speed equal if not superior to that of the express trains."

Fogg made a bargain with Mr. Mudge, who was very confident of reaching Omaha, Nebraska, in time. The wind was, then, fresh and favorable—blowing from the west. Also the snow had hardened, like ice. Fogg, Fix, Passepartout, and Aouda boarded the iceboat and huddled under blankets against the cold. Fogg had offered to leave Aouda at Fort Kearney, under the care of Passepartout, but she refused. The distance between Fort Kearney and Omaha is about 200 miles. The iceboat was capable of sailing at

40 mph, so the trip might take as little as five hours. " 'If nothing breaks,' says Mudge, 'we shall get there!' "

Fogg had but two things to fear: an accident, as mentioned, but also decreasing winds. Nevertheless, writes Verne, "the breeze, far from lessening its force, blew as if to bend the mast, which, however, the metallic lashings held firmly. These lashings, like the chords of a stringed instrument, resounded as if vibrated by a violin bow. The sledge slid along in the midst of a plaintively intense melody."

The only words Fogg uttered during the voyage was to comment on the noise of the wind in the rigging: " 'These chords give the fifth and the octave.' "

Passepartout, with "natural buoyancy of spirit," was invigorated by the passage. He began to hope that they would reach New York, if not by the morning of the eleventh, then by the evening, which might be in time. He also recognized clearly his profound respect for Phileas Fogg. "One thing, however, Passepartout would never forget, and that was the sacrifice which Mr. Fogg had made, without hesitation, to rescue him from the Sioux. Mr. Fogg had risked his fortune and his life. No! His servant would never forget that!" pens Verne.

The plain, Verne writes evocatively, "was absolutely deserted. . . . From time to time they sped by some phantom-like tree, whose white skeleton twisted and rattled in the wind. Sometimes flocks of wild birds rose, or bands of gaunt, famished, ferocious prairie-wolves ran howling after the sledge. . . ."

Finally, after five long hours, Mudge announced, " 'We have got there!' " Fogg rewarded him handsomely for his trouble, as was his way.

The station was "in daily communication by numerous trains, with the Atlantic seaboard!" Verne writes. Boarding one, they traveled into Iowa and rapidly passed such cities as Council Bluffs, Des Moines, and Iowa City. They crossed the "mighty" Mississippi at night at Davenport. Here the first bridge to span the Mississippi River had been constructed in 1856. Across the

Mississippi, the train entered Illinois at Rock Island. It arrived at Chicago on the evening of December 10.

Nine hundred miles away was New York. "Trains are not wanting in Chicago," Verne writes. They boarded one immediately. "It traversed Indiana, Ohio, Pennsylvania, and New Jersey like a flash, rushing through towns with antique names, some of which had streets and car-tracks, but as yet no houses. At last the Hudson came into view; and at quarter past eleven in the evening of the eleventh, the train stopped in the station on the right bank of the river, before the very pier of the Cunard line."

However, the *China,* heading for Liverpool, had departed forty-five minutes before. It was the seventieth day of Fogg's travels. Tick-tock.

If Fogg were real and could peer 121 years into the future, he'd see we were struggling too. Doubtless, this would be little consolation.

# In which
# my loose lip
# nearly sinks our ship

I had never joined this trip thinking I was going to make money; however, there was always some vague talk that there might be a large pot of gold at the end of the rainbow if we were successful. First there was PMU, a French lottery organization, that put up $1 million. As noted, that prize disappeared. While we sailed, the Trophée Jules Verne Committee was working on finding another sponsor. Later, a large French cigarette company proposed a $100,000 prize. Bruno refused it, however, believing he could get more from someone else. He wasn't sharing his financial machinations with any of us, however; and I didn't learn about this overture or Bruno's refusal of it until after the voyage had ended. Unfortunately, there were no other offers.

Marc, who had a new baby, a wife who wasn't working as a result of the new baby and his absence, and large debts incurred from getting his helicopter pilot's license, canvassed the crew about a petition he wished to present to Bruno. It was, in essence, a legal document that said if we were successful in beating the record and there was prize money, it would be distributed in some equitable manner *after* Bruno had paid all his debts.

The document seemed appropriate to me, as it did to the rest of the crew: Jacques and Chinois. Everyone in the sailing game has been taken advantage of at one time or another, because there typically aren't contracts. Marc, for example, sailed around the world with a notable sailor who wouldn't pay him his share of the prize money, because he worked for a sailmaker. My only caution to Marc was not to piss Bruno off.

It took Marc a couple of days to steel his courage, but one day as I was driving *Commodore Explorer* off the coast of Brazil, he presented the petition to Bruno, who was, as usual, beavering away in his office in the starboard hull. Marc was gone for more than an hour. Bruno was furious, less because of the document, I think, than of the fact that he was being asked to put it in writing. Between Bruno and Marc, a chill developed that even the equator—the endless summer in the center of our planet—couldn't thaw.

From the Horn, it took us more than a week to get to Recife, where Brazil bulges into the Atlantic Ocean. Recife is at 6 degrees south latitude. Arriving there on April 6, our sixty-fifth day at sea, we broke a running-backstay fitting. We were on-the-wind—that dreaded beating orientation—and the hulls and mast were working in many directions but rarely together. In the waves that smashed us again and again, one hull would go at one speed and the other hull would go at another speed, until the beams brought the hulls back together. It was parallelogram-rectangle parallelogram-rectangle. This geometry was ceaseless, and at the same time, the 102-foot mast was drawing endless ellipses in the sky.

Then a titanium piece that joined the two runners broke, despite the fact that its safe working load was supposedly 25,000 pounds. The break wasn't that serious, but it served as a warning that the boat was fatigued. The next day we changed the other runner and began to patrol the boat more vigorously, looking for signs of wear.

After this, Bruno established a speed limit. Twenty-three knots was as fast as you were allowed to go. Above that you got a "speeding ticket."

The clouds blowing off Brazil picked up huge quantities of water from the rain forests. So dramatic were they, they seemed more animated than real. They were huge cumulous clouds—cottonballs—that seemed to come to life in the equatorial heat. Some of them were stable, and under these was an umbrella of light winds. Others bubbled and spun toward the heavens into anvil-shaped thunderheads. Often there would be chaos under them in the form of squalls—rain and wind, lightning and thunder—but it never lasted very long. The boat would sprint, and then, after they passed, just amble along.

That night we saw the lights of Recife, which has a population of about 1.3 million. As we passed I wondered what the lives of the people who made these lights were like. Were they reading, or talking, loving, or watching television? Was there television? This was like the game I used to play as a child, looking at maps and wondering what the people and lands were like. The population of Recife is largely African; many of them descendants of slaves brought to Brazil to work in the sugarcane plantations. I also wondered what they would think of us if they could see us.

This night, April 6, I remember we had a full moon. I mention this because it was a perfectly wonderful moon and a magical night—other than the Cape Verde Islands and Cape Horn, we'd seen no land since we left. I also mention this because Easter Sunday follows the first full moon on or after March 21. It was this moon. That meant next Sunday, April 11, would be Easter Sunday.

In the light of this full moon, I said something about the Easter bunny. My remark was met with shock by my French shipmates. While I didn't know this until then, the word *rabbit*, or *lapin* in French, is considered ill-luck aboard a French ship. From what I gather, a rabbit allowed to run loose on the deck of some significant ship ate through the rigging, dismasting it. While not particularly superstitious, I hoped my loose lip wouldn't sink this ship.

On April 8, our sixty-seventh day at sea, we crossed the equator. The sun had passed this way, heading in the same direction, on March 20, some 19 days before. This signals spring in the northern hemisphere—fall in the southern—which occurs on or about March 21; this year, it was March 20.

At this point I was starting to look toward home to New England, to the northwest, where Molly and my family waited. My French shipmates were, doubtless, looking northeast toward France and home. A day later, April 9, I saw the North Star. It seemed like an old friend, welcoming me home. Not only does the North Star shine, however, faintly only over the northern hemisphere—it is a second magnitude star—but it was the first star used in celestial navigation to determine latitude.

Determining latitude with the North Star works this way: the angular distance of this star above the horizon during morning or evening twilight is measured with an angular-measuring device, like a sextant. The star is so many degrees above the horizon—the horizontal line where the sea meets the sky.

At Newport, where I then lived, which is about 41 degrees north latitude, the North Star is at about 41 degrees above the horizon, plus or minus a small correction. The correction is necessary because the North Star is not directly over the North Pole; rather it circles it on a small radius. If you were at the North Pole, or at 90 degrees north latitude, the North Star would be very close to 90 degrees, or directly overhead. At the equator or south of it, the North Star is below the horizon and invisible.

Since the North Star is not visible in the southern hemisphere, a second method for determining latitude was developed by Prince Henry's cosmographers in the fifteenth century. Determining latitude by the sun takes place at local apparent noon, or high noon. Local apparent noon occurs at around 1200 hours, or 12:00 P.M., when the sun crosses an observer's longitude, or meridian. At that instant, which varies depending on where the observer is in the time zone, the sun is directly due north or due south. Then its angle above the horizon, or *altitude*, is measured with a sextant. It is then converted to zenith angle, which is 90 degrees minus altitude. This, then, is combined with the sun's declination (which can be thought of as the latitude of the sun, which varies, as described, from 23$^1$/$_2$ degrees south latitude on or about December 21, to 23$^1$/$_2$ degrees north latitude on or about June 21). The sun's declination is provided in tables, first determined by Prince Henry's cosmographers. Then latitude could be computed with a formula, (that is, Latitude = Zenith +/− declination).

(In the next chapter, Phileas Fogg, a man of endless surprises, will take a sun sight after assuming command of the *Henrietta*.)

By the year 1500—eight years after Columbus "discovered America"—charts showed accurate latitude scales, or north-south lines. Navigators would sail north or south to the latitude of their destination, and then "run down the latitude," or "parallel sail," as this was called, until, it was hoped, they bumped into their east-west destination. This was how Columbus was able to find the "New World"—or whatever he called it—four times.

It was east-west longitude that proved difficult to compute. To hurry that science along, the British Parliament offered a £20,000 prize in 1714 to the person who could find a practical method to determine longitude at sea. John Harrison, a carpenter from Yorkshire, England, produced a chronometer—an accurate timepiece—denoted as H.4 (Harrison's fourth clock) in 1759, which garnered the prize for him.

The chronometer allows the navigator to find his longitude this way: In more basic piloting, the navigator measures an angle with a compass to an object, like a lighthouse, and *if* that object is on the chart, draws that line on the chart to the angle measured. A second line to a second charted object, a buoy, for example, allows the two lines to cross. Where the two lines of position cross, the navigator has a "fix"—a longitude as well as latitude, or a unique address.

In celestial navigation, one is offshore, without landmarks. Thus, the sun or a select group of stars, the "navigational stars," are used as "landmarks." However, since the earth spins, these landmarks rise in the east and set in the west—thus, they are moving targets. Tables in the *Nautical Almanac* tell the navigator exactly where the sun or stars are at any instant. This, then, is the significance of a chronometer, or timepiece, and of the aforementioned Greenwich Mean Time (GMT) and more recently Universal Time (UT). The movements of the sun and stars are given in one time.[1]

---

[1] While we carried a sextant aboard *Commodore Explorer,* as a backup, we never used it. The modern celestial navigator has a much easier time of it, as time from most accurate atomic clocks comes to him over the shortwave radio on stations WWV and WWVH. Also, sight-

Today navigators depend less on chronometer time and the angular measurement of the sun, other stars, and the moon but more on man-made moons, or satellites. It is this method, called GPS, or Global Positioning Satellite, that we used on *Commodore Explorer*. More than two dozen satellites circle the earth at an altitude of about 600 miles (964 km). As the satellite passes overhead, its position from an observer at sea is measured by the Doppler effect—a shift in the frequency of radio signals transmitted from the moving satellite.

When the GPS aboard *Commodore Explorer* said we had crossed the equator—yeah, I know, Jacques, there are several equators out here—France lay about 3,300 nautical miles away to the northeast, at least as the crow flies. How fast would *Commodore Explorer* fly? I wondered, as we had 13 days to reach the finish to break the 80-day record. It was going to be close. Very close. Tick-tock.

From the equator we headed northwest under storm jib and three reefs. That seemed unlikely garb for what should have been the doldrums. As I wrote in my log entry of April 9: "We had 30 knots of northeast trades on the nose. Hard to sleep last few off-watches as the boat is jerking, bouncing, and shaking. Like sleeping in a strange motel bed with a strange woman who has put too many quarters in the shake machine. But you don't have a woman, and there's water rushing by in a roar. . . .

"The weather, however, is warm—a pleasant change from the deep raw cold days of the south, and sailing naked is not uncommon." Then I finished with the words: "In good shape physically and mentally, and boat without a catastrophe is going well. Keep the mast up and avoid gravity storms. Remember, gravity storms give no warn-

---

reduction trigonometry is handled by computers or programmable calculators.

ing.[2] Also as we enter the North Atlantic, the junkyard of millions, we have to hope not to hit anything. Time to make lunch. *Lapin*, anyone?"

On April 10, the next day, I was hanging up my washing on the martingale forward on a beautiful morning as the cat purred along easily at about 14 knots. The equatorial weather had given us an opportunity, at last, to wash our clothes and bodies and bake a bit in the summer sun. Suddenly there was a huge collision—you could hear carbon-fiber shattering—and the boat slowed precipitously. I grabbed the headstay to steady myself. I couldn't understand what we'd hit, as I'd looked forward but seconds before. Then, I ran aft to the starboard cockpit. Behind the boat I saw an upwelling of water, brown blood, and guts, and two whales surfaced. Bruno's worst fears had been realized: I guess the world was a smaller place than he'd figured when he waved me off the whale-avoidance system, because we'd collided with two leviathans. They must have surfaced directly under the hulls of *Commodore Explorer*.

Bruno ran from his office in the starboard hull and grabbed the video camera and started taping. He got about three seconds' worth of tape before the spent battery shut it down.

[2] Before any Jimmy Buffett fans accuse me of stealing the phrase *gravity storm*, know it is the other way around. I got to know Buffett during the America's Cup of 1988, when I sailed with Dennis Conner. Conner and Buffett were friends, dating back to the America's Cup of 1987, in Perth, Western Australia. One day in San Diego, Buffett asked me how it was going. I said fine except for the "gravity storm" that had attacked us the day before when we'd lost the mast on one of Conner's catamarans. Buffett liked the line enough that he used it in his book *Tales from Margaritaville* and later in his song "Gravity Storm." In 1992, he performed a concert in San Diego, during the America's Cup. Before singing the song, he said, "I'd like to thank my friend Cam Lewis for this."

From a hundred yards away, the whales—to me they looked like sperm whales by the inverted canoe–like shape of their heads—started to chase us. In one world cruise, we'd gone from Verne's mostly joyful *Around the World in Eighty Days*, to Conrad's terrifying *Typhoon*, to Melville's equally terrifying *Moby-Dick*. However, *Commodore Explorer* was faster than Captain Ahab's *Pequod*, to be sure—and after ten minutes or so, the whales veered off toward the Caribbean.

By this time, Jacques and Chinois were on deck too. I went to the port hull and tried to lift the port dagger board. It wouldn't go up or down. I looked over the side and could see an eight-foot gash at the waterline. Jacques donned a mask and snorkel and dropped over the side. He needed a bath anyway. He was tethered to *Commodore Explorer* by a harness. Jacques concluded the crack was only a compression ding. When we checked from the inside, it hadn't, seemingly, penetrated the port hull. The dagger board, however, was hanging on by a few threads of fiberglass. Jacques said wait awhile, and it will surely fall off. A couple hours later, after the excitement had passed, and I was in my bunk trying to sleep, I heard the broken-bottom section of the dagger board bounce aft a couple of times against the hull. When the dagger board's bottom broke off, what remained was removed and replaced with the undamaged one from the starboard side. Since that was the last dagger board we had, I hoped we wouldn't hit anything else.

Some magician, I thought: I'd turned a rabbit into two whales.

# In which Detective Fix realizes the error of his ways, but it is too late for Phileas Fogg

"The *China*, in leaving, seemed to have carried off Phileas Fogg's last hope," writes Verne. "None of the other steamers were able to serve his projects." Fogg knew this having consulted *Bradshaw's*, a publication that listed the daily departures of transatlantic steamers.

Passepartout blamed himself for the many delays. "Instead of helping his master, he had not ceased putting obstacles in his path!" This was all the more painful as they'd only missed the *China* by three quarters of an hour. Fogg, however, wasn't outwardly troubled by this. " 'We will consult about what is best tomorrow. Come,' " he said.

His party took rooms at the St. Nicholas on Broadway. Fogg slept "profoundly," while Passepartout and Aouda slept little—so upset were they by the apparent loss of the wager.

Fogg woke up on December 12, 1872, and departed alone for the Hudson River docks. However, he told Passepartout to await his return and asked Aouda to be ready to leave at a moment's notice. From 7:00 A.M., that morning, he had exactly 9 days, 13 hours, and 45 minutes to reach the Reform Club in London.

Many vessels were ready to depart, but they were sailing vessels and thus not fast enough for Fogg's purposes. However, he eventually spotted the *Henrietta*, "a trading vessel, with a screw, well-shaped, whose funnel, puffing a cloud of smoke, indicated that she was getting ready for departure." The boat was iron hulled with a wood superstructure.

Fogg hailed a water taxi and soon found himself aboard the boat. The captain, a man of about fifty, was "a sort of sea-wolf, with big eyes, a complexion of oxidized copper, red hair and thick neck, and a growling voice." Fogg learned from the captain, Andrew Speedy, an American, that he was departing for Bordeaux, France, in an hour's time without cargo and without passengers. " 'Never have passengers. Too much in the way,' " he said.

Fogg asked the captain if his boat was fast. "Between eleven and twelve knots," the appropriately named Speedy assured him. Even though the boat was empty, Fogg's entreaty to carry him and three others to Liverpool was refused. " 'Money,' Fogg assured Speedy, 'is no object.' "

(Why, one wonders, was Fogg planning on four passengers, rather than three: Passepartout, Aouda, and himself? It was, of course, Detective Fix who was the fourth. Was it Fix's ability at whist that had gotten him included?)

" 'To Liverpool? Why not to China?' " said Captain Speedy.

" 'I said Liverpool,' " Fogg rejoined.

" 'No. I am setting out for Bordeaux and shall go to Bordeaux.' "

Up to this point, money, of course, had smoothed Fogg's way around the world. He next offered to pay the freight rate to Liverpool and finally to purchase the vessel. All of which were refused. Fogg asked to make his proposition to the vessel's owners; Captain Speedy said he was the sole owner. In exasperation Fogg finally said, " 'Well, will you carry me to Bordeaux?' "

" 'No, not if you paid me two hundred dollars.' "

" 'I offer you two thousand.'

" 'Apiece?' " said Speedy.

" 'Apiece.' " Every man has his price, and for $8,000 Captain Speedy speedily acquiesced. This conquered, writes Verne, "the repugnance he had for all kinds of passengers. Besides, passengers at two thousand dollars are no longer passengers, but valuable merchandise."

Captain Speedy gave Fogg thirty minutes to return with his party. "To disembark from the *Henrietta*, jump into a hack, hurry to the *St. Nicholas*, and return with Aouda, Passepartout, and even the inseparable Fix, was the work of a brief time, and was performed by Mr. Fogg with the coolness which never abandoned him."

So Fogg paid $2,000 for Detective Fix, who meant to arrest him as soon as Fogg set foot on English soil. Of course, Fogg didn't know this, but Passepartout did. Why he didn't intervene, Verne doesn't explain. Verne's only explanation, "the inseparable Fix," seems insufficient.

The "inseparable Fix," who occasionally was struck by the incongruity of his accepting Phileas Fogg's unstinting generosity, wasn't troubled by it this time. His only worry was for his patron, the Bank of England, which "would certainly not come out of this affair well indemnified," thought the detective. "When they reached England, even if Mr. Fogg did not throw some handfuls of bank-bills into the sea, more than seven thousand pounds would have been spent!"

After her departure, the *Henrietta* passed the lighthouse that marked the entrance to the Hudson River. Missing, of course, at the entrance of the Hudson was the Statue of Liberty, a gift of the French people to mark America's centennial in 1876—some four years after Fogg's fictitious travels. The 151-foot statue opened in 1886.

The *Henrietta* then turned the point of Sandy Hook and entered the Atlantic Ocean, passing New York's Long Island and then

Fire Island, before turning to the northeast for Liverpool, not Bordeaux!

We learn of the course change when at noon the next day a "man mounted the bridge to ascertain the vessel's position." It wasn't Captain Speedy, as might be supposed; rather, it was Phileas Fogg. This trick of trigonometry, seamanship, and the use of a sextant, called a "sun sight," while not the navigator's highest art, as discussed in the previous chapter, is still well beyond the skills of the uninitiated. How had Phileas Fogg come to know this?

In the first chapter, Verne poses the question: "Had [Fogg] travelled? It was likely, for no one seemed to know the world more familiarly; there was no spot so secluded that he did not appear to have an intimate acquaintance with it. He often corrected, with a few clear words, the thousand conjectures advanced by members of the [Reform] club as to lost and unheard-of travellers, pointing out the true probabilities, and seemingly as if gifted with a sort of second sight, so often did events justify his predictions. He must have travelled everywhere, at least in the spirit." Verne could be talking about himself there.

Fogg had taken control of the *Henrietta* by passing out banknotes to sailors and stokers. We learn these seamen were "only occasional crew" and not on the best terms with Captain Speedy. While Verne does not say it, mutiny, be it aboard a military or a civilian ship, was a very serious offense. It was punishable by death in the United States, which Fogg had just left, and in Britain, where he was heading. For example, thirty years prior to the fictitious Fogg-inspired mutiny on the *Henrietta*, a mutiny on the *Somers*, a U.S. naval brig, culminated in the hanging of the son of Secretary of War John Canfield Spencer. Spencer worked in President John Tyler's administration.

It was very apparent, Verne writes, "to see Mr. Fogg manage the craft, that he had been a sailor. . . . Never had the crew seen so jolly and dexterous a fellow. He formed warm friendships with the sailors, and amazed them with his acrobatic feats. He thought they managed the vessel like gentlemen, and that the stokers fired up like heroes. His loquacious good-humour infected everyone. He had forgotten the past, its vexations and delays. He only thought of the end, so nearly accomplished, and sometimes he boiled over with impatience, as if heated by the furnaces of the *Henrietta*."

As for the ungrateful Detective Fix, he now realized that Fogg was both a bank robber and a pirate and worried about Fogg's true plans for the ship. At any moment, he expected Fogg to change course, to head for parts unknown. Parts where his warrant would be worthless.

As Captain Speedy promised, the *Henrietta* cruised at about 12 knots, and at that speed, might be able to "cross the three thousand miles from New York to Liverpool in nine days, between the twelfth and the twenty-first of December," says Verne. Actually the distance between New York and Liverpool is 3,107 nautical miles, which represents another 10 hours of steaming. "No matter, it's enough to mention the error."

During the first few days, "The wind seemed stationary in the north-east," writes Verne, "the sails were hoisted, and the *Henrietta* ploughed across the waves like a real transatlantic steamer." As they neared the Grand Banks off Newfoundland, the barometer began to drop, the cold became sharper, and "the wind veered to the south-east. Mr. Fogg, in order not to deviate from his course, furled his sails and increased the force of the steam; but the vessel's speed slackened, owing to the state of the sea, the long waves of which broke against the *stern* [author's emphasis]." How can headwinds generate waves that break against the stern of the boat? This is a mistake by the translator, because in the French the word is *étrave* meaning "stem," which is the bow or front of the boat.

Then Verne describes Fogg's demeanor when the going got rough: "Phileas Fogg was a bold mariner, and knew how to maintain headway *against* the sea; and he kept on his course without even decreasing his steam."

On December 16, the seventy-fifth day, half of the transatlantic course was completed. The engineer came on deck and brought more bad news to Fogg. " 'Since we started, we have kept up hot fires in all our furnaces, and though we had coal enough to go on short steam from New York to Bordeaux, we haven't enough to go with all steam from New York to Liverpool.' " Fogg said he would reflect on the matter.

If up to this point, the clock had been ticking gently in the background, it was here tolling like the bells of Big Ben in London's Westminster Palace. Back in London when this very bell chimed half-past eleven, Phileas Fogg would have been departing for his beloved Reform Club. That now seemed a lifetime ago.

Passepartout, who overheard this conversation about the dwindling coal supply, related it to Detective Fix. Fix said, " 'Then you believe that we really are going to Liverpool?' "

" 'Of course,' " said the Frenchman.

" 'Ass!' " swore the detective.

Verne writes that "Passepartout was on the point of vigorously resenting the epithet, the reason of which he could not for the life of him comprehend; but he reflected that the unfortunate Fix was probably very much disappointed and humiliated in his self-esteem, after having so awkwardly followed a false scent around the world, and refrained."

After due consideration Fogg announced, " 'Feed all the fires until the coal is exhausted.' " And two days later, on the eighteenth, the coal was about exhausted. This was the seventy-seventh day. After checking his position, Fogg asked Passepartout to bring him Captain Speedy. The Frenchman was unenthusiastic about this errand, however: " 'He will be like a madman!' " Nevertheless, an order is an order, and "in a few moments, with cries and oaths, a bomb appeared on the poop-deck." The "bomb," of course, was Captain Speedy.

It took him several minutes to compose himself sufficiently to spit out one question: " 'Where are we?' he said, with purple face."

" 'Seven hundred and seventy miles from Liverpool,' " answered Fogg with "imperturbable calmness."

" 'Pirate!' " cried Captain Speedy.

" 'I have sent for you, sir—'

" 'Pickaroon!'

" '—Sir . . . to ask you to sell me your vessel,' " continued Fogg.

" 'No! By all the devils, no!'

" 'But I shall be obliged to burn her.'

" 'Burn the *Henrietta!*'

" 'Yes; at least the upper part of her. The coal has given out.'

" 'Burn my vessel,' replied Captain Speedy, who could scarcely pronounce the words. 'A vessel worth fifty thousand dollars!'

" 'Here are sixty thousand,' replied Fogg, handing the captain a roll of bank bills. This had a prodigious effect on Andrew Speedy. An American can scarcely remain unmoved at the sight of sixty thousand dollars. "The captain forgot in an instant his anger, his imprisonment, and all his grudges against his passenger. The *Henrietta* was twenty years old; it was a great bargain. The bomb would not go off after all. Mr. Fogg had taken away the match."

Before agreeing to the proposal Captain Speedy asked if he might reclaim the vessel's iron hull and engines. Fogg agreed and the deal was struck.

Detective Fix, however, was "apoplectic" about Fogg's latest extravagance, as his reward ("five percent on the sum that might be recovered") was diminishing to nothing as rapidly as the coal supply.

Then Fogg sent Passepartout for the wood, which the Frenchman attacked with an ax and with relish. First to feed the hungry boilers were the seats, then the bunks, and frames. Next went the poop deck, cabins, more bunks, and the spare deck [whatever that is?]. Then went the masts, rafts, spars, railings, fittings, the greater part of the deck, and topsides.

It was a beast feeding upon itself. By the twentieth of December, on the seventy-ninth day, the *Henrietta* was reduced to nothing but a hull. However, this day they sighted Fastnet Rock and the Irish coast. "By ten in the evening they were passing Queenstown. Phileas Fogg had only twenty-four hours more in which to get to London; that length of time was necessary to reach Liverpool, with all steam on. And the steam was about to give out altogether!" Tick-tock!

Even Captain Speedy, "who was now deeply interested in Mr. Fogg's project," was saddened by the impossibility of completing the journey in time. "I really commiserate you. Everything is against you. We are only opposite Queenstown."

Fogg wondered if they could enter this harbor. Captain Speedy said they must wait three hours for high tide. " 'Stay,' " replied Fogg calmly.

You will recall that Verne said of Fogg, "There was no spot so secluded that he did not appear to have an intimate acquaintance with it." Fogg had one more inspiration. "Queenstown," Verne writes, "is the Irish port at which the transatlantic steamers stop to put off the mails. These mails are carried to Dublin by express trains always held in readiness to start; from Dublin they are sent on to Liverpool by the most rapid boats, and thus gain twelve hours on the Atlantic steamers.

"Phileas Fogg counted on gaining twelve hours in the same way. Instead of arriving at Liverpool the next evening by the *Henrietta*, he would be there by noon, and would therefore have time to reach London before a quarter before nine in the evening."

At one o'clock in the morning, Fogg and his party departed the *Henrietta* in Queenstown Harbor, near Cork. He had 19 hours and 45 minutes to reach the Reform Club.

Now on English soil, we expect Detective Fix to arrest Phileas Fogg; however, he hesitated. "Why?" Verne poses. "What struggle was going on within him? Had he changed his mind about 'his man'? Did he understand that he had made a grave mistake? He did not however, abandon Mr. Fogg."

Fogg's party of four boarded the train for Dublin, which arrived there at dawn on the final day. From the train, they immediately boarded the steamer for Liverpool. They arrived in Liverpool at twenty minutes before twelve. They were only six hours distant from London. That would put them in London before six in the evening, two hours and forty-five minutes before the witching hour of eight forty-five.

At that moment, however, Detective Fix intervened. " 'I arrest you in the Queen's name!' " he said.

Fogg went calmly and was imprisoned in the Custom House in Liverpool. He was to be transferred to London the next day, after the time limit had expired.

Verne writes: "Passepartout, when he saw his master arrested, would have fallen upon Fix, had he not been held back by some policeman. Aouda was thunderstruck at the suddenness of an event which she could not understand. Passepartout explained to her how it was that the honest and courageous Fogg was arrested as a robber. The young woman's heart revolted against so heinous a charge, and when she saw that she could attempt or do nothing to save her protector, wept bitterly.

"The thought then struck Passepartout that he was the cause of this new misfortune! Had he not concealed Fix's errand from his master? When Fix revealed his true character and purpose, why had he not told Mr. Fogg? If the latter had been warned, he would no doubt have given Fix proof of his innocence, and satisfied him of his mistake; at least, Fix would not have continued his journey at the expense and on the heels of his master, only to arrest him the moment he set foot on English soil. Passepartout wept till he was blind, and felt like blowing his brains out."

While Aouda and Passepartout wept, Fogg sat in his jail cell seemingly unperturbed, as was his way. Verne writes, "Mr. Fogg carefully put his watch upon the table, and observed its advancing hands. Not a word escaped his lips, but his look was singularly set and stern. The situation, in any event, was a terrible one, and might be thus stated: If Phileas Fogg was honest, he was ruined. If he was a knave, he was caught."

At thirty-three minutes past two, Fogg heard a noise outside his cell. The iron door swung open, and there was Passepartout, Aouda, and Detective Fix. Said Fix, " 'Sir—forgive me—a most—unfortunate resemblance—robber arrested three days ago—you —are free!' "

Phileas Fogg walked toward the detective and looked at him directly. "And with the only rapid motion he had ever made in his life, or which he ever would make, drew back his arms, and with the precision of a machine, knocked Fix down.

" 'Well hit!' cried Passepartout. 'Parbleu! That's what you might call a good application of English fists!' "

Fogg's party of three now went immediately to the train station. It was two-forty. TICK-TOCK!

Asked if there was an express train for London, Fogg learned it had left thirty-five minutes before. He ordered a special train; however, railroad regulations would not allow it to leave until three o'clock. Even then the journey to London might be possible; however there were "forced delays."

When they arrived, at last, in London, all the clocks there "were striking ten minutes before nine," writes Verne. As clocks normally strike four times an hour, every fifteen minutes beginning on the hour, even the translator has to chuckle in a footnote: "A somewhat remarkable eccentricity on the part of the London clocks?"

Nevertheless, "Having made the tour of the world, he was behind-hand five minutes," says Verne. "He had lost the wager!"

Clocks don't lie. Or do they?

# In which we
# hear music worthy
# of the gods
# and dream of home

There was no Easter bunny for us on Sunday, April 11, 1993; nor was there any wind. What there was, however, was a swimming party. We all dove in naked as *Commodore Explorer* drifted ever so slowly toward France. The feeling was sublime as Mother Ocean closed around me and started lapping away at the grease and gristle that had accumulated over the past 70 days, despite my best efforts.

For several minutes that day we were suspended in time and space: We'd stopped racing, as in the dearth of wind there was really nowhere to go. Also, the still water ran deep. The bottom was 14,000 feet beneath us. That's a fact that can rivet your attention. Further, South America, the closest land, was 960 nautical miles to the southwest; the Cape Verde Islands were 1,080 miles due east; and should we miss them if adrift, which seemed quite likely, it was 1,560 miles to Africa.

However, we were all tied to the boat with harnesses in case it bolted for the barn. Even then, I felt like a stranger in a strange land, as man does not belong out at sea frolicking in a bottomless blue void.

There's a story—perhaps apocryphal—about a large yacht found adrift in the Mediterranean and abandoned. When the yacht was found, the original theory was the party had been murdered by pirates and dumped overboard. Another theory was that they'd had a spontaneous swimming party. Everyone dove in but they'd neglected to lower the swim ladder. Without it, they just couldn't get back aboard.

To test this theory a water-polo team was enlisted to try to board the boat from the water without the benefit of a ladder. While no one swims more strongly or more vertically than a water-polo player, not one of them could make it back aboard. *Commodore Explorer* did have handrails on the transom that made for solid hand and footholds, but I thought of that story then.

The swim also gave us a chance to look at the crack on the port hull, courtesy of Moby-Dick and friend, which, as far as cracks go, was truly impressive. For a moment I had that giddy sense of peering over the edge of Grand Canyon —thinking about how little separated us from the edge.

Easter Sunday we did a painfully slow 240 miles; probably as punishment for my "faux pas"—yes, my French was improving. The next day, April 12, was even worse, as we did about 170 miles. The third day we did 180 miles. Tick-Tock.

On this day, we played boccie, or boules, a game we'd played from time to time when the going got slow. The "target jack" was a funnel, used to feed the diesel heaters. You'd throw it the length of the boat, and the pointy end would often stick in the trampoline. Rather than "boules," or balls, we used the thermoses that I used to make, eat, and store hot food. It was hard to make them roll straight toward the target jack, but the game proved a pleasant enough diversion on a summerlike day near the center of the planet. While we had miles and miles to go, we had no way to get there at that moment. Like Fogg, one must be realistic.

At this point, Bruno bet his fortune, or lack of one, by heading well to the west. His hope was that we'd avoid the headwinds of the northeast trades that seemed bent on blocking us from France. By heading northwest on those three painful days, we kept the wind off the bow. More to the point, Bruno hoped that once we got far enough north we could ride the prevailing westerlies that blow from America to Europe. He also hoped to hitch a ride on the Gulf Stream—that meandering river of warm water in the ocean that travels in the same direction as the westerly winds—toward France. If you've ever wondered why there are palm trees in the Isles of Scilly, some 25 miles (40 km) from the southwest corner of England, look to the Gulf Stream. For those three glacially slow days, it looked as if we'd lost the bet. Tick-Tock!

April 15, our seventy-fourth day at sea, began with a bang, not a whimper. You are but half asleep in a passage like this, and anything that goes bump in the night—or day —awakens you instantly with an adrenaline rush. It must be what life is like along the San Andreas Fault.

As I slept in the port hull, I heard a crash, and the boat ground to a halt. I was on deck in an instant. Five days after we'd hit two whales, our dagger board had struck a semisubmerged log but, amazingly, didn't break. Without the directional stability of our last dagger board—the one borrowed from the starboard hull—we'd never have gotten home to France. The log was twenty feet long and three feet around. We wrestled the boat off it and continued on, but worried what else lay in wait, as we were obviously and lamentably sailing in modern man's garbage dump.

It was a bad start to the day, but things later changed. The longed-for westerlies began to blow, from America toward Europe. With them, Bruno made a gradual right-hand turn to the northeast. Our track now paralleled that of Phileas Fogg's Atlantic crossing. On this day, our seventy-fourth, we did 480 nautical miles. It was pure pedal-to-the-metal speed, and with it our spirits soared.

All of us, I know, were dreaming of home. Molly would be waiting for me in France, as would my father and stepmother. Nikki, Chinois's wife, would be waiting for him. Molly and Nikki had discovered they were pregnant at the same time, and I wondered what they'd look like. Michelle and Antoine, Marc's wife and new son that he had barely seen before we left, would certainly be waiting for him, as would Bruno's girlfriend, Catherine. Who would be waiting for Jacques? I wondered, as his girlfriend lived in Boston. Jacques didn't have any money—he'd just recently received his first credit card—and his girlfriend, Sherri, who was a student and working three jobs, had no extra cash either. She'd telexed Jacques to say that she couldn't afford the airplane fare; I'd found this message when paging through some computer files.

Without telling Jacques, I got Bruno, Marc, and Chinois to chip in with me to buy Sherri an airplane ticket to France. I called my sisters in Boston and New York on the SSB radio and asked them to organize it, which they did. This wasn't easy to do because Sherri was a moving target, and so were we. It would, I hoped, be a nice surprise for Jacques.

Another day, another 507 nautical miles!—our best speed to date. Thus in two days, we had traveled almost a thousand miles, for an average speed of just under 21 knots. In answer to Bruno's prayers—all of our prayers—the westerlies were roaring, as was our little kitty cat.

In the sun this day, April 17, Bruno had Beethoven's *Ninth Symphony* cranked up on the boat's CD. Whatever your musical tastes might be, to hear the orchestra, the solo baritone, and chorus perform it and not to get chills, you'd have to be dead or deaf. I can't listen to it without thinking, at least for a moment, what a wonderful creature is man. Or at least was Beethoven. It is music worthy of the gods—music of a conquerer. "With whom need I be afraid of measuring my strength?" Beethoven once asked.

Bruno was obviously moved by the music. He told me that when he was ten years old, he accompanied his mother to the symphony in Paris. As a captain in the merchant marines, his father was often away from home. Bruno and his mother heard Beethoven's *Ninth Symphony*. He said that this was the first time he ever saw his mother cry.

From this conversation, I thought about my mother too. It was at the University of Virginia that my mother—a "faculty brat" and one of very few females on campus—and my father, George Lewis, met.

After they were married, they moved to Sherborn, Massachusetts, where my father had grown up. His mother was a Saltonstall (Muriel Gurden Saltonstall Lewis). She had lived there along with her two brothers, Leverett and Richard Saltonstall. Leverett, as mentioned, was governor of Massachusetts for six years, 1938–44. Before him, eight other ancestors had served as governors of Massachusetts. Leverett was next a U.S. Senator for 23 years, 1944–67, as well as the Republican whip. Richard Saltonstall invented mutual funds in 1924 with two friends, Paul Cabot and Richard Paine.

Like Bruno, I know when I first saw my mother cry. I was about twelve, and she announced that she and my father were getting a divorce. I begged her not to do that, as we had, at least in my eyes, such a wonderful family. She had tears in her eyes, and so did I. When my mother and father divorced, she moved into a house on the pond, not a quarter mile from my father's house.

I attended boarding schools through my formative years. However, when I was home I'd live with whichever parent I thought would give me the most freedom—allow me to have the most fun. After the strict regimen of boarding school, I thought I deserved fun. An idea I haven't completely shaken to this day. There was really no rhyme or reason as to which parent I stayed with; it was all pleasure-driven.

My mother was a tall woman, five feet eleven inches, consistent with her family's warrior past, and, outwardly at least, extremely sunny. However, she was what was then termed a "manic-depressive." Today, there's a fancier name for it—"bipolar disorder"—and a fancier drug to treat it: Prozac. Then they prescribed Valium, which, sadly, my mother mixed with alcohol.

When I was seventeen, I was home for a weekend from Middlesex, my prep school in Concord, Massachusetts, and staying at my mother's house, as was my youngest sister, Lynnie, then aged eleven, who lived with Mother. A girl-friend, Amy Wood, and I were going to the movies, and my mother wished to go too. Sister Lynnie would be going to dance class with our neighbor Louisa Browne, who taught the class. However, my mother had had a few drinks, and I asked her not to drink anymore. When she mixed alcohol with her medications, she wasn't that easy to be around. She continued drinking, however, so I told her she should stay home.

When I returned after the movie, there were an ambu-lance and police cars, with those awful flashing lights, in the driveway. Despite my mother's warrior forebears, she had lost her greatest battle. She had died of an overdose.

She'd been discovered by my sister Lynnie and our neighbor Louisa Browne, when they returned from dance class. I had to call my older brother, George, who was attending the University of Virginia—the school my father and mother had attended and where they had met, and which my sisters would later attend. He was at a fraternity party at the time and not wholly there. "George" I said, "Mom has died. You better come home."

Then I had to call my father, who was out of town. However, he wasn't far from my sister Lisa, who was at school outside of Hartford, Connecticut. He told her of Mother's death and brought her home.

Next, I had to figure out how to handle Lynnie, who was devastated by my mother's death and by the fact that she had discovered it. I was seventeen and had to try to make sense of this. To her and to me. None of us had ever really understood our mother's disease and how difficult her life was. She fought hard, but just couldn't stay balanced. Manic depression is a horrible, devastating, family-wrecking, genetically transmitted defect in our family, and all I hope is that my relatives, offspring, and I can be spared.

My innocence ended that night. While this wasn't my mother's first suicide attempt, I've often wondered if I'd allowed her to go to the movies, would she still be alive?

My mother's death left me with an overwhelming sense of how short and precious our journey on this planet is. I wish to do and see as much as I can. While I can.

Or as John Donne once put it so much better: "No man is an island entire of itself; . . . any man's death diminishes me, because I am involved in mankind; and therefore never send to know for whom the bell tolls; it tolls for thee."

# In which Aouda seizes the moment and her man, and Fogg wins his bet after all

---

The bells had certainly tolled for Phileas Fogg. Nevertheless, he "bore his misfortune with his habitual tranquility," writes Verne. That said, the author next summarizes his situation, which appears bleak. "Ruined! And by the blundering of the detective! After having steadily traversed that long journey, overcome a hundred obstacles, braved many dangers, and still found time to do some good on his way to fail near the goal by a sudden event which he could not have foreseen, and against which he was unarmed; it was terrible! But a few pounds were left of the large sum he carried with him. There only remained of his fortune the twenty thousand pounds deposited at Barings, and this amount he owed to his friends of the Reform Club. So great had been the expense of his tour, that, even had he won, it would not have enriched him. . . ."

Yet despite being "ruined!"—a word we will hear often in this chapter—Fogg still worried about Aouda's comfort. A room was set up for her at his mansion on Saville Row. Aouda was, we learn, still overwhelmed by grief for her protector.

Passepartout first went up to his room, to turn off the gas that had been burning at his expense for the past 80 days. "He had found in the letter-box a bill from the gas company, and he thought it more than time to put a stop to this expense, which he had been doomed to bear."

Once he turned the gas off, the Frenchman worried about Fogg committing some self-destructive act. "Knowing that Englishmen governed by a fixed idea sometimes resort to the desperate expedient of suicide, Passepartout kept a narrow watch upon his master, though he carefully concealed the appearance of so doing."

Throughout that first night back in London, Passepartout watched "like a faithful dog, at his master's door." Thus, he had no sleep. Aouda slept not at all either.

In the morning, Fogg told Passepartout to prepare his breakfast, a cup of tea and a chop, and breakfast for Aouda, to be served later. He would not join her for breakfast or dinner, "as his time would be absorbed all day in putting his affairs to right." He wished to have a private conversation with her that evening, however; and asked Passepartout to convey that message to her.

Passepartout was consumed with guilt, primarily because of his failure to warn Mr. Fogg about the rat in their midst: Detective Fix. Writes Verne: "Yes! if he had warned Mr. Fogg, and had betrayed Fix's projects to him, his master would certainly not have given the detective passage to Liverpool and then—"

Passepartout's guilt bubbles over at this instant: " 'My master! Mr. Fogg! Why do you not curse me? It was my fault that—'

" 'I blame no one,' returned Phileas Fogg, with perfect calmness. 'Go!' "

The Frenchman went to Aouda's room, to deliver Fogg's message. " 'Madam,' he added, 'I can do nothing myself—nothing! I have no influence over my master; but you, perhaps—'

" 'What influence could I have? . . . Mr. Fogg is influenced by no one. Has he ever understood that my gratitude to him is overflowing? Has he ever read my heart? My friend, he must not be left alone an instant! You say he is going to speak with me this evening?'

" 'Yes, madam,' " said the servant. " 'Probably to arrange for your protection and comfort in England.' "

This was Sunday, Verne tells us, and on any other Sunday— indeed any day—Mr. Fogg would have departed for his club when the Westminster clock struck half-past eleven. Things were very different now, Verne writes: "Why should he present himself at the Reform? His friends no longer expected him there. As Phileas Fogg had not appeared in the saloon on the evening before (Saturday, the twenty-first of December, at a quarter before nine), he had lost his wager. It was not even necessary that he should go to his bankers for the twenty thousand pounds; for his antagonists already had his check in their hands, and they had only to fill it out and send it to the Barings to have the amount transferred to their credit."

As Fogg busied himself in his room, Passepartout kept ascending and descending the steps, making sure his master was all right. He'd occasionally listened at the door, even spied on his master through the keyhole.

At about half-past seven that evening, Fogg sent for Aouda. She found him in a chair, near the fireplace. He sat for several minutes before speaking. Finally he turned his eyes on Aouda and said, " 'Madam . . . will you pardon me for bringing you to England?'

" 'I, Mr. Fogg!' replied Aouda, checking the pulsations of her heart.

" 'Please let me finish,' returned Mr. Fogg. 'When I decided to bring you far away from the country which was so unsafe for you, I was rich, and counted on putting a portion of my fortune at your disposal; then your existence would have been free and happy. But now I am ruined.'

" 'I know it, Mr. Fogg . . . and I ask you, in my turn, will you forgive me for having followed you, and—who knows?—for having, perhaps, delayed you, and thus contributed to your ruin?' "

Fogg continued in his gallant way: " 'Madam, you could not remain in India, and your safety could only be assured by bringing you to such a distance that your persecutors could not take you.'

" 'So, Mr. Fogg,' resumed Aouda, 'not content with rescuing me from a terrible death, you thought yourself bound to secure my comfort in a foreign land?'

" 'Yes, madam; but circumstances have been against me. Still, I beg to place the little I have left at your service.'

" 'But what will become of you, Mr. Fogg?' "

Fogg answered, " 'I have need of nothing.' "

Aouda suggested that Fogg's friends or relatives might be willing to help him. Fogg said he had neither.

" 'I pity you, then, Mr. Fogg, for solitude is a sad thing, with no heart to which to confide your griefs. They say, though, that misery itself, shared by two sympathetic souls, may be borne with patience.'

" 'They say so, madam.' "

Then Aouda, rising in passion, seized Phileas Fogg's hand and the moment. " 'Mr. Fogg . . . do you wish at once a kinswoman and friend? Will you have me for your wife?' "

Fogg stood too. There was an unusual light in his eyes, and his lips trembled in a passion heretofore thought impossible. Aouda stared at his face, and Verne describes what Fogg suddenly saw there with the clarity of dawn: "The sincerity, rectitude, firmness, and sweetness of this soft glance of a noble woman, who could dare all to save him to whom she owed all, at first astonished, then penetrated him." Fogg said, " 'I love you! Yes, by all that is holiest, I love you, and I am entirely yours!' "

Passepartout was called. As he entered the room, he saw that Mr. Fogg and Aouda were holding hands and understood all. Passepartout's "big round face became as radiant as the tropical sun at its zenith," writes Verne. For Passepartout and Fogg and Aouda, this is obviously "high noon."

Fogg asked his servant if it was too late to ask the Reverend Samuel Wilson, of Marylebone parish, to officiate at the ceremony. " 'Never too late,' " said Passepartout. It was then five minutes past eight. " 'Will it be for to-morrow, Monday?' " the Frenchman asked Mr. Fogg. Both Fogg and Aouda agreed that the wedding would be "to-morrow, Monday."

Then Verne shifts scenes. Unbeknownst to Fogg, the London newspapers had covered his journey. First, it had been followed like a horse race, and many a wager for or against Fogg had been placed by the sporting public. These bets became known as "Phileas Fogg bonds." Then when the public learned that the authorities had linked Fogg to the robbery at the Bank of England, it was written about as if it were a crime story with the criminal on the lam. With the arrest and confession of the real robber, a James Strand, the newspapers and the public began focusing again on the sporting nature of the proposition. "The 'Phileas Fogg bonds' again became negotiable and many new wagers were made," writes Verne.

The public, Verne tells us, had heard nothing of Fogg, since the real robber's arrest on December 17 and hungered for news of him. "Was he dead? Had he abandoned the effort, or was he continuing his journey along the route agreed upon? And would he appear on Saturday, the twenty-first of December, at a quarter before nine in the evening, on the threshold of the Reform Club saloon?

"The anxiety in which, for three days, London society existed, cannot be described. Telegrams were sent to America and Asia for news of Phileas Fogg. Messengers were dispatched to the house in Saville Row morning and evening. No news. The police were ignorant of what had become of the detective, Fix, who had so unfortunately followed up a false scent. Bets increased, nevertheless, in number and in value. Phileas Fogg, like a race-horse, was drawing near his last turning point."

On the evening that Fogg was expected a curious and substantial crowd formed around the Reform Club. The police had to be called in to control them. Fogg's five "antagonists," writes Verne, awaited him in the saloon of the club. When the clock in the club indicated "twenty minutes past eight," Andrew Stuart, the engineer, announced, " 'Gentlemen, in twenty minutes the time agreed upon between Mr. Fogg and ourselves will have expired.' " Actually, this entire sequence is mistranslated as in the French version, Verne notes the time as *"huit heures vingt-cinq"* [8:25] and the time limit as in *"vingt* [20] *minutes."*

" 'What time did the last train arrive from Liverpool?' " asked Thomas Flanagan, a brewer.

" 'At twenty-three minutes past seven,' " said Gauthier Ralph, the director of the Bank of England, where the very robbery that had so much affected Fogg's fortunes had transpired. We learn the next train does not arrive until ten minutes after twelve.

" 'Well, gentlemen,' continued Stuart, 'if Phileas Fogg had come in the 7:23 train, he would have got here by this time. We can therefore regard the bet as won.' "

Samuel Fallentin, another banker, cautioned them not to be too hasty. " 'You know that Mr. Fogg is very eccentric. His punctuality is well known; he never arrives too soon, or too late; and I should not be surprised if he appeared before us at the last minute.' "

When the hands of the clock at the Reform Club said twenty minutes to nine, five minutes before the witching hour, Mr. Fallentin proposed a rubber of whist. Verne describes their painful waiting: "Certainly, however secure they felt, minutes had never seemed so long to them!" They couldn't keep their eyes off the clock and their minds on the game. They also listened to the telltale TICK-TOCK! of the clock.

" 'Sixteen minutes to nine!' said John Sullivan, in a voice which betrayed his emotion." The £20,000 wager would be won or lost in the next minute. They suspended their card game and "counted the seconds."

Verne writes, "At the fortieth second, nothing. At the fiftieth, still nothing.

"At the fifty-fifth, a loud cry was heard in the street, followed by applause, hurrahs, and some fierce growls. . . .

"At the fifty-seventh second the door of the saloon opened; and the pendulum had not beat the sixtieth second when Phileas Fogg appeared, followed by an excited crowd who had forced their way through the club doors, and in his calm voice, said, 'Here I am, gentlemen.'"

Do clocks lie? How had Phileas Fogg snatched victory from the jaws of defeat? Verne describes the dénouement this way:

When Passepartout was sent for the Reverend Samuel Wilson to officiate at the marriage, it was five minutes past eight. Passepartout had to wait twenty minutes for Reverend Wilson to appear. He left the Reverend's house at thirty-five minutes past eight and was on the run. "He ran along the street as never man was seen to run before, overturning passers-by, rushing over the sidewalk like a waterspout." He reached Fogg's house, by thirty-eight minutes past eight.

Immediately, he delivered this message: " 'My master!' gasped Passepartout—'marriage—impossible—'

" 'Impossible?'

" 'Impossible—for to-morrow.'

" 'Why so?'

" 'Because to-morrow—is Sunday!'

" 'Monday,' " punctiliously replied Mr. Fogg.

" 'No—to-day—is Saturday.'

" 'Saturday? Impossible!'

" 'Yes, yes, yes, yes,' cried Passepartout. 'You have made a mistake of one day. We arrived twenty-four hours ahead of time; but there are only ten minutes left!' " [Actually, there were only seven minutes left—a mistake in both the French and the English. But "no matter; it's enough to mention the error."]

Passepartout seized Fogg by the collar and dragged him along the street. They flagged down a carriage and promised the driver £100 to get them to the Reform Club—rather than the church—on time. In this mad dash, they ran "over two dogs and overturned five carriages."

Thus, Phileas Fogg traveled around the world in 80 days and won his wager of £20,000.

Verne summarizes Fogg's and presumably the reader's confusion. "How was it that a man so exact and fastidious could have made this error of a day? How came he to think that he had arrived in London on Saturday, the twenty-first day of December, when it was really Friday, the twentieth, the seventy-ninth day only from his departure?

"The cause of the error is simple.

"Phileas Fogg had, without suspecting it, gained one day on his journey, and this merely because he had travelled constantly *eastward*; he would, on the contrary, have lost a day, had he gone in the opposite direction, that is, *westward*."

Because he had traveled eastward toward the rising sun, "the days diminished for him as many times four minutes as he crossed degrees in this direction. There are three hundred and sixty degrees on the circumference of the earth; and these three hundred and sixty degrees, multiplied by four minutes, gives precisely twenty-four hours—that is, the day unconsciously gained. In other words, while Phileas Fogg, going eastward, saw the sun pass the meridian *eighty* times, his friends in London only saw it pass the meridian *seventy-nine* times. This is why they awaited him at the Reform Club on Saturday, and not Sunday, as Mr. Fogg thought."

And what of Passepartout's family watch that always kept London time? It "would have betrayed this fact, if it had marked the days as well as the hours and minutes!" This feature, of course, is common today on the meanest quartz watches that cost a couple dollars.

So Phileas Fogg won £20,000 pounds, or about $60,000. His expenses, we learn at this point, had been £19,000. Writes Verne, "His object was, however, to be victorious and not to win money. He divided the one thousand pounds that remained between Passepartout and the unfortunate Fix, against whom he cherished no grudge. He deducted, however, from Passepartout's share the cost of the gas which had burned in his room for nineteen hundred and twenty hours, for the sake of regularity."

Later that evening, Mr. Fogg asked Aouda if their marriage was still agreeable to her. " 'Mr. Fogg' replied she, 'it is for me to ask that question. You were ruined, but now you are rich again.'

" 'Pardon me, madam; my fortune belongs to you. If you had not suggested our marriage, my servant would not have gone to Reverend Samuel Wilson's, I should not have been apprised of my error, and—'

" 'Dear Mr. Fogg!' " said Aouda.

" 'Dear Aouda!' " Fogg responded with equal tenderness.

Their marriage took place forty-eight hours later. Passepartout gave the bride away, which was only appropriate, as he had saved her life.

# In which a voice on the radio said, *"Fini"*

On April 17, 1993, our seventy-sixth day at sea, all that separated us from France was about 1,000 nautical miles. In the early morning watch, confused 20-foot seas lapped at Chinois and Jacques in the cockpit of *Commodore Explorer*. One broke aboard and smacked Chinois, who was wet and shaken but unharmed.

After this, Jacques relieved Chinois at the wheel. Suddenly, another wave broke aboard, hurling both Jacques and Chinois toward the back of the boat. Before his harness could arrest him, Jacques's head smashed into the back beam. There was blood everywhere. He was taken below, where his wound was cleaned and his head bandaged.

All of this had taken place while Marc and I slept. When we got on deck to relieve them, Jacques was sporting a bandage under a cap. He told us what had happened. Apparently there was a lot of blood, typical of a head wound, but fortunately not much damage. Then I noticed Jacques was wearing the polar-fleece baseball-style cap that I'd given to Molly for Christmas. "Hey, Jacques! That's Molly's hat!" I said. He said, "Oh, I found it in the house. It looked warm so I took it."

The big days that had started when we reached the westerlies continued unabated. On April 17, the day Bruno and I listened to Beethoven's "Ode to Joy," we did 507 nautical miles, our best speed to date. That is an average speed of 21 knots. At one point, I steered the catamaran at a solid 29 knots. Bruno came on deck to give me a "speeding ticket" and to relieve me—that was my punishment. I went below-decks to cook but noticed on the repeater down there that Bruno was doing 32 knots! What we had here was a high-seas drag race between a Frenchman and an American.

I had a couple of other tricks in my repertoire, however. On one watch, on this day, I flew the windward hull for almost the entire time. It was analogous to flying a hull on a 16-foot Hobie Cat; however, this "Hobie Cat" is 86 feet long, 45 feet wide, and has a wing mast that towers 110 feet in the air. By now, having girded most of the globe, *Commodore Explorer* felt as familiar and as nonthreatening to me as a Hobie.

For the modern voyager, "Water, water, everywhere/ Nor any drop to drink" is no longer a problem, due to the desalinator, which uses reverse osmosis to turn salt water into fresh water. At least most of the time. During this watch, the desalinator stopped working. This was more a nuisance than life threatening, as we had sufficient water for drinking and cooking to make it back to France. However, if we wanted to look sharp when we returned to civilization—none of us was sure we wanted to—we needed water for sink baths and, perhaps, shaving. So Chinois carefully took the desalinator apart. It took him about two hours to do this.

Once he was into the guts, however, he found nothing

amiss. Then he pondered it for a while, shifting from micromechanics to macromechanics. He realized that by flying the hull, as I had been doing, I had raised the water-intake valve out of the water. Thus, the desalinator had been sucking air, not water. Exasperated, Chinois put the desalinator back together and told me to put the hull down at least long enough for him to make water. The "rain-maker," as I thought of it, worked fine after that.

In hindsight, this drag race or game of chicken was crazy, as we could have so easily broken the boat when we were so near to success. Boys will be boys, after all, and it was irresistible if irresponsible. It was just time to kick up our heels.

At the same time as we played these adolescent, macho games, I worried—we all did—about hitting something. From whales to logs, this was beginning to seem almost a daily occurrence. Also, we worried about the mast falling down, as it had on Philippe Poupon's *Fleury Michon* in the Vendée Globe Race that had finished in France the month before. Then we worried inordinately about the wind shutting down. Fogg could burn his boat *Henrietta*, when he ran out of coal in the North Atlantic. Without an engine, however, we could burn nothing, except, of course, precious time. Besides, if we had had an engine to turn on, it would have been a violation of the rules. Fogg had no such rules to constrain him.

The first tangible evidence of home arrived on April 18, our seventy-seventh day at sea, in the form of a French naval frigate. It had been looking for us. The Navy launched a helicopter that spent several hours filming us between fuel stops. It was pretty interesting to see these guys, just playing around, burning up taxpayers' francs. Is France a great country, or what?

The presence of this behemoth was strange, however. It seemed as if we were playing a pilot fish to a shark; however, the pilot fish had become the star attraction. Yet the attention was welcome at the same time. Do animals in zoos feel this same sort of ambivalence? I wondered. Are they happy for the attention, yet at the same time are they made wary and uncomfortable by it? At times this got awkward—particularly since there was a "lack of accommodations" on *Commodore Explorer*.

As we closed on the finish, messages continued to pour in on the fax and telex. Radio France, one of our sponsors, asked its listeners to send messages of encouragement to us. By the time we finished, there were 10,000 of them. Radio France sorted through them and sent us the ones it thought most interesting. We later saw all of them at a reception that Radio France hosted for us back in France.

One that made the cut was from a famous French woman marathoner who wrote about not quitting; it was reminiscent of the Robert Service poem "The Quitter" that had arrived earlier and anonymously. The runner wrote that once she was in a marathon and couldn't imagine finishing. She didn't feel very well. Finally, she crested a hill that seemed to be sucking the life from her, and there she saw a friend who encouraged her to go on—to keep putting one foot in front of the other. She did that and not only finished the race but won it.

Bruno also received words of encouragement from a fisherman, who wrote about his father, a fisherman, too, who had been injured in a fishing accident, and as a result had been bedridden. He hadn't walked in six years. However, for the first time since the accident, he'd gotten out of bed to turn on the television to find out how we were doing—whether we were going to make it in under 80 days. This message really moved Bruno. Later, when we entered the Bay of Biscay and passed right by this fisherman's boat, Bruno got on the radio, and the two of them started yammering away as if they were best friends. There were other fishing boats out there, and they took a break from their work to sound their horns and to give us waves of encouragement. In France there is a great affinity between fisherman and sailors—particularly multihull sailors.

Bruno also received more telexes from his homeless friend, offering us words of encouragement. This guy couldn't afford to put a roof over his head, but found the money and method to send us messages on the telex.

Early on our seventy-ninth day at sea, another helicopter arrived carrying members of the press. They wanted to burn some film on us, but were nearly out of fuel. The captain of the French destroyer invited them to land on their flight deck to refuel. And to have coffee and baguettes. This they did. Believe me, such hospitality is uniquely French. Once aloft again, they filmed us, and then Bruno gave a representative of Radio France, who was also aboard the helicopter, an interview.

Later on this day, a 200-foot ferryboat joined us. It carried some journalists, but many more interested spectators. They had come from France to see us break the fictitious record of Jules Verne. Though the wind was dying, the seas were sloppy and considerable. It had to be uncomfortable, and a number of them were making "wild vomits," as author Richard Henry Dana, Jr., described it, into the sea. Nevertheless, they had taken the trouble to come out here and to wave at us, and we all waved back. I was beginning to have a sense of what a big story this was back in France.

In due time, we started hamming it up for the hometown crowd. We played some boules, or boccie, as described, and then Jacques and I played some soccer, on our floating tennis court, using a plastic fuel can for the ball. The spectators on the ferryboat seem to enjoy the effort we made for them, if not the skill we possessed. Meanwhile, fixed-wing aircraft, carrying photographers and journalists, and sportfishing boats, carrying similar passengers, had started to arrive too. As the still cameras snapped and video cameras whirled, Bruno was having us change gear and clothes to satisfy sponsors who had given us their stuff. This is why we appeared in so many ensembles in the various pictures that were published and videos that were shown on television in France. It was amusing and at the same time bothersome to have to change clothes so often.

As the day wore on, the wind grew tired. I held a large sign up to the ferryboat asking if they wanted us to put up a spinnaker. I wrote "Spinnaker?" Yes, my French was improving. Actually the French word for spinnaker is *spinnaker*. Aboard the ferryboat binoculars were raised to try to read my sign and to discern my meaning. Eventually the passengers understood and started cheering. We hoisted the big blue masthead spinnaker. It took us five minutes to get the sail flying—a far better effort than our initial hour-and-a-half attempt when we'd left France 79 days before.

As we neared the Créac'd lighthouse on Ouessant, there were hundreds of boats buzzing us and planes and helicopters above us. I looked for familiar faces on the boats: I saw Florence Arthaud and Jane Redford, who were on the loosely defined Trophée Jules Verne Committee. Florence, a tremendous sailor in her own right, had had aspirations to do this circumnavigation too. Only a pregnancy had prevented it. I kept searching for Molly and my father and stepmother, but couldn't find them in the madding crowd. I had no idea where they were. I was videotaping the scene, but then decided I'd prefer to experience it rather than record it for posterity, and put the camera down.

For Phileas Fogg and Jean Passepartout the finish line was the stuffy Reform Club in London's Pall Mall district. For us, it was between the lighthouse at l'île d'Ouessant, which we could see, and the lighthouse on the Lizard in England. That's a distance of close to 90 nautical miles; as such, it has to be the world's longest starting and finishing line.

As we neared it, the sun was setting behind us. The wind ceased to blow with the exit of the sun. As it died, it went aft, and we were in danger of not crossing the line. So we jibed—or turned the back of the boat through the wind— one last time. After that, we lit red flares to mark the boat's position in the dark, but mostly for the utter joy of it. As Phileas Fogg burned his boat, the *Henrietta*, we burned flares.

We crossed the finish line on Tuesday, April 20, at 19:18:23 GMT. On the radio a voice simply said: *"Fini."* And we were.

It had taken us 79 days, 6 hours, 15 minutes, and 56 seconds to sail around the world. While 121 years separated us, we'd beaten Phileas Fogg and Jean Passepartout —they seemed real to me by this time—by a mere 17 hours, 44 minutes, and 4 seconds.

We'd also beaten the fastest sailing circumnavigation, done by Frenchman Titouan Lamazou, in *Ecureuil d'Aquitaine II*, in the 1989–90 Vendée Globe Race by 30 days, 2 hours, and 33 minutes. That is a 27 percent improvement.

# In which
# I kiss Molly and the
# ground—in that order

Following that simple French word, *"Fini,"* I let out a sigh. It occurred to me then that I'd been holding my breath—however slightly—since we'd left l'île d'Ouessant some 1,902 hours ago. Actually it had begun in November, on Thanksgiving Day, when my father broke into tears after Thanksgiving dinner and told me, for the very first time in my life, "Be careful." Since then I'd asked Molly to marry me, and we had made a baby. For all of them I'd wanted to be careful.

With such a high-strung boat traveling so fast over such unsympathetic waters, I never felt wholly comfortable. I never felt that we were on anything but thin ice. We survived and conquered the world because we were extremely lucky and, forgive my immodesty, extremely good. For 1,902 hours, however, we were on guard. This was true awake or asleep.

As we crossed the finish line, I also felt a tingling pass

through my entire body, like an internal lightning bolt, but one of immense pleasure. It was an amazing emotion. I could have cried for joy, but not before this crowd. Then boat horns began to blast in welcome, and people walked on one another in French on the radio. I didn't understand any of it, but it sounded to me like music—music of the gods.

We'd sailed 27,372 nautical miles to round the world. In that distance, we'd done 568 maneuvers: tacks, jibes, and sail changes. Marc kept a record of each one.

Fogg's voyage around the world was, Verne tells us, "twenty-six thousand" miles. As noted earlier, it was actually closer to 24,000 statute miles or 20,870 nautical miles. That is an average speed of 10.9 knots. Our average speed, again, was 14.3 knots. So one difference between the world in 1872 and 1993 was 3.4 knots. When viewed that way, it isn't much, really. Finally, there wasn't that much difference between a fictitious voyage in 1872 and a real one in 1993.

Once across the finish line, we took the spinnaker down. Two boats came alongside and tossed bottles of beer and champagne to us. Without wind and without an engine, we worried about running aground on the rocks that guard Ouessant, where ferocious currents run. Recall the French saying: Who sees Ouessant sees his blood.

However, we managed to sail into a little protected cove and were joined there by a couple of motorboats and a big ferryboat. Bruno's girlfriend, Catherine, and Chinois's wife, Nikki, came aboard bearing gifts: pâté, baguettes, and rare roast beef, and Champagne. Good, sure, but what I really longed for was *le cheeseburgeur et pommes frites.* Catherine also brought a bagful of Sector watches, a company that Bruno and Michel Horeau had secured as sponsors as we sailed. A spinnaker with their name came aboard, too, which we would hoist the next day and fly appreciatively.

One of the photographers who came aboard was Kéruzoré, whom we had dropped off at the Cape Verde Islands the first week. He was wearing my red foul-weather-gear pants. "Like your pants," I said to him. He just laughed and said that I looked none the worse for wear. Kéruzoré told me that since the storm at Cape Horn, we'd been constantly in the news in France.

Apparently, Michel Horeau, our press agent, had made considerable journalistic "hay" during our Cape Horn hurricane. A picture of a world-weary Chinois, in the midst of the storm, was transmitted by satellite back to France. It was published in practically every newspaper and magazine there, including the cover of *VSD*, the French weekly newsmagazine. Chinois was even dubbed "Face of the Month." Another Fujix photograph, taken by Bruno around the same time, of the crew off Cape Horn, was sent digitally by computer from *Commodore Explorer* to France and similarly was published everywhere.

Kéruzoré gave me a copy of *L'Équipe*, the French daily sports newspaper, that had our picture plastered across the top of the front page.

Marc and I asked Bruno where Michelle and Antoine—Marc's family—and Molly and my family were. We learned that the original plan, concocted by Bruno and Michel Horeau, had been for a private rendezvous for the crew at Belle-Île before facing the nation. Molly, Michelle, and Antoine had gone there in a helicopter. The plans had changed, but too late to include our loved ones.

After the press got their stories, most of them disappeared. Nikki left too; being pregnant like Molly, she didn't wish to stay aboard overnight. Catherine and a few journalists stayed aboard, however. One of them told me an odd story. How on this day, April 20, the actor Cantinflas had died. He had played Passepartout in the Mike Todd–produced Academy Award–winning 1956 Best Picture, *Around the World in 80 Days*. While he played a Frenchman, he was actually from Mexico; his real name was Mario Moreno Reyes. Perhaps, I wondered aloud, he'd waited to see if we were going to break "his" record before moving on?

The journalist also told me how the day before, April 19, U.S. federal agents had stormed the heavily armed compound of a religious sect, the Branch Davidians, led by a David Koresh, in Waco, Texas, and seventy-five of the cult members died, including seventeen children.

Since I had left France nearly 80 days before, things had changed: there was a new president, Bill Clinton, in America, and there was a new prime minister, Edouard Balladur, in France and a new government, the Union for France coalition.

I felt like Rip Van Winkle, having just woken up after a long, long nap; this seemed a little too much too soon. I also felt like Bernard Moitessier, the notable French sailor, who would likely have won the Golden Globe Race in 1969 —the first nonstop solo race around the world. Moitessier had decided, however, to continue sailing in the deep-south latitudes, or the "Roaring Forties," leaving the race, the win, considerable fame, and indeed some fortune to Robin Knox-Johnston, our friend on the departed *ENZA New Zealand*.

As Moitessier wrote, "I have no desire to return to Europe with all its false gods. It is difficult to defend oneself against them—they eat your liver and suck your marrow and brutalize you in the end. . . ." Hearing this, his wife commented that he must be temporarily insane. Perhaps not, I considered for a moment.

After the rendezvous, we set sail for le Pouliguen, where Bruno lives. It was 120 miles away. There was no wind; indeed, there was no real wind at the finish line for the next two days. If we hadn't finished on April 20, we might still be out there.

We drifted toward le Pouliguen in the dark at 2 knots. Finally Bruno got on the radio and arranged for a tow. The tow, however, couldn't go faster than 6 knots. It was better than going 2 knots but not much. At that speed, it would take us 20 hours to get ashore, where, I knew, my loved ones—Molly, our baby-to-be, my father and stepmother— waited. Even after an around-the-world sail—or especially after—it seemed much too far.

I went below to sleep. However, a journalist had made himself at home in my bunk. I wasn't going to sleep with some dirty-smelly, bunk-thieving journalist. (Don't misunderstand me, I don't think all journalists are dirty-smelly and bunk-thieving; this one just happened to be.) And so, disgusted, I went forward and dropped into the forward hatch, where the spinnakers lived. I fell asleep on some damp sail bags there. At some point that night, we traded our 6-knot tow for the real thing.

As the sun rose the next morning, the wind filled in where we were, at least sufficiently to sail. After sailing around the world, Bruno did not wish to be towed ignominiously into port by the nose. We set sail and cast the tow loose. After sailing for a while, we were met by three multihulls: Bruno's old catamaran, now called *Club Explorer*, sailed by family and friends; and two 60-foot trimarans, Laurent Bourgnon's *Primagaz* and Bruno's brother Loïck with his *Fujicolor*. Bruno, you will recall, had originally hoped this would be a trip for the brothers Peyron: Loïck, Stéphane, the transatlantic windsurfer and now a television producer, and himself. Loïck had professed to be interested in this, too, but actually Bruno discovered he'd been organizing his own program. The two brothers were somewhat estranged at this point, but

Loïck's welcome-home seemed a nice gesture. The four multihulls sailed together like birds of a feather.

While I didn't know it then, little more than a year later, I would be racing across the Atlantic with Bourgnon on this *Primagaz* against Loïck Peyron and crew on *Fujicolor*. We would beat Loïck by 80 minutes and set an east-to-west double-handed transatlantic record of 9 days, 8 hours, and 58 minutes. This broke the previous record by more than 38 hours.

By midafternoon the breeze was up to 15 knots; it was springtime in France and a beautiful sailing day. There were puffy white clouds that punctuated the perfect blue sky.

Our escort continued to increase in size throughout the day until it numbered about 300 spectator boats. We were the Pied Piper of le Pouliguen. We'd slow down and let them catch up to us, only to trim the sails and just blast away. It was great fun, at least for us. At one point, I heard my father's voice on the radio. Before I could talk to him, dozens of other voices broke in, speaking French. And he was gone.

When we got to le Pouliguen, we didn't go right in. Rather we were having too much fun doing speed burns back and forth along the beach. This is what sailing's all about, and it wasn't diminished by a tour of the world. It was a Wednesday in France, and the crowd on the beach was estimated by one newspaper to be 100,000. The beach at le Pouliguen is 10 miles long. At low tide, it is about a mile wide.

Then I got word that Molly was waiting for me at the dock, so at my behest we headed in. We had to be towed into the harbor. In fact, *Commodore Explorer* was too long to make the clubhouse turn into the harbor without assistance from two rubber boats, pushing the bow and stern in opposite directions. Once we made the turn, it was like athletes coming into a packed stadium. People were lined up wall-to-wall on either side of the harbor to see us.

I could see my father, incongruously waving an American flag. Next to him was Molly and Emmy, my stepmother. Also, there was Bruno's seven-year-old daughter Alexandra, holding a bouquet of flowers for her papa. Chinois's Nikki was there, looking a little bit pregnant. Also there were Marc's Michelle and Antoine, his new son. As we were towed by the dock where my father stood, I couldn't grab Molly, so I grabbed his American flag and waved it enthusiastically. Jacques and I went to the bow of *Commodore Explorer* and tried to get the French crowd to do the wave cheer—the one you see so often in American stadiums. This doesn't translate easily. It took time and patience but they got it. And got into it.

As we pulled into the dock, a journalist jumped aboard and put a headset on me and began an interview. In the midst of this, I saw that Molly had made her way to the dock and was about to board the boat. I ran across the boat to greet her, forgetting that the headphones were still on my head. I ran right out of them—they nearly took off my head—and grabbed her and hugged and kissed her. She looked beautiful to me. Then I grabbed my dad and Emmy as they stepped aboard.

Later, surrounded by my family—Molly, our baby-to-be, my father and stepmother—we all walked up the ramp from the dock to land. I dropped to my knees and kissed the earth, in a gesture I hoped would be amusing. (The next day a French newspaper wrote I appeared to be drunk.) It was good to be back.

French novels often have a dénouement—a working out of the plot, or final scene. In *Around the World in Eighty Days*, Verne poses the question: What did Phileas Fogg gain by his adventure?

The author writes: "Phileas Fogg had won his wager, and had made his journey around the world in eighty days. To do this, he had employed every means of conveyance—steamers, railways, carriages, yachts, trading vessels, sledges, elephants. The eccentric gentleman had throughout displayed all his marvellous qualities of coolness and exactitude. But what then? What had he really gained by all this trouble? What had he brought back from this long and weary journey?

"Nothing, say you? Perhaps so; nothing but a charming woman, who, strange as it may appear, made him the happiest of men!

"Truly, would you not for less than that make the tour around the world?"

That answer applies to me too. I gained "a charming woman," who became my wife, and then a son, Max Cameron, who was born exactly nine months to the day after we departed Brest. They have made me "the happiest of men."

You want more? I believe life should be lived ". . . like a mighty rushing wind," as Hugh Robert Mill wrote about Sir Ernest Shackleton, the great polar explorer. For seventy-nine days in 1993, it was for me and for four Frenchmen who I came to regard as brothers.

# AFTERWORD

M olly and I were married a month later, on May 22, 1993. Bruno Peyron was my best man. There were about a hundred people there, including *Commodore Explorer* crew members and their mates: Chinois and Nikki Despaigne and Marc and Michelle Vallin. (Jacques Vincent was sailing in the Around Europe Race.)

Our wedding was at the Newport station of the New York Yacht Club. Molly got her diamond ring, and I didn't have to sell my mountain bike or Rollerblades to finance it. I used the money that Bruno paid me, all of it, to buy the ring. Also, in keeping with my wishes, we didn't have a tent for the reception, as I hate tents. May in Newport can be more winter than spring; however, we had, for the most part, a beautiful day. It rained a little, however, when a squall passed. The yacht club overlooks Newport Harbor from a high hill. As soon as it started raining, several of the guests, dressed in jackets and ties or dresses, grabbed trays and started sliding down the hill.

Jacques Vincent, who accurately calls the sea his home, sailed in the Whitbread Round the World Race beginning in September 1993, as a watch captain for America's Cup skipper Chris Dickson, on *Tokio*. They were leading the race when this Whitbread 60 was dismasted on the second-from-last leg, from Punta del Este, Uruguay, to Ft. Lauderdale, Florida. Jacques, incidentally, was met by his girlfriend, Sherri, at the end of our voyage, but as these things sometimes go, they've both gone their own ways.

Marc Vallin is continuing to pursue a career as a helicopter pilot and has continued to race sailboats when he can. His wife, Michelle, has gone back to work as a flight attendant with Air France. The two of them are kept busy by their son, Antoine.

Olivier "Chinois" Despaigne went back to work at Multiplast, the boat builder who had made *Commodore Explorer*, or *Jet Services V*, as she was then called. While Nikki, Chinois's wife, and Molly were pregnant at the same time, Nikki and Chinois lost the baby. They now have a baby girl. In addition to being a mother, Nikki, who's from Scotland, has become a teacher and a translator.

Bruno Peyron went on to fame in France but, sadly, not fortune, which, I believe, he absolutely deserved. Commodore International, Ltd., the computer company that sponsored *Commodore Explorer*, went out of business in 1994. A bank ultimately took the boat *Commodore Explorer* from Bruno, but he later got it back. Bruno continues to pedal a bicycle around le Pouliguen and Paris, where he spends most of his time with his girlfriend, Catherine. I gave him a new bicycle, a classic American cruiser bicycle with fat tires and even an imitation gas tank, for being my best man. He continues to design his 123-foot Clipper Cat and to organize "The Race." This race around the world will start the last day of this century. I'd like to be there for that one too.

Since the day Marc presented Bruno with the petition, they don't speak much anymore. For reasons I don't fully understand, my relationship with Bruno is strained too. This is my sole regret of the voyage and of the friendship that we shared, but I'm sure to sail with him again.

In the world of adventuring, it's always best, I believe, to be first—the one who proves that something is possible. Since Sir Edmund Hillary, of New Zealand, and Tenzing Norgay, a Nepalese Sherpa tribesman, became the first to reach the summit of Mount Everest, in 1953, the 29,028-foot (8,848 m) mountain, between Tibet and Nepal, has been climbed hundreds of times. Since Roald Amundsen reached the South Pole on December 14, 1911, thousands have visited there. Indeed, there's even a U.S. base there, the Amundsen-Scott Base. Dozens of planes fly from New York to Paris every day, but practically everyone remembers that Charles Lindbergh was the first man to make this historic flight alone, on May 21, 1927. His name is even on the airport in San Diego.

Records are made to be broken, and our record of 79 days, 6 hours, 15 minutes, and 56 seconds lasted only one year. After we finished in 1993, Peter Blake, the coskipper of *ENZA New Zealand,* that had dropped out of this race, said, "It was more a Christopher Columbus, rather than a Jules Verne, undertaking last time. Nobody knew whether 80 days was possible, and there were the skeptics who said it was foolhardy to take a big racing catamaran into the Southern Ocean. Eighty days was proved achievable."

Blake and his coskipper, Robin Knox-Johnston, suited deeds to words. The next year, they sailed around the world in their now lengthened 92-foot cat *ENZA New Zealand* in 74 days, 22 hours, 17 minutes, and 22 seconds. They had the benefit of a race; *ENZA* raced against the newly lengthened and newly named *Lyonnaise des Eaux Dumez* (the old *Charal),* skippered by Olivier de Kersauson. Who? *Lyonnaise des Eaux Dumez* beat our 79-day record too; her time was 77 days, 8 hours, 3 minutes, and 7 seconds. It was this same Peter Blake who led New Zealand to victory in the 1995 America's Cup.

By the time we arrived in France, we had accumulated seventy-nine bags of garbage, one for each day. All of us aboard *Commodore Explorer* had a strong sense that we were guests on this beautiful planet and didn't wish to leave our garbage behind us. The bags, packed in the back of either hull, were removed the next day and disposed of properly.

In early 1994, I was named the 1993 Rolex Yachtsman of the Year Winner in America for sailing on *Commodore Explorer.* Due to a snowstorm, however, I missed the presentation in New York City. Molly and I left Newport and moved to Maine, where we eventually purchased forty-six acres and live in a house beside a lake. In the attic there, I have a five-liter jerrycan of Cape Horn water. Last time I looked, it was frozen solid. I don't have a clue what to do with it. So much for acorns and trees.

We live there with our son, Max Cameron, who is a year old as I write these last words. He has the looks of his mother and the size and strength of his father. But so far he hasn't uttered a word.

Cam Lewis
Michael Levitt

# APPENDIX

## FOGG'S FICTITIOUS VOYAGE IN 1872

| From | To | Statute Miles | Nautical Miles |
| --- | --- | --- | --- |
| London | Dover, England | 68 | 59 |
| Dover | Calais, France | 25 | 22 |
| Calais | Paris | 173 | 150 |
| Paris | Turin, Italy | 360 | 313 |
| Turin | Brindisi | 612 | 532 |
| Brindisi | Port Said, Egypt | 1,064 | 925 |
| Port Said | Suez | 115 | 100 |
| Suez | Aden, Yemen | 1,506 | 1,310 |
| Aden | Bombay, India | 1,898 | 1,650 |
| Bombay | Banaras | 828 | 720 |
| Banaras | Calcutta | 506 | 440 |
| Calcutta | Singapore | 1,875 | 1,630 |
| Singapore | Hong Kong | 1,656 | 1,440 |
| Hong Kong | Shanghai, China | 981 | 853 |
| Shanghai | Yokohama, Japan | 1,185 | 1,030 |
| Yokohama | San Francisco | 5,199 | 4,521 |
| San Francisco | New York | 2,438 | 2,120 |
| New York | Queentown, Ireland | 3,157 | 2,745 |
| Queenstown | Dublin | 130 | 113 |
| Dublin | Liverpool, England | 134 | 119 |
| Liverpool | London | 176 | 153 |
| TOTAL | | 24,086 | 20,945 |

# BIBLIOGRAPHY

Books:

Amundsen, Roald. *The South Pole,* trans. A. G. Chater. London: John Murray, 1913.

Amundsen, Roald. *My Life as an Explorer.* New York: Doubleday, Page & Co., 1927.

Bathe, Basil W. *The Visual Encyclopedia of Nautical Terms Under Sail.* New York: Crown Publishers Inc., 1978.

Born, Franz. *Jules Verne: the Man Who Invented the Future,* trans. Juliana Biro. Englewood Cliffs, N.J.: Prentice-Hall, Inc., 1964.

Brown, Joe David, and the editors of *Life. India.* New York: Time, Inc., 1961.

Byrd, Admiral Richard E. *Alone.* New York: G. P. Putnam's Sons, 1938.

Calder, Nigel. *The English Channel.* New York: Viking Penguin, Inc., 1986.

Chester, Jonathan. *Antarctica: Beauty in the Extreme.* New York: Running Press/Friedman Group, 1991.

Coleridge, Samuel Taylor. "The Rime of the Ancient Mariner." *A Book of Famous Verse,* ed. Agnes Repplier. New York: Houghton Mifflin Co., 1982.

Cross, Milton, and David Ewen. *The Milton Cross New Encyclopedia of the Great Composers and Their Music.* New York: Doubleday & Co., Inc., 1953.

Dana, Richard Henry, Jr. *Two Years Before the Mast.* New York: Dodd, Mead & Co., Inc., 1946.

Day, George, and Herb McCormick. *Out There.* Newport, R.I.: Seven Seas Press, 1983.

Du Bois, Cora. *Social Forces in Southeast Asia.* Cambridge: Harvard University Press, 1959.

Eliot, T. S., from the poem "The Hollow Men," 1925.

Fessler, Loren, and the editors of *Life*. *China*. New York: Time, Inc., 1963.

*Grolier 1995 Multimedia Encyclopedia*. Danbury, Conn.: Grolier Electronic Publishing, Inc., 1994. Also, the 1992 version.

*Hammond Citation World Atlas*. Maplewood, New Jersey: Hammond, Inc., 1976.

Henry, Thomas R. *The White Continent*. New York: William Sloane Associates, 1950.

Holms, Donald. *The Circumnavigators: Small Boat Voyagers of Modern Times*. New York: Prentice-Hall, Inc., 1974.

Howe, John. *History of Virginia*. Charleston: W. R. Babcock, 1849.

Hoyt, Edwin Palmer. *The Last Explorer: The Adventures of Admiral Byrd*. New York: The John Day Company, 1968.

Huxley, Elspeth. *Scott of the Antarctic*. London: Weidenfeld and Nicolson, 1977.

Karnow, Stanley, and the editors of *Life*. *Southeast Asia*. New York: Time, Inc., 1962.

Knox-Johnston, Robin. *A World of My Own: The Single-handed, Nonstop Circumnavigation of the World in* Suhaili. New York: Morrow, 1970.

Lazarus, Emma. "The New Colossus," sonnet written for the inscription on the Statue of Liberty, 1886.

*Life Pictorial Atlas*. *Life* and Rand McNally, eds. New York: Time, Inc., 1961.

MacLeod, Norman, D. D. *Days in North India*. Philadelphia: J. B. Lippincott & Co., 1870.

May, John. *The Greenpeace Book of Antarctica*. New York: Doubleday & Co., Inc., 1989.

*Mercantile Marine Atlas of the World*. New York: C. S. Hammond & Co., 1914.

Mill, H. R. *The Life of Sir Ernest Shackleton*. London: W. H. Heinemann, Ltd., 1923.

Moody, Lieutenant Commander Alton B. *Navigation and Nautical Astronomy, Dutton,* 9th ed. Annapolis: United States Naval Institute, 1948.

Muller, Robert A., principal academic advisor. *Physical Geography Today.* Del Mar, Cal.: CRM Books, 1974.

Peyron, Bruno. *Tour du Monde à la Voile en Quatre-Vingts Jours.* Paris: Livres Hachette, 1993.

Ralling, Christopher, ed. *Shackleton: His Antarctic Writings.* London: British Broadcasting Corporation, 1983.

Ransome, Arthur, *Racundra's First Cruise,* New York: Hippocrene Books, 1984.

Service, Robert, "The Quitter," a poem from *Rhymes of a Rolling Stone,* New York: Dodd, Mead and Co., 1916.

Shackleton, Sir Ernest. *South.* London: Century Publishers, 1983.

Shakespeare, William. *The Complete Works of William Shakespeare.* London: Abbey Library, 1974.

Siedensticker, Edward, and the eds. of *Life. Japan.* New York: Time, Inc., 1961.

Slocum, Joshua, *Sailing Alone Around the World,* New York: Sheridan House, 1954.

Stone, Robert. *Outerbridge Reach.* New York: HarperPerennial, 1992.

Swinglehurst, Edmund. *The Romantic Journey: The Story of Thomas Cook and Victorian Travel.* London: Pica Editions, 1974.

Tomalin, Nicholas, and Ron Hall. *The Strange Last Voyage of Donald Crowhurst.* New York: Stein and Day Publishers, 1970.

Turley, Charles. *The Voyages of Captain Scott.* London: Smith, Elder & Co., 1914.

Verne, Jules. *Le Tour du Monde en Quatre-Vingts Jours,* Paris: Editions Gallimard, 1977.

Verne, Jules. *Le Tour du Monde en Quatre-Vingts Jours,* Paris: Hachette, 1977.

Verne, Jules. *Around the World in Eighty Days*, trans. George
     Makepeace Towle. New York: Bantam Books, Inc.,
     1984.
Periodicals:
Associated Press article, "Chunnel: Ready to Roll?" pre-
     sumably by Patrick McDowell and Dirk Beveridge,
     published in *The Providence Journal-Bulletin*, April 24,
     1994.
Bowermaster, Jon, "Has the Great Lamazon Missed the
     Boat?" *Outside*, November 1993.
Chiodi, Charles K., "The Man Who Vanished," *Multihulls*,
     March/April 1993.
Février, Christian, "Around the World in 80 days (or less),"
     *Multihulls*, April/May 1993.
Gliatto, Tom, Bryan Alexander and Vickie Bane, "I Am
     Alive," *People*, April 18, 1994.
Kramer, Jane, "Dirty Hands," *The New Yorker*, March 28,
     1994.
Rosenow, Frank, "The Fire Still Burns," *Sail*, May 1990.

# INDEX